GOOD NEWS STUDIES

Consulting Editor: Robert J. Karris, O.F.M.

Volume 34

The Book of Revelation

The Open Book of Prophecy

Charles Homer Giblin, S.J.

A Michael Glazier Book
THE LITURGICAL PRESS
Collegeville, Minnesota

A Michael Glazier Book published by The Liturgical Press

Cover design by David Manahan, O.S.B.
About the cover: detail of a panel in ivory from a fifth-century reliquary, Museo Civico, Brescia, Italy.

1   2   3   4   5   6   7   8   9

Library of Congress Cataloging-in-Publication Data

Giblin, Charles Homer.
    The book of Revelation : the open book of prophecy / by Charles Homer Giblin.
        p.   cm. — (Good news studies ; v. 34)
    "A Michael Glazier book."
    Includes bibliographical references.
    ISBN 0-8146-5005-8
    1. Bible.   N.T.   Revelation—Commentaries.   I. Title.
II. Series.
BS2825.3.G53   1991
228'.077—dc 20

91-12958
CIP

CONTENTS

ABBREVIATIONS

Bib	*Biblica*
CBQ	*Catholic Biblical Quarterly*
HUCA	*Hebrew Union College Annual*
Int	*Interpretation*
JBL	*Journal of Biblical Literature*
JSS	*Journal of Semitic Studies*
Neot	*Neotestamentica*
NRT	*Nouvelle Revue Théologique*
NTS	*New Testament Studies*
RevThom	*Revue Thomiste*
StTh	*Studia Theologica*
VigChr	*Vigiliae Christianae*

FOREWORD

For most people, John's Book of Revelation (Apocalypse) is anything but open, clear, and worth close attention. Snatches here and there seem to be intelligible and even moving. The book as a whole, however, even with its salient emphasis on "the end of everything," strikes the average reader as befuddling, lacking both unity and coherence. John himself must have thought otherwise. For, unlike other apocalyptic writers, notably Daniel (Dan 12:9), he regarded his work as a message both for his own day and for all the time left to the world. At its close (Rev 22:10), he recounts being instructed to let his book stand open, "unsealed."

The aim of this commentary on John's Book of Revelation is to render it readable for a Christian—or anyone, for that matter—who has had the equivalent of some college-level education, particularly in humanities. Built around the orderly presentation of the author's translation of John's Greek text, the commentary strives to enable the reader readily to perceive the literary unity, coherence, and emphasis of John's composition. Intended strong points are a comprehensible analysis of the carefully-wrought literary structure of John's work, the eschatological framework of John's thought, and the dominant thematic aspects couched in his unusual theological language, apocalyptic.

Another volume, the Bible, should serve as needed or useful background reading. Although Revelation never really quotes the Bible, it refers to or alludes to biblical passages more often than does the rest of the New Testament as a whole. John supposed that his hearers were familiar with it, especially with the prophetic books. References to biblical texts, however, have been used somewhat sparingly in this commentary, so as to further and not to impede the reader's progress through John's own work.

Similarly, the introduction has been restricted to a clear-cut treatment of key issues that should be addressed first, for subsequent, easier comprehension of the structure, eschatology, and thematic thrusts of Revelation. The interpreter's task is to read the text aright and, at the same time, to enable his audience to assimilate and savor the text which John has laid out before us. The truth of any interpretation remains always asymptotic. Even so, the validity it has lies in the better understanding of the composition which it attempts to open up more fully. Of the success of that attempt, the attentive reader himself will have to judge.

INTRODUCTION

Most introductions to commentaries on Revelation deal extensively with questions concerning authorship, place and date of publication, and some general themes of the work. They treat quite summarily its literary structure and the most unifying themes of its major vision (Rev 4–22). In line with the scope of this commentary, however, the emphasis has been altered. Following a minimal treatment of author, date, and place of composition, this introduction will highlight the literary structure of Revelation, its apocalyptic eschatology, and its reworking of the major biblical theme of God's Holy War.

I. Author, and Circumstances Affecting His Composition

The author of the Book of Revelation (also known, from its first word in Greek, as the Apocalypse) has left us his name, John (1:19; 22:8). He claims to be no more than a prophet, a member of the Christian community (cf. 1:1, 9; 19:10; 22:6-10). From ancient times, there were some, like Dionysius, a third century bishop of Alexandria,[1] who rightly refused to accept him as the same person who wrote the Gospel and Epistles of John. Although the isle of Patmos appears to be his place of (temporary) exile, and does not designate his origin, that locale for his vision may serve to designate this particular prophet as "John of Patmos." His

---

[1]Cf. Eusebius, *Ecclesiastical History,* VII.25.

social identity, as distinguished from his personal identity, includes his knowledge of at least two Semitic languages as well as Greek, his Jewish-Palestinian background, and his role as an itinerant prophet, functioning on his own rather than as the head of a prophetic school.[2]

Revelation as we have it probably dates from A.D. 95, during the reign of Domitian—a view proposed as early as Irenaeus. John may well have made use of earlier sources. The scope of this commentary, however, precludes giving more than a few examples, notably in John's allusion to Roman Emperors (17:9-11). Domitian's persecution of Christians was probably not universal.[3] Nonetheless, like that of Nero (A.D. 67) before it, Domitian's hostility vividly raised the prospect of what Christians could expect from Rome. Furthermore, worldwide Roman imperial policy, with its deification of the Emperor, provided a ready example of colossal opposition to God. The world-reign of God, which was the quintessence of apocalyptic concern, could in John's day find no better counter-image than caricature of Rome. Lastly, no doubt in his own experience as in that of fellow believers who shared John's urban environment, social discrimination and occasional violence (like the murder of Antipas, 2:13) easily gave rise to a perception of ongoing oppression. This, in turn, fostered the prophetic-apocalyptic desire for a definitive manifestation of God's justice on the "sinful structure" of pagan society.[4]

The immediate audience for which John wrote lived in seven major cities in the Province of Asia, the far western portion, along the Aegean Sea, of what is now Turkey. Most of these communities faced internal problems as well as those arising from their pagan environment. John regards as particularly insidious some teachers and / or prophets known as Nicolaitans (2:6, 15), whom John types as "Balaam" and "Jezebel" (2:14, 20). His proph-

---

[2]For the discussion, cf. A. Y. Collins, *Crisis and Catharsis: The Power of the Apocalypse* (Philadelphia: Westminster, 1984) 33–50. According to Steven Thompson, the primary source of Semitic influence on Revelation is biblical Hebrew, and biblical Aramaic; *The Apocalypse and Semitic Syntax* (Cambridge: University Press, 1985) 107.

[3]Cf. A. Y. Collins, *Crisis and Catharsis*, 55–77.

[4]For a discussion of the social context of Revelation, see A. Y. Collins, ibid., 84–107.

ecy as a whole, however, attends both to particular situations in individual communities and to a worldwide vision. Attesting this complexive viewpoint is the complementarity of the two major parts of Revelation (1:9–3:22 and 4:1–22:6, 8-11) which follow the prologue (1:1-8) and precede the epilogue (22:7, 12-21).

The first part (1:9–3:22) contains John's inaugural vision and the so-called "letters," divine proclamations of the risen Jesus, which John is directed to send to the seven churches. These missives look particularly to the current state of the religious health of each of the Christian communities. At the same time, each of the written communications will be read in all the churches (plural, 2:7a, as reiterated at the close of each of the remaining communications). Moreover, the number seven, as well as the varied characterizations which emerge in the whole set, suggest that John has in mind an even wider compass of Christian communities, equivalently "the Church" as he knew it.' The second part (from 4:1 into ch. 22) complements the first by introducing both fuller emphasis on the future and what is clearly a worldwide, expressly cosmic perspective.

Explanation of the scope and of the articulation of each of these parts requires first and foremost a careful reading of John's own composition. A detailed explanation cannot be provided, without provoking both annoyance and confusion, until the reader will have become familiar with John's translated text. Accordingly, the explanation will emerge in the commentary proper. More thorough attention to the links between the first and second parts of Revelation will be deferred to an appendix.

At this juncture, it should suffice to survey the extensive outline of the work which appears below. Unlike similar portions of the table of contents, the outline contains annotations designed to enable the reader to grasp John's elaborately integrated composition. The reader may find it convenient to peruse first the

---

'John never employs the singular, *ekklēsia* ("assembly"), of the "Church universal." His vocabulary remains limited to dealing with local communities. John's conception of Christian unity, however, extends to all the faithful on earth and, indeed, covers those in heaven as well. It finds its fulfillment in the New Jerusalem. John's equivalent expression for the "communion of saints" seems to be the priestly kingdom (Rev 1:5b-6; 5:9-10; 20:4-6; and 22:3b-5).

capitalized divisions and then read them a second time together
with the sentence-style summary of each in turn.

II. Outline-Précis of Revelation

1:1-8   **Prologue**

A dialogue-style introduction, involving the community, a presiding member of the community, and a
reader (lector), presents John's letter-style greeting
(1:4-5a) and states the scope of his communication.

1:19-3:22   **The First Major Part: John's Inaugural Vision and the
Seven Proclamations to the Churches**

1:9-20   *John's Inaugural Vision*
John recounts his vision of the risen Lord, received on
a Sunday while he was in exile on Patmos. The vision
(with auditory, then visual components) covers the
scope of the whole apocalypse, but focuses in particular on written communications to the seven churches.

2:1-3:22   *The Seven Proclamations (or so-called Letters) to the
Seven Churches*
Each proclamation contains variations of the same precise structure: the address and the command to write
a named community (Ephesus, Smyrna, Pergamum,
Thyatira, Sardis, Philadelphia, Laodicea); the Lord's
self-identification; the body of the edict, stating what
the Lord knows and, accordingly, his words of praise
and / or blame; concluding challenges (to heed) and
promises (to the victor). Although they envisage each
individual church, these missives are intended to be
heard by all the churches.

4:1-22:11   **The Second Major Part:[6] John's Heavenly, Universal
Vision of Things to Come Hereafter**

This part proceeds in seven principal sections of un-
equal length but, all in all, in climactic order. Each sec-

---

[6]At its end, the second major part dovetails with the conclusion or
"epilogue" to Revelation and, together with the epilogue, harks back
to the prologue. See below, pp. 17-18; detailed analysis has been reserved
to the commentary.

tion is tightly latched on to what precedes it by various interlocking verbal devices. As a whole, this part commences with John's vision of the heavenly throne and the Lamb (Jesus Christ as risen from the dead) and entails a panorama of the forthcoming Day of the Lord (God's Holy War), which culminates in the utter destruction of evil (the type of which is Babylon) and, at the same time, in the advent of God's new creation for his saints (the heavenly Jerusalem, the bride of the Lamb).

4:1–5:14	*§I. Heavenly Acclaim of God and the Divine Redeemer*
4:1-11	A celestial court (the 24 elders) and figures representing creation (the 4 living beings) adore the Creator, the Enthroned.
5:1-5	John beholds with consternation a sealed book by the throne, which an interpreting elder then discloses can be opened by the victorious Lion of Judah, the root of David.
5:6-14	This sacrificial Messiah, the redeeming Lamb (slain and risen), is acclaimed together with the enthroned Creator by all the celestial court and by all creation, including hosts of angels.

6:1–8:5   *§II. The Seven Unsealings*

This first of three major series of seven numbered events consists of a *preview* of victory but at the same time of worldwide suffering (the first four unsealings), then of suppliant martyrs to be rewarded and complemented by more martyrs (the fifth unsealing), then of those terrified at the coming Day of the Lord and, conversely, of those delivered through trial (the sixth unsealing and its enlargement) and, lastly, with a dramatic silence in heaven, of the forthcoming engagement. During the silence, the seven angels before the throne are given seven trumpets, and another performs two, related symbolic actions: offering up at the altar the prayers of the saints (incense) and casting fire upon the earth.

8:6–15:18   *§III. The Seven Trumpet-Blasts*

This section, with striking elaborations, depicts the engagement, the actual conflict between God and his wicked, unrepentant foes, and climactically (in the last three of the trumpet-blasts, the three woes), demonic forces and their social embodiments. At the same time, it portrays the heavenly triumph of the saints, the followers of the Lamb, who are saved through their unwarlike but determined resistance in God's Holy War on their behalf. In its conclusion, this section introduces the last of the three numbered septenaries of this part of Revelation, namely, the seven angels with the final plagues.

8:6-13   • THE FIRST FOUR TRUMPET-BLASTS AND THE AN-
NOUNCEMENT OF THREE FORTHCOMING WOES

The first four trumpets cover cosmic portents on earth, sea, fresh waters, and heavenly bodies. Following them, an eagle introduces three woes, each corresponding, respectively, to the events staged with the fifth, sixth, and seventh trumpet-blasts.

9:1–15:8   • THE THREE WOES (AFTER THE FIFTH, SIXTH, AND SEV-
ENTH TRUMPET-BLASTS)

9:1-12   *The fifth trumpet-blast:*
A demonic locust-plague upon pagans brings out the long period of hopelessness, their frustration with life and their despair during "five months."

9:13–11:14 *The sixth trumpet-blast and its enlargement:*
The so-called "interlude" is actually an enlargement, looking ahead, as do the enlargements under the sixth unsealing and the sixth of the last plagues. A hellish plague from the Euphrates afflicts sinners (pagans); the survivors remain unrepentant.

• John is told that the climactic moment is at hand, and is instructed to consume the opened, proclaimed booklet and to prophesy again.

• He is also instructed to measure God's secure heavenly sanctuary. The unmeasured forecourt (the earth) is the theater of persecution. In the latter (the world-city), identically-twinned, prophetic witnesses (symbols of authentic, biblical Christian testimony to the world) are slain by the demonic beast; at their resurrection-ascension, however, the majority of their enemies are converted.

11:15–15:8 *The seventh trumpet-blast:*
A sevenfold scenario of creation-wide conflict is set forth in concentric order:

11:15b-19 A. A canticle celebrates the advent of the messianic kingdom.
The sanctuary in heaven then opens, disclosing the ark of the covenant.

12:1-18 B. Two contraposed signs in heaven (the pregnant woman and the dragon) are followed by an attack on the woman's messianic offspring; then by angelic conflict in heaven and a canticle of victory and woe; and lastly by the dragon's attack on earth against the woman and her other progeny.

13:1-18 C. Two beasts, both mutants of the dragon (and the second identified as the false prophet) dominate the earth. Between the portrayals of the first beast and of the second, a wisdom-utterance (13:9-10) defines the trial the saints must undergo. A closing wisdom-saying (13:18) identifies the first beast.

14:1-5 D. The Lamb on Mt. Zion is followed by 144,000 celibates (representing the redeemed), who sing a unique (but unquoted) canticle of victory.

14:6-20 C'. Three angels herald, respectively, the eternal gospel, the fall of Babylon, and the penalty for worshippers of the beast. Four angelic figures then deal with the harvesting of the earth (two concerned with reward, two with condemnation). Between the two sets of angelic figures, a wisdom-utterance (14:12-13) defines the present reward for deceased Christians.

15:1 B'. John sees another sign in heaven, the seven angels with the last plagues, who will consummate God's wrath.

15:2-8 A'. A canticle (that of Moses and the Lamb) celebrates God's triumph in judgment and the worldwide prospects for the salvation of the nations.
The sanctuary of the tent of testimony then opens in heaven to disclose the seven angels as ready (vested, and holding libation-bowls) to execute God's wrath, as the sanctuary remains temporarily inaccessible.

16:1-21   §*IV. The Seven Libation-Bowls of God's Final Wrath*

After the command from the sanctuary which "activates" these seven angels (16:1), the first four plagues strike earth, sea, fresh waters (whose guardian voice, seconded by the altar, affirms God's judgments), and the sun. The fifth strikes the throne of the beast, whose realm it plunges into darkness. The sixth dries up the Euphrates, preparing for invading hordes, and its enlargement concerns the Lord's coming at the consummation of the Holy War. The seventh smites the air, highlights a voice from the throne solemnly declaring the fulfillment of God's final wrath ("Done!" *[gegonen]*, 16:17b), and then immediately describes the utter devastation of Babylon.

17:1-19:10   §*V. Angelic Interpretation-Scene Regarding the Fall of Babylon*

17:1-3a   The introduction describes the *angelus interpres* as one of those who had the libation-bowls. John is ecstatically transported to a wilderness to behold the judgment on the great harlot (Babylon).

17:3b-18   A.   The angel interprets John's vision of the woman and her entourage, especially the beast with seven heads and ten horns.

18:1-24   B.   John has visions of judgment-oracles and lamentations concerning Babylon's fall.

19:1-8   C.   John hears jubilant rejoicing of a heavenly multitude, affirmed by the heavenly court (three alleluias), a voice from the throne calling for praise of God, and, again, a heavenly multitude voicing a climactic alleluia and announcing the wedding of the Lamb.

19:9-10   The conclusion of the interpretation-scene affirms the truth of the whole passage and forbids worship of the angel.

19:11-21:8   §*VI. Narrative Regarding Other Eschatological Adversaries (besides Babylon) and the New Creation*

19:11-21   X.   The King of Kings conquers the beast, the false prophet, and their allied, earthly kings.

20:1-10   Y.   Victory over Satan, along with the demonic horde of Gog and Magog, is achieved at the climax of

	Christ's millennial reign with the saints (which is the first resurrection, the heavenly reward of the saints prior to the "general resurrection").
20:11–21:8	Z. The Enthroned judges men according to their works as he also vanquishes Death and the Grave (Hades). John then beholds the new heavens and earth and the New Jerusalem. In the second, auditory portion (21:1ff.) of this vision, a voice from the throne enunciates God's rewards. The Enthroned himself then declares his fulfillment of these events (which occur, theologically, at the same eschatological moment as the fall of Babylon: "Done!" *[gegonan]*, 21:6a), and concludes with words of promise and warning.
21:9–22:11	§*VII. Angelic Interpretation-Scene Regarding the Heavenly Jerusalem*
21:9-10a	The introduction again (*cp.* § V) describes the *angelus interpres* as one of those who had the libation-bowls. John is ecstatically transported to a high mountain to behold the coming of the bride of the Lamb, the holy city, Jerusalem.
21:10b-14	A. The angel shows John the holy city. The perspective is general, but highlights at the outset the light of God's glory.
21:15-27	B. The angel measures the city, its walls, and its gates. The perspective is detailed, with special attention to numerically symbolic features and, at the close, highlights the replacement of the sanctuary by God and the Lamb, who provide the city's glorious illumination.
22:1-5	C. The angel shows John the river of life and the tree of life (the fruits of which conclude the numerical symbolism). John then describes the worship of God and the Lamb and, for a third time, God's illumination.
22:6-11	The conclusion of the interpretation-scene affirms the truth of the whole passage and forbids worship of the angel, repeating and developing elements of the conclusion of §V. This conclusion also harkens back to the prologue (in 22:6b, cp. 1:1; 22:10b, cp. 1:3b) and dovetails (22:7, cp. 22:12ff.) with the epilogue.

22:7, 12-21   **Epilogue**

Partly fused with the end of §VII (by 22:7, and also by elements in vv. 6b, 9, 10) this passage concludes John's entire apocalypse. It presents in a kind of liturgical dialogue or ordered set of "interventions" statements of Jesus, declarations by the presiding member of the assembly, a prayerful response by the whole community, and John's own concluding testimony and final salutation.

III. The Eschatology of John's Apocalypse

"Eschatology" may be defined as the understanding of the final and definitive stage of religious experience and, in the biblical sense, of religious history as well. Biblical eschatology is always historically oriented and endowed with a social, not just individual, dimension. Christian eschatology encompasses a coherent period of time which, however, is not defined in terms of clock-and-calendar computation. Its beginning is marked by Jesus Christ's coming into the world to save mankind from sin and death; its consummation occurs with his second coming (parousia) and the general resurrection.

Some NT authors, like Luke, complexively include under Jesus' coming his conception, birth, and early years, his public ministry, and his death-resurrection-ascension. Others, like Paul and John of Patmos, concentrate their attention almost exclusively on the central mystery of the Gospel (paramount in the theological perspective of all NT authors), Jesus Christ's death and resurrection for the forgiveness of sins and the communication of new life to believers. They mention very little (or, in the case of John of Patmos, nothing) about Jesus' earlier activity. The period from Jesus' first coming to his second marks the "eschaton" or endtime. Although the beginning of the eschatological period may be dated by historians, its consummation cannot be calculated or temporally delimited. For the consummation occurs with Jesus' parousia as the unforseeable moment of the final judgment of (physically) living and dead human persons. In the case of every NT author, eschatology is defined not temporally (that is, in a chronological sense) but Christologically; Jesus Christ is the Alpha and the Omega, the beginning and the end, of the end-time (Rev 22:13).

Luke's Gospel and Acts, especially because Luke writes as a religious historian, may be termed "salvation history." They present multiple stages of the eschatological period in broad stretches, as it were. John's Apocalypse does not proceed in the same way. It marks but three major "moments" or foci of attention: what was, as John has beheld it in Christ; what is; and what is coming hereafter (1:19; cf. 4:1). What "was" amounts to the decisive event of Jesus' death and resurrection, his becoming (in functional terms of his acquiring full exercise of power as man) the Lord of God's creation and in particular the Lord of the churches. John perceives this mystery in his inaugural vision of the risen Lord on the Lord's Day, and expresses it anew in the throne-vision of Revelation 4-5. What "is" centers upon the situation of the churches in John's purview, with express consequences for the future, both proximate (like their current trials, moral conduct, repentance, and the like) and less proximate (like ongoing aspects of trials, symbolically represented as "ten days," for example [Rev 2:10]). "The things to come hereafter" cover the execution of the divine plan for the world, particularly for the faithful, as a result of the Lamb's death and resurrection. "The things to come" include both the destruction of evil and rewards for the saints (holy persons), the latter conceived both "vertically" (as heaven) and horizontally (as the new heavens and the new earth). The "less proximate consequences," in particular, cannot be compartmentalized and thus distinctly separated from "the things to come hereafter," for the end-time is a continuum. Not exclusively, but with express emphasis, "the things to come hereafter" are set forth in Rev 4-22.

In the second major part of Revelation (Rev 4-22), the execution of the Creator's plan, unfolded with the scroll which the Lamb alone can and does unseal, seems to contain multiple moments. Actually, these can be reduced to two foci of attention: the proximate future, as John can grasp it, which is growing out of the present, and its end-result(s). The cascading visions of the three septenaries connect the proximate future to its ultimate resolution. That resolution has two correlated aspects: the fulfillment of God's wrath upon evil (cf. *gegonen,* "It has taken place" [or, "Done!] in 16:17a) and his new creation (cf. *gegonan,* "They have taken place" [or, "Done!"] in 21:6a). His wrath, targeted against the whore, Babylon, nonetheless proves to cover the destruction of other eschatological adversaries (Satan, the beasts, Death and the Grave) as well. His new creation, the Lamb's bride, Jerusalem, comes to earth simultaneously. The nature of imaginative, apocalyptic description, however, requires a sequence of visions to render unified and coherent the multiple, interrelated elements of God's achievement and their relevance to the faithful. The panoply of serialized events (seals, trumpets, libation-bowls—to mention only the most evident) does not, strictly speaking, entail "recapitulation" of the same events. For the vision entails an overall progression, with ever more complicated orchestration. At the same time, basic themes do recur, sometimes in prospect (like the image of the redeemed in Revelation 7) and sometimes in partial retrospect as well (like the 144,000 with the Lamb in 14:1-5).

Certain particular "moments" in the vision which spans the proximate future and its end result(s) can be paralleled from the schema of God's Holy War (see below, IV, pp. 25–34ff.). Though sequential—again in the sense that one vision requires another for clarification—these particular "moments" are not tied to any chronology. Even numerical expressions like 1260 days (and its variables) or the "thousand years" (the millennium) are both symbolic and metahistorical, beyond the reach of clock-and-calendar computation.

The foregoing survey of John's eschatology has already moved into the sphere of *apocalyptic* eschatology. Eschatology need not be apocalyptic at all, any more than salvation-history, for example, need be. No apocalyptic writing, however, can fail to be eschatological in some real sense.

Apocalyptic, at least in the biblical tradition, is a kind of theological language, of prophetic provenance, which makes use of highly imaginative, even bizarre imagery (notably in image-clusters) to express the coming worldwide-reign of God and its attendant circumstances. A case in point is the image of the slain Lamb, standing, who is also the Lion of Judah, who alone can open the sealed book. That apocalyptic must devise "out-of-this-world" kinds of symbolic imagery arises mainly from its endeavor to present the working-out of a mystery. A mystery is an event (or, conceptualistically, a "set of truths") which transcends human comprehension yet at the same time admits of solid insights and some understanding of its fascinating depths. Unlike a problem (e.g., knotted shoelace, which can be untied or cut to resolve the obstacle) a divine mystery is never "resolved" and never fails to afford new insights. To express its other-worldly character, beyond the range of merely human experience, the apocalyptist must reach beyond the everyday, merely human universe of discourse. This means, concretely, that he will have to avail himself of other-worldly language, especially of prophetic provenance (and, therefore, of inspired, divine origin), as his own creative imagination can adapt it so as to make himself intelligible to his readers.

In contrast to apocalyptic, "apocalypticism"[7] names a kind of socio-religious movement characterized, almost by definition, as an ideological excess. Apocalyptic is not necessarily escapist, though it may find its origin in a certain disillusionment with historico-political circumstances.[8] It need not seek to evade, through a dream world of ancient "science-fiction," what must be coped with in daily social and moral life. John's Apocalypse, as the seven communications to the churches attest in a clear-cut way, does not merit classification as an instance of apocalypticism.

The term "apocalypse" labels the literary genre or form of a composition. Because of sharp differences between biblical apocalypses (like Daniel and Revelation) and non-biblical, notably "intertestamental" apocalypses (like *1 Enoch* and *2 Esdras*), as well as between canonical apocalypses themselves, like Daniel and Revelation, definition remains a vexing problem.

Every literary genre may be defined, to cite J. J. Collins,[9] as "a group of written texts marked by distinctive characteristics which constitute a recognizable and coherent type of writing." The very phrase *"type* of writing," which nearly begs the question, shows how almost irreducible the notion is. One is dealing with a kind of writing which stands out as something unusual, yet at least recognizably quite similar to things which are compared with it. Different scholars, however, single out different

---

[7]David Aune, "The Apocalypse of John and the Problem of Genre," *Early Christian Apocalypticism: Genre and Social Setting, Semeia* 36 (1986) 65–96, 67.

[8]Cf. Paul D. Hanson, "Old Testament Apocalyptic Reexamined" [= his article in *Int* 25 (1971) 454–479] in *Visionaries and Their Apocalypses,* ed. Paul D. Hanson (Philadelphia: Fortress, 1983) 37–60, 48–58; *The Dawn of Apocalyptic* (Philadelphia: Fortress, 1975) 402–413.

[9]J. J. Collins, "Introduction: Towards the Morphology of a Genre," in *Apocalypse: The Morphology of a Genre, Semeia* 14 (1979) 1–20, 1.

characteristics when they try to determine what they (and others, even those who disagree on many of their points) recognize as an apocalypse.[10] At least one characteristic that many regularly adduce, pseudonymity, does not hold of John's Revelation. For, although Revelation is outstanding in that it is expressly entitled an apocalypse (Rev 1:1), its author clearly writes under his own name. Another criterion finds more general acceptance, namely, an at least occasional reference to ecstatic states (e.g., Rev 1:19; 4:1-2) and / or to being transported to an appropriate site (as in Rev 17:1-3a; 21:9-10a). One may also safely list related series of visions, otherworldly, usually angelic figures (particularly as interpreters), eschatological crises, and a keen concern for God's ultimate justice in his cosmically-conceived worldwide rule *(Weltherrschaft Gottes)*. Not all texts that can be classified as apocalyptic are necessarily apocalypses. This becomes evident, for instance, in passages like the Synoptics' presentation of Jesus' baptism (Mark 1:8-11 and parallels) and Paul's argument in Rom 5:12-21.

We may forego here the attempt to itemize the formal characteristics of the genre of what almost everyone concedes is an exceptionally good example of an apocalypse, namely, John's Book of Revelation. Worth special consideration, however, is the relationship of John's apocalypse to the "genre" known as gospel, particularly as gospel is expressed canonically (viz., in the NT). Canonical gospel form (that is, the enunciation of the good news about Jesus Christ—normative for faith—as found in the collection of inspired books) is not limited to the four story-form Gospels. It must also include the earlier, kerygmatic (or "headline") formulations of it, like the summary story-form used by

---

[10]To date, the best definition, though lengthy, is that offered by D. Aune, "The Apocalypse of John and the Problem of Genre," 65: "In *form,* an apocalypse is an autobiographical prose narrative reporting revelatory visions experienced by the author and structured to emphasize the central revelatory message. The *content* of an apocalypse is the communication of a transcendent, often eschatological, perspective on human experience. In *function,* an apocalypse legitimates the transcendent authority of the message by mediating a new revelatory experience for the audience to encourage them to modify their cognition and behavior in conformity with transcendent perspectives."

Peter to instruct Cornelius (Acts 10:34-43) or the credal-like statement of which Paul reminds the Corinthians (1 Cor 15:1-11, esp. vv. 3-5). Furthermore, in the light of Rom 1:15-17, which governs the series of expositions and controversies in Rom 1:19–8:39, the gospel can be set forth in argumentative terms which are quite different from any story-form presentation of it.

On the other hand, there is only one Gospel, as Paul himself affirms in Gal 1:7, 9, even as he recognizes that it would have to be adapted to different fora of apostolic endeavor (cf. Gal 2:7-8). Gospel "genre," therefore, stands out independently of any fixed literary mode of expression.[11] In this respect, it may well be unique among literary genres. Its essential features lie in its attested proclamation (attested both by its basis in Scripture, God's promissory word, and also by apostolic testimony) of the death and resurrection of Jesus Christ for the forgiveness of sins (and its corollary, salvation in his life-giving Spirit) as a call to faith in the Lord. John's Revelation supposes and recasts in apocalyptic prophecy the one Gospel. For attestation, he draws on his own prophetic experience (1:9-20) rather than on direct reference to apostolic tradition, though he surely supposes the latter (21:12). Thus, John's own contribution to the genre recognizable as "apocalypse" is innovatively to include in its very fabric another "genre," the Gospel of Jesus Christ.

Not a few have found Revelation to be at odds with the Gospel on the score of its alleged failure to stress the love of God, particularly as reflected in Christians' expected love of others, even of their persecutors. To many, indeed, Revelation seems to be vindictive (cf. 18:24), though it is hardly more so than some statements attributed by the Evangelists to Jesus Christ himself (e.g., Matt 23:34-36). One should not feel surprised to find no mention of love for one's enemies. For John's Gospel is also silent on this point, although it stresses the disciples' love for one another as the hallmark of Christianity and part of its testimony to the world (Jn 13:35). Revelation clearly acknowledges Jesus' sacrificial love for believers (1:5b-6; 3:9; 20:9) and for the saints in heaven (20:9), and expects Christians to love God (2:14, 19) even more than their own lives (12:11). Furthermore, in accord

---

[11]Cf. C. H. Giblin, "Confrontations in John 18, 1–27," *Bib* 65 (1984) 210–232, 210 n. 1.

with Christian tradition elsewhere, love of God supposes a practical love for one another (2:4, 19), for the Lord does not address a particular community as though it were a kind of "sandbox" of individual grains. What accounts for the absence of love for persecutors must be John's preoccupation with God's justice, particularly against the unrepentant.

As John uses the term, the "gospel" stresses the mystery of God as he announced it to (literally, as he "evangelized,"[12] *hōs euēggelisen)* his servants the prophets (10:7). That mystery, as the structure of Revelation discloses, precisely in the events introduced by the *blast of the seventh trumpet,* with which this mystery is identified (10:7), essentially includes a call to repentance. Thus, the angel flying in mid-heaven while holding the everlasting gospel *(euaggelion)* to announce *(euaggelisai)* to those dwelling on the earth, who are identified as all humanity (14:6), proclaims the message to fear and glorify the Creator, whose judgment is at hand (14:7). Since God's judgment stands as an essential feature of his kingly sway over the world, John's message accords quite well with that of Jesus himself (Mark 1:14-15). God's persistent offer of forgiveness is attested by unrepentance in spite of the signs of his judgment (9:20-21; 16:9, 11) and by actual conversions through the resurrection-ascension of his prophets (11:11-13). Forgiveness remains a possibility, hoped and prayed for by the saints victorious in heaven (15:2-4), up to the moment of the utter ruin of Babylon (19:17-21).[13] Lastly, the faithful, even in heavenly glory, do not gloat over the damnation of individuals. The vindication they deserve is achieved by the Lord, not by themselves. Fuller understanding of God's "vindictive" justice (as a rightfully wrathful, victorious achievement over evil— the root meaning of this word for retributive justice) requires that we survey a dominant, unifying theme of the major vision: God's Holy War of Liberation.

[12]For the transitive sense of this verb, cf. S. Thompson, *The Apocalypse and Semitic Syntax,* 22-23. Theologically, the transitive sense fits quite well, for, in receiving the gospel, the prophets are not just "spoken to" but are also moved, and undergo in their inaugural experiences a kind of religious conversion.

[13]Cf. C. H. Giblin, "Revelation 11. 1-13: Its Form, Function, and Contextual Integration," *NTS* 30 (1984) 433-459, 446, 450-454.

IV. The Holy War in Rev 4-22

Religious demagogues (and journalists) have recently popularized a notion of "Holy War" that bears little or no relation to the biblical concept of Holy War. In biblical terms, the focal point of that conflict is God's own, unaided defeat of the wicked oppressors of his people and his securing for them a lasting inheritance according to his promises. In its classic example, the Exodus,[14] God's people do not engage in belligerent action at all. Their role is to follow God's directives, and their physical activity amounts to little more than local motion from one dwelling to another. Elsewhere in the historical books, the people take a more active role, but their participation never amounts to Cromwellian self-justification over their foes. Insistently, warlike conduct finds its rationale, even if through controlled ritual, in God's own initiative and guidance. The theme of Holy War rises to a more transcendent expression in prophetic literature, notably in the Divine Warrior Hymns. There, God alone is exalted as combatant and victor.

Roland de Vaux pointed out that nowhere in the accounts of the early wars of Israel does there occur one in which all the several elements of the Holy War appear.[15] Nevertheless, he is able to amass from a number of the stories the characteristics of this in-

---

[14]Millard C. Lind holds—quite solidly—that the particularly Israelite view of the Holy War is found in Israel's experience of the Exodus, God's miraculous deliverance of his people through the prophet Moses. Israel's emphasis on the lack of human participation in battle is not a late theological reflection; *Yahweh is a Warrior: The Theology of Warfare in Ancient Israel* (Kitchener, Ont.: Herald, 1980) 170.

[15]Roland de Vaux, *Ancient Israel. Its Life and Institutions,* trans., J. McHugh (London: Darton, Longman & Todd, 1961), "The Holy War," 225-267. He also takes care to point out that Israel's Holy War was not a war of religion, that is, an attempt to impose its faith on others. R. de Vaux's summary is heavily indebted to G. von Rad's monograph (*see below,* note 16). More recent studies of aspects of God's Holy War as "wars of Yahweh," which move beyond "institutional" or even "cultic" facets of its theological thematic are also necessary. For example, Rudolf Smend speaks of Yahweh's deciding from the heavens the fight which was conducted on earth; *Yahweh's War and Tribal Confederation* trans. M. G. Rogers (Nashville: Abingdon, 1970) 27.

stitution.[16] The Book of Revelation remarkably contains a high percentage of them, perhaps all of them, if one makes necessary allowance for an apocalyptic transposition of the theme of Holy War. Moreover, as will emerge below, these elements occur in a similar narrative sequence, which imparts to the theme and to the vision of Revelation 22:4-22 itself a certain narrative coherence of no little importance.

The key elements of the Holy War, as inferred from the historical books of the OT, stand as follows:

1) The combatants, as God's people, had to be assembled and "made holy"; this consecration entailed remaining continent (chaste).

2) Oracles expressing the decision of Yahweh and sacrifices preceded the conflict.

3) The ark of the covenant, the visible sign of God's presence, figured as the palladium in the battle, and its presence was accompanied by the battle-cry *(t^{e}rû'āh)*.

4) In a number of passages, notably, at the fall of Jericho (Jos 6), horns or trumpets were sounded. Their principal function was to stress the religious character of the war, as God's people were remembered before the Lord (Num 10:9; 31:6).[17]

5) Faith on the part of God's people was the indispensable condition for victory.

6) During the battle, Yahweh fought for his people, calling into service the elements of nature and throwing the enemy into confusion by a divine terror.

[16]The basic monograph concerning the Holy War remains that of Gerhard von Rad, *Der Heilige Krieg im alten Israel* (Zürich: Zwingli, 1951).

[17]Significantly, this notion becomes prominent in the Qumran War Scroll (1QM); cf. Yigael Yadin, *The Scroll of the War of the Sons of Light Against the Sons of Darkness,* trans. B. and C. Rabin (Oxford: University Press, 1962) 113. The Qumran War Scroll, antedating John's Apocalypse by only a few decades, helps one understand why John places such emphasis on the trumpet septenary. John need not have known the work; the notion attested by 1QM was probably shared beyond the confines of Essene settlements near the Dead Sea.

7) The Holy War culminated in the *ḥērem,* the anathema executed on the vanquished enemy and his goods.

8) Ultimately, God's defense of his people resulted in secure possession of the land to which he had brought them (Deut 6:18; 7:1f.; 19:1), and which, of course, he had promised them.

In his ground-breaking study of the Holy War, Gerhard von Rad pointed out that the concept found new life even after the period of the last (historical) holy wars (Pss 44; 60; 18; 20) and underwent a "spiritualization" in post-exilic times (2 Chron 20:1-30; Pss 33:16-18; 147:10-11).[18] The "war-shout," for instance, becomes a hymn of praise (cf. 2 Chron 20:19).[19]

In a further study,[20] relying heavily on Isaiah 13 and 24, Ezekiel 7, and Joel 2, von Rad established the Holy War as the original context for the prophetic motif of the Day of the Lord. More recent investigations,[21] have enlarged the importance of the theme in later prophetic (very early apocalyptic) works of the OT, where it appears as the "Divine Warrior Hymn." Regular aspects of the hymn (as in Isa 26:16–27:6, for instance) include crisis (threat), war, victory, and feast (often expressed as rejuvenation of the land). This kind of hymn makes considerable use of mythological imagery. The "Day of the Lord" motif is obvious in Rev 6:12-17 (the fifth unsealing)—to cite but one text. A. Y. Collins has also found the features of the Divine Warrior Hymn in many pasages of Revelation,[22] although she tends to confuse a hymnic, "lyrical" motif with a structural analysis of John's *narrated* visions. Her observations, however, serve at the very least to show

[18]G. von Rad, *Der Heilige Krieg,* 80–83.

[19]Ibid., 81.

[20]G. von Rad, "The Origin of the Concept of the Day of Yahweh," *JSS* 4 (1959) 97–108.

[21]Cf. F. M. Cross, *Canaanite Myths and Hebrew Epic: Essays in the History of the Religion of Israel* (Cambridge: Harvard University Press, 1973) 79–90, 169–177; P. D. Hanson, "Zechariah 9 and the Recapitulation of an Ancient Ritual Pattern," *JBL* 92 (1973) 54–59; *The Dawn of Apocalyptic, passim;* William D. Millar, *Isaiah 24–27 and the Origin of Apocalyptic* (Missoula: Scholars, 1976) 104 ff.

[22]Adela Yarbro Collins, *The Combat Myth in the Book of Revelation* (Missoula: Scholars, 1976) 211–234.

that the theme of the Holy War, in its prophetic-apocalyptic trans-position, pulsates in John's thought and suffuses John's lengthy vision of God's battle for his people.

From the period immediately preceding the destruction of Jerusalem in A.D. 70, the War Scroll *(1QM)* of the Essene community at Qumran attests the importance of the Holy War thematic well into the first century of the Christian era. What is more, this document, for all its anti-gentile, nationalistic belligerence, and concrete, military expertise,[23] has a pervasively apocalyptic character. Most strikingly, perhaps, it expresses the theme of Holy War in a narrative (not declamatory or hymnic) manner—for all its concerns with specific directives—and describes a kind of militancy which offers profitable contrasts with that expressed in Revelation.[24]

Given the wide biblical background of the Holy War and its recurrence as an apocalyptic motif and narrative-style scenario of the end-time close to the period in which John wrote, John's use of it should not come as a surprise. Like other biblical data, however, the thematic of the Holy War is reborn in John's Christian perspective and according to his own creative genius.

That Revelation employs the notion of the Holy War has not passed unnoticed among recent commentators. The concept is evident in 6:17 (which speaks of the Day of Wrath of God and the Lamb) and 16:14 (the Great Day of God). R. Bauckham, for instance,[25] has carefully treated salient features of the Holy War in a number of particular passages:

1) John's representation of the conquering Messiah (the Lion of Judah, 5:5-6)—not to mention 19:11-31 (the Word of God on the white horse) which bears out 16:14 (the announcement of Armageddon).[26]

2) The messianic army in 7:2-14: the 144,000 numbered as in a census, which was a counting-up of the military strength of a nation or people.[27]

---

[23]Cf. Y. Yadin, *The Scroll of the War of the Sons of Light,* 114–197.

[24]R. Bauckham, "The Book of Revelation as a Christian War Scroll," *Neot* 22 (1988) 17–40, 30–34.

[25]Ibid., 30–34.

[26]Ibid., 19–21.

[27]Ibid., 21–28.

3) The army of celibates in 14:1-5, a metaphor for a characteristic of Christian life (fidelity), but recalling the OT requirement of "being undefiled by women" to be worthy soldiers of the Lord during the Holy War.[28]

In all these instances, of course, Revelation deliberately transposes physically belligerent conduct or preparedness in order to enunciate a spiritual thesis of suffering witness. Bauckham proves this thesis repeatedly. The triumph of God's army and that of the Lamb lies through its participation in Christ's death and resurrection, not in any physical combat of a destructive nature. At the same time, there is a real combat, not merely "passive resistance." The martyrs do overcome evil (cf. 12:11).

The theme of God's Holy War does not appear, however, only here and there in Revelation, nor according to just a few of the aspects considered basic to articulating this religious institution. In the major vision (4–22), the Holy War theme in *all* its essential institutional features *structures the entire course of events.*[29] Its various components also cohere strikingly with the literary structure of Revelation as already outlined in this introduction.

Thus, §I represents in its central portion (5:1-5) the elder's reassurance to John that the Lion of Judah, the conquering root of David, is able to open the sealed book of destinies. Although Jesus Christ, the Lion, derives this power from his being the sacrificial Messiah, slain and risen (the slain Lamb standing, 5:6-7), it is precisely in terms of warlike, royal supremacy that he is introduced

---

[28]Ibid., 28–30. Sexual relations were forbidden for those to be engaged in God's Holy War. Hence, the victorious army of Revelation is represented as celibates. Allusion to the Holy War helps also to dissipate the problem many may have in supposing "sexism" or "male chauvinism" in 14:4a.

[29]The theme may also be discerned somewhat in the inaugural vision, which presents the risen Lord with the two-edged broadsword as his word (1:16), and also in the seven proclamations, which conclude with promises to the "victor." These promises, most of which John later depicts as verified in a heavenly state after death and / or in the new creation (the heavenly Jerusalem manifested at the general resurrection) serve to predict the "promised land," which is the positive result or fruit of the term and goal (*telos*) of the Holy War.

into the major vision. The Lamb's seven horns and seven eyes then underscore the motif of sovereign power and dominance.

§II (the unsealings) contains the equivalent of "oracles" for the coming events. After announcing the theme of victory and of ongoing, earthly tribulations (the four horsemen), this section enunciates the crisis in terms of the martyrs' call for vindication (the fifth unsealing) and (with the sixth unsealing and its enlargement), God's response to it: the coming Day of the Lord and the triumph of the assembled army of the saints. The "purity of the army," since it is viewed spiritually as effected through the "combat" itself (7:14)—an important theological modification perhaps proper to John's presentation of the Holy War—is only proleptically noted at this point. The same "purity" will be described expressly in the re-presentation of the 144,000 victors in 14:1-4. The "panic striking the foe" is also depicted quite adequately under the sixth seal (6:15-17), and reappears later as the trumpet-septenary escalates: with the fifth trumpet (= the first woe), 9:6—and probably with the enlargement of the sixth as well, 11:13a (but with the enemy's "surrender" in repentance). With the seventh unsealing, a "sacrifice" is enacted: the offering to God of the prayers of the saints in conjunction with the ominous casting of fire upon the earth, and the readying of the angels to sound the trumpets for the great engagement.

§III heralds the engagement itself (the first six trumpets) and brings it to its climax (the seventh). In this septenary, John begins to attend to God's power over the forces of nature. This power was implied, of course, as early as the epiphanic manifestations of voices, thunders, and lightnings from the throne in 4:5, and in what was "given" to various preliminary figures (the four horsemen), strikingly in the role of Death and Hades, 6:7-8. It was vividly sketched in the sixth unsealing, which expressly stated the motif of the Holy War. Nevertheless, the expanded description of God's power over the elements commences formally with the septenary of the trumpets, and recalls in many ways the plagues with which God smote the Egyptians prior to the Exodus. Manifestations of God's power over nature will continue in Revelation until the manifestation of the new creation (21:5-6), the apocalyptic version of the promised land. The seventh trumpet ushers in the "great tribulation" (as the elder explained in 7:14). The unfolding elements of the sequence of "signs" occur "in the days of the sound of the seventh angel, when he blows his trumpet," as the angel swore in 10:7, and they fulfill the gospel mystery of the advent of God's kingdom (with its urgent summons to repentance as the alternative to wrath—another characteristically Johannine modification of Holy War imagery).[30]

At the outset of the seventh trumpet, the "victory shout" appears as a declaration of God's worldwide kingly sway and as a prayerful thanksgiving (11:15-18). In conjunction with this—also as part of §*A*—the ark of the covenant, the palladium of God's Holy War, is made manifest in heaven (11:19) with heavenly portents (v. 19b) that will reach their consummation in the *ḥērem* (ultimate annihilation) inflicted upon Babylon (16:18, 21). At the close of the seventh-trumpet events (§*A'*), God's "tent of testimony" appears in heaven (15:5), recalling in a promissory way his dwelling with Israel after delivering them from Egypt. The consummation of the New Exodus itself has just been celebrated in the same sub-section (§*A'*, 15:2-4; the victory hymn of Moses and the Lamb). The passages framed by §§*A* and *A'* depict, through expressly labeled "signs," key figures in the cosmic conflict that moves from heaven to earth (§*B*, 12:1-18) and to its coming resolution upon earth (§*B'*, 15:1). Within these signs are counterpoised the scenarios of earthly oppression (§*C*, 13:1-18) and heavenly-sent portents of reward and requital (§*C'*, 14:16-20). At the center of each of these counterpoised sections, John notes correlated aspects of the saints' patient endurance: their need to be ready to suffer (§*C*, 13:9-10) and the Spirit's assurance of their reward (§*C'*, 14:13), Lastly, strategically situated at the very center of the whole concentric, (*ABCDC'B'A'*), format of the events proclaimed "in the days of the seventh angel" who has sounded his trumpet, stands the precious vignette of the victorious army of the Lamb (§*D*, 14:1-5). The army's fruit of victory lies in a heavenly state (cf. 7:1-17), which will later be described as the millennium, the first resurrection (20:4-6).

[30]One may find this motif adumbrated in OT prophetic literature, notably in early apocalyptic (Joel 2:12-29; cp. Ps 7:12). For John, however, there is no distinction within the true Israel between Jews and Gentiles, and the latter are not reduced to tributaries of the former. In this connection, the Holy War "ultimatum" expressed in Psalm 2 (esp. v. 11) is most illuminating. I am indebted to Luis Alonso-Schökel for the apt term, "*ultimatum*."

The ultimate resolution of the entire Holy War requires a two-fold event consequent upon the battle, namely, the annihilation *(ḥērem)* inflicted on the corrupt (and, in John, culpably unreformable) foe or set of foes as the negative corollary of God's people's secure inheritance of the promised land. Accordingly, §IV (the sequence of libation-bowls) depicts the last plagues on the unrepentant, focusing (in the seventh) upon Babylon, but also announcing (in the sixth plague) the forthcoming battle of Armageddon (depicted at the beginning of §VI, 19:11-21). In §V (17:1-19:10), an interpretation-scene retrospectively views the ruin visited upon Babylon. The progressive narrative, resumed in §VI (19:1-21:8), deals with the remaining eschatological adversaries and moves from Armageddon to the creation of the new heavens and earth to the new Jerusalem. The intrinsic complementarity of the ultimate resolution of the Holy War is evidenced by the two, paired interpretation-scenes (§§V and VII) which focus, respectively, on the *ḥērem* inflicted on the whore, Babylon, and on the new creation, the New Jerusalem as the bride of the Lamb.

Angelic interpretations at the conclusion of the Holy War (i.e., §§V and VII) as well as interpretations by angelic equivalents (the elders in §I, 5:5, and in §II, 7:13-17, and still again in §III, 11:16)[31]

---

[31]The actions of the elders are limited to the ambience of the heavenly scene, as befits a royal-priestly cortege that is privy to "what is actually going on" in the heavenly court. Hence, they can reassure or inform John of exceptionally important events which he must grasp (5:5; 7:13-14a). Angels, on the other hand, regularly perform some action before they explain anything, and conversely, their explanation almost always concerns something in which they have been involved. This can be seen even in the case of the "libation-bowl angels" of §§V and VII. (In §VII, the angel can show John the New Jerusalem because its appearance is the intrinsic result of the last plagues, in which he was instrumental).

The earthly *engagement* does not really begin until the casting of fire to earth and the trumpet septenary. Angels, not elders, figure in that engagement. Except for their "interpretative" heavenly hymns (11:16; 19:4) and their helping to define (by their own presence) that Mt. Zion is heaven (14:3), the elders do not appear after Revelation 7:13-17. Thus, they do not figure in the earthly engagement in the way the angels do, but function as God's wise courtiers.

Their number, "twenty-four" (a doubling or "superlative" of twelve) do not figure as incidental additions to John's dramatic, visionary narrative. Indeed, they seem essentially to articulate the pervasive motif of the Holy War. Other angelic speakers do the same. In §III (10:2, 5-8), the altogether awesome "world-angel" (standing on earth and sea, haloed by the rainbow, and having a face like the sun), apparently a "stand-in" for the Lord Jesus Christ, commands attention. He proclaims the coming climax of the engagement (viz., the events ushered in by the seventh trumpet) and John's sweet-but-bitter task of prophesying it. Like the elder in 5:5, who consoles John, this angel furthers John's understanding of the well-integrated series of visions of the Holy War, and does not interrupt it (as if introducing a new, distinct "part" of the visionary continuum). John, too, must suffer (albeit little more, symbolically, than "indigestion") to achieve his Christian witness as a prophet. In §IV (16:5-6), the third libation-bowl angel, interpreting his own action (as angel of the fresh waters), proclaims a fitting realization of God's holiness as the Almighty, the king of the nations (cf. 15:3-4), shown in his vindication of the prayers of the martyrs (6:10—setting up the vision of the coming Day of the Lord in 6:12–7:17). Accordingly, the (angel of the) altar, featured (silently) in the fiery sacrificial omens of 8:3-5 at the moment the trumpet-angels had been readied, appositely adds his endorsement (16:17) of the angel of the waters. Lastly, angels

may perhaps represent their being heavenly representatives of a cosmic or universal Israel of God.

The elders before whom the Lord manifests his glory (Ps 47:8-10) in the Holy War (Isa 24:23) may be representations of the nations (*Völkerwelt*), according to Hans Wildberger, *Jesaja 2 (Jesaja 13–27)* (BKAT X, 2; Neukirchen: Neukirchener Varlag, 1978) 949–950. But this does not explain the *number*. Now, given the elders' association with the four living beings, which are colored by astrological allusions, their own number, "twenty-four," probably alludes (as Gunkel suggested long ago) to the twenty-four stars beyond the zodiac, half in the north, half in the south, those visible assigned to the world of the living and the rest to the world of the dead, and all of them called "Judges of the Universe" (*dikastai tōn holōn*); cf. Diodorus Siculus, *World History (Bibliothēkē)*, II, 31. In Revelation, the twenty-four enthroned elders declare with thanksgiving the time of God's judgment for the living and the dead (Rev 11:16-18). As usual, John creatively blends OT imagery with pagan imagery in a Christian fresco of God's world-encompassing reign.

stand out prominently in heralding Armageddon (§VI, 19:17-18; and perhaps the meaning of the holy city, 21:3-4) as well as within the first of the paired angelic interpretation-scenes (§V, 18:1-3, 21-24), which deals with the ruin of Babylon. The sequence of prayers in Revelation moves from voices celebrating creation and then redemption (4–5)[32] to a plea for vindication (6:10). This prayer of complaint evokes, with the next unsealing (6:12ff.), the first unambiguous preview of the Holy War.[33] Subsequent praise of God or affirmations of his justice always occur only on or from the heavenly plane and articulate God's triumph in the Holy War (notably: 11:15-18; 12:10-12; 15:3-4; 16:5-8; 19:1-4, 6-8). Significantly, no canticles follow the alleluias of Rev 19:1-4, 6-8. For, with the celebration of the inseparably two-fold event of the ruin inflicted on the whore and of the wedding of the Lamb (to the bride, the New Jerusalem), the theme of God's War on behalf of the faithful has reached its intended term.

V. *Concerning the Translation*

Following the text of Nestle-Aland's twenty-sixth edition of the Greek NT, the translation given in the following pages strives both to be very exact and also to remain quite readable. Where necessary for idiomatic English, words not in the Greek text have been

[32]Cf. Klaus-Peter Jörns, *Das hymnische Evangelium. Untersuchungen zu Aufbau, Funktion und Herkunft der hymnischen Stücke in der Johannesoffenbarung* (Gütersloh: Mohn, 1971) 40–42. Jörns stresses (in Revelation 4) the theme of divine judgment. This theme, on the contrary, does not appear in any of the hymns or prayers until the martyrs call for judgment in 6:10. The *potential* for judgment surely lies in the setting of the scene and, subsequently, in the Messianic Lion's ability to unseal the book (Revelation 5). The unsealing will disclose both God's wrath and that of the Lamb (6:16-17). But the opening scene (§I, 4:1–5:17) paints in ever-widening circles (cf. *kyklothen,* "roundabout," 4:3; 4:6; 5:11) centered on the Enthroned (4:1-2 ff.) and the Lamb (5:6, 13) a kind of liturgical worship in the heavenly sanctuary (*naos*—so denominated when the victorious martyrs are pictured as having entered it, 7:15).

[33]For the four horsemen, evoked by the four living beings, representatives of creation, have only a general scope, as "preliminaries" to the Day of the Lord, first announced clearly under the sixth unsealing.

added in parentheses. Square brackets have been used to enclose an alternative expression or to indicate a very literal rendering of John's Greek. The whole text appears in a kind of "video-format." That is, by spacing between lines and by a minimal use of indentations of lines or groups of lines, the literary unity, coherence, and emphasis of John's visions has been made to emerge more clearly. The attentive reader can thus "see" the structure of John's orderly visions and comments. By measured, oral reading, one can also better "hear" the text. A general overview precedes each portion of the translated text, and particular comments follow it. The latter are not given according to what von Dobschütz (even in 1909) lamented as "the old, glossatorial method," which still governs most commentaries, but are offered by way of paragraph-style clarification.

THE PROLOGUE (1:1-8)

John's written communication to the Seven Churches has been placed within a liturgical dialogue.[34] This dialogue appears in the first eight verses (for the text, *see* below) and will reappear again only at the close of Revelation (22:6b-21). In the Prologue (1:1-8), a speaker (who seems to function as a kind of "president of the assembly") announces the subject, the audience, and the author of the communication (vv. 1-2) and pronounces a blessing (the beatitude in v. 3) on the lector and on the attentive audience (the community). The lector then reads aloud John's letter-style greeting (vv. 4-5a) and the community responds (vv. 5b-6) with a doxology based on the redemption already accomplished for them. The speaker then announces the further coming of the crucified one (v. 7), to which the community responds with an "Amen" (v. 7c). Lastly, the speaker pronounces an oracle in the Lord's name (v. 8), enlarging the statement (cf. v. 4c) in John's own greeting. The liturgical dialogue then yields to the actual reading of John's own communication (1:9).

Recognizing this dialogue-setting should enable the reader to perceive that the Book of Revelation is John's letter as read to and accepted by a group of Christians assembled to hear the word of the Lord. Unlike other apocalypses, whether they be biblical books like Daniel or the many intertestamental works, the Book

[34]Cf. Ugo Vanni, *L'Apocalisse: Ermeneutica, esegesi, teologia* (Bologna: Dehoniane, 1988) 73-97, 101-114.

of Revelation has a more definable context. It was received not just by the Seven Churches addressed at its outset, but by the Christian community of a subsequent time that recognized it as a prophetic message addressed to itself.

1:1-8

1 ¹   A revelation of Jesus Christ
which God gave him
to show to his servants what must soon happen;
and he made (it) known
by sending his angel to his servant John
² who bore testimony to the word of God
and to the testimony from [of] Jesus
Christ (amounting to) all that he saw.
³ Blessed is he who reads (aloud)
and those who listen to the words of this prophecy
and keep the things written in it;
for the time is near.

⁴ John to the seven churches in (the Province of) Asia:
grace to you and peace
from who is and who was and who is coming
and from the seven spirits before his throne

⁵ and from Jesus Christ
the faithful witness
the first-born from the dead
and the ruler of the kings of the earth.

To him who loves us
and who has redeemed us from our sins by his blood—
⁶ and he (actually) made us (to be) a kingdom,
priests to his God and Father—
to him (is) glory and dominion for ever and ever. Amen.
⁷ Behold,
he is coming with the clouds
and every eye will see him,
even all those who pierced him,
and all the tribes of the earth will mourn because of him.
Yes; Amen.

8   I am the Alpha and the Omega, says the Lord God,
    who is and who was and who is coming,
    the Almighty [*ho Pantokratōr*].

The speaker announces the subject of John's communication
as an awe-inspiring manifestation ("apocalypse/revelation") of
Jesus Christ. The revelation concerns Jesus Christ but, more precisely, the genitive ("of/from") indicates in this context that it
has been given by him. He has received from the Father a disclosure intended for his servants, the Christian community, about
the imminent future. The temporal perspective here is not that
of clock-and-calendar time, but that which deals with the fulfillment of Christian life in the "last days," the end-time of religious history in this creation. The disclosure is made to John not
by Jesus as physically present in the proper, flesh-and-blood
sense—for that will occur with the parousia or second coming
itself—but in sign-form. Jesus has made the revelation known
(literally, "signified it," *esēmanen*) by sending his angel to John
(cp. 22:16). The term "angel" here builds upon OT usage of "the
angel of the Lord" not as a distinct person but rather as the Lord
himself in a certain visible form proper to visionary experiences.
Making known or "signifying" the events to come will entail both
vision and interpretation (cf. Dan 2:45 [LXX]). In receiving the
revelation (v. 2), John has borne a twofold witness: to God's own
word and to the testimony, the sworn, unalterable assurance of
Jesus Christ himself.
    The speaker then pronounces a blessing both on the lector and
on the audience listening to this prophecy. In 1 Cor 14:26-32, St.
Paul indicates that various communications formed part of the
early Christian liturgy. Among them was an "apocalypse" (1 Cor
14:26), which he seems to equate with a form of prophecy (vv.
29-30). Clearly, the length of an apocalypse like that to which
Paul refers would not run to the length of Revelation, which would
take days to read aloud. John's Apocalypse, however, seems to
be a highly developed orchestration of the kind of thing to which
Paul refers, and also to find its proper setting as a liturgical communication in which the prophet is God's spokesman. The close
of the beatitude repeats the theme of events close at hand (cp.
v. 1). In large measure, the insistence on imminence serves to make
the audience attentive to what is certain to affect their own lives.

In short, "imminence" is a way of expressing, in the standard perspective of apocalyptic, "immediate relevance." No actual computation of time is ever given in Christian apocalyptic literature. The end is near, for Christians live in the "end-time," but the day and hour are not matters for human disclosure or human knowledge, even for that of Jesus as the Revealer.[35]

John's epistolary greeting (vv. 4-5), read by the lector, is directed to seven churches located clockwise along the post-road in the westernmost Roman province ("Asia") of what is now Turkey. The greeting "grace and peace," highlighting God's personal favor (grace) and the theme of messianic reconciliation (peace) may be indebted to Paul, at least remotely. The source of this particular greeting, a form of blessing, initially strikes one as unusual. First, John refers to God the Father (using deliberately a grammatical solecism) as "he being and he was and he coming"—

---

[35]Cf. Mark 13:32; Matt 24:36. "No one knows x except. . . ." describes idiomatically (in a manner closely paralleled in Revelation 2:17b and 19:12-13) the personal prerogative and / or "business" of the one who *does* know x or concerning x. To devise a homely illustration: "Concerning shoemaking no one knows, neither the butcher nor the baker (but only the shoemaker)." Luke certainly interpreted the Marcan saying in the sense that the times were none of the disciples' business. For he avoids repeating in his own Gospel Mark 13:32, only to rewrite it in Acts 1:7.

Inevitably, a believing human's imagination will suggest either that the Day of the Lord will occur soon in chronological time or that it will not. In neither case, however much one's imagination holds sway, is the validity of faith itself in question. Most early Christians, especially in their "first fervor," must have been strongly under the impression that the Lord would return within one (or two or perhaps three) biological generations. St. Paul himself evidently shared this view, at least prior to writing 2 Corinthians 5:1-10. But this wishful thinking was erroneous. Nonetheless, as long as Christians held to the truth that they *did not know* (cf. Rev 16:15; 1 Thess 5:1-2), their faith was fully intact. In some cases, of course, when there was question of fidelity to apostolic tradition, their temporal perspective had to be corrected (2 Thess 2:1-17; 2 Pet 3:1-13). To some degree, even adult believers have been like schoolboys who think that the shorter the absence of the teacher from the classroom the sooner he will return, and the longer his absence, the longer it will take him to return—if, indeed, they should worry about his sudden re-entry at all. Actually, they *do not know when*. . . .

which has to be translated idiomatically as "who is and who was and who is coming." John does so in order to present the eternal, historically active Christian God in a way which polemically counters a pagan; pantheistic notion of Isis, "all that has been and is and will be."[36] God is not "all," and he will not just "be," but will come, that is, will personally manifest himself in judgment and salvation. Second, John speaks of a greeting from the seven spirits before God's throne. Although many have attempted to see in these seven spirits the fullness of the Holy Spirit, the phrase fits better with apocalyptic imagery when construed as "the angels of the presence," that is, as representing God's heavenly court and his omniscient and effective contact with the whole of his creation. They stand obediently in the service of God ("before his throne," 1:4; 4:5) and become the instruments of Jesus Christ as well (3:1; 5:6).[37] Third, John conveys a greeting from Jesus Christ with a threefold emphasis. He is the faithful witness (that is, the exalted Christ, the one believers can rely upon because he has proved himself true by confirming God's work through his death). He is the first to rise from the dead (cf. Rom 8:29; Col 1:15) and thus the one who guarantees the resurrection of those who acknowledge him. Consequently, he is also the universal messianic Lord (cf. Isa 55:4b).

[36]Plutarch, *De Iside et Osiride,* 9, records the inscription on the statue of Isis in Sais: "I am everything that has been, is, and will be" (*egō eimi pan to gegonos kai on kai esomenon*). Cf. W. C. van Unnik, "A Formula Describing Prophecy," *NTS* 9 (1962 f.) 86–94, 91.

[37]John understands the Holy Spirit as the one who speaks to and through the prophets, not as an attendant in the heavenly court. Besides, the order in which the seven spirits are placed in this greeting seems to be at odds with John's relating the Spirit to the Father and to Jesus as its source (19:10b; 22:6b). The "seven spirits before his throne" (1:4) reappear in 8:2 in a new guise for a further, new function as "the seven angels who stand before God." One is hardly to suppose that John had failed to mention them earlier, in his elaborate description of the throne vision. Besides, the definite article supposes they have been mentioned earlier. The importance of the trumpet angels in Revelation (from 8:1 through 15:8 [cf. 10:7, ". . . in the days of the seventh angel, when he is going to blow his trumpet. . . ."]) helps account for their special mention in the salutation of 1:4. *John's opening greeting reflects his standpoint as a witness of what he has seen in his heavenly visions.*

Responding to this greeting (vv. 5b-6) the community glorifies
Jesus Christ as the eternal Lord, His love is present and enduring; he has freed us from our sins by his passion; he has made
us to be a royal power as priests to his God and Father. The royal
power or "kingdom" describes here the present status of the faithful on earth. John derives the text from the promissory covenant
of Exod 19:3-6, and will refer to it subsequently at least twice
more, apropos of the saints in heaven (5:10; 20:6). The theme
of the priestly kingdom figures prominently in Revelation. Exod
19:3-6 is the only OT text which John employs more than once.
In using it, he does not intend to speak of a ministerial priesthood but of the "redeemed" as sharing Christ's own triumph.
Ultimately, the status of the faithful derives from their baptism.
Nevertheless, as the later instances make clear, especially 20:6,
the "priestly kingdom" covers the whole "communion of saints"
and implies that its members will have lived out their redemption
by sharing in tribulations for the Lord's sake and by therefore
enjoying with him, even before the general resurrection, a heavenly
"first resurrection."

The speaker of the assembly then cites a combination of scrip-
tural passages (v. 7: Dan 7:13; Zech 12:10) which announce the
coming of the Lord both as triumphant Son of Man and as identified with the crucified one. John's emphasis falls on this identification and on the world-wide recognition of it (note the
insistence on the words "*every* eye," "*all* the tribes of the earth"),
not on the aspect of mourning. Probably, John hopes for the conversion of the world (cp. 14:6-7; 15:4b). "Mourning" is mentioned
to identify the triumphant Lord as the one who was the Suffering Servant as well. The community responds with an "amen"
both in Greek and in Hebrew, attesting God's promissory word
and their trust in it.

In v. 8 the speaker concludes with an oracle reaffirming the
opening phrase in John's written greeting (v. 4): ". . . who is
and was and is coming." The oracle adds two elements. First,
at the beginning, the speaker declares that God is the beginning
and end of all communication (the first and last letters of the
Greek alphabet, *alpha* and *omega,* standing for the beginning and
the end of whatever can be said or written).[38] Second, at the end,

[38]At a later time, they were taken to refer to elements of the universe.
In John's context, the implied reference to "whatever can be said or writ-

he underscores God's power as almighty *(ho Pantokratōr).* The "Almighty" will repeatedly be hailed as such in Revelation (1:8; 4:8; 11:17; 15:3; 16:7, 14; 19:6, 15; 21:22). *Pantokratōr* is the term regularly used in the Greek Bible [LXX] to translate the Hebrew word *ṣᵉbā'ôt* ("armies") in the phrase "Lord God of hosts [armies]." The imagery is that of Yahweh the Warrior as commanding the hosts of heaven (an angelic army) in the Holy War. Cf. 2 Sam 5:10; 7:8-11; Jos 4:13; Amos 4:13 (where it is clearly tied to God's being the Creator); Mic 4:1-4 (of the ultimate goal of peace). Appositely, then, Rev 1:8 states the cohesive thematic of the entire apocalypse as God's coming in the Holy War. Jesus applies to himself the title "Alpha and Omega" and, equivalently, the whole verse (1:1) when, at the close of the apocalyptic prophecy, he announces his own coming (22:13). This is John of Patmos's way of saying that Jesus and the Father are One. The oracle does not call for a response (even an amen) other than the further reading of John's own prophetic vision, which begins with v. 9.

ten" surely looks primarily to the eschatological message which John has heard and has written down. In the epilogue to Revelation, Jesus predicates Alpha and Omega of himself (22:13), affirming the scope of John's revelation, as finalized in the parousia (22:7, 12). The expression also reveals (in anti-magical polemic) that Yahweh cannot be controlled; *see below,* note 103.

THE FIRST MAJOR PART (1:9-3:22)

The Inaugural Vision (1:9-20)

John recounts his experience on Patmos on the Lord's Day, the regular Sunday feast celebrating the resurrection of Jesus Christ.[39] He had a mystical experience (v. 10: "I was in the Spirit") and had a twofold vision. The first part (vv. 10-11) is auditory, commanding him to write seven Churches. The second part (vv. 12-20), which is visual, complements the first, but is clearer and more imposing. The visual part encompasses the awesome sight of the triumphant Son of Man (vv. 12-16), John's reaction (v. 17a), the Lord's reassurance and his amplified command to write (vv. 17b-20). A customary apocalyptic format appears: after a visionary experience, the seer feels overwhelmed, incapacitated (cp. Dan 7:15; 8:15-19). Here, John's reaction recalls the OT axiom that one cannot see God and live; he falls down "as if dead" (v. 17a). With the Lord's strengthening reassurance, however, the meaning and scope of the vision are interpreted—here, by the very one who has been heard and seen. John's experience falls into the category of "inaugural prophetic experiences" (cf. Isa 6:1-13; Ezek 1:1-3:27; Jer 1:4-19), but stands out as unique. He sees the triumphant, risen Christ, described in terms borrowed from OT images of God himself as well as of the Son of Man in Dan 7. The message is urgent, covering what John has just seen (the risen Lord), the current situation (namely, the needs of the seven

[39]For the discussion, cf. U. Vanni, *L'Apocalisse,* 87-97.

44

churches), and what will occur hereafter (suggesting not only the future of each but also, as Rev 4:1 will make clear, a world-wide vision for all the churches) (v. 19). For the speaker, like God the Father (1:8), is "the first and the last" (1:17b; cp. 22:13).

1:9-20

9   I, John,
> your brother,
> and a sharer with you in tribulation, kingdom,
>> and patient endurance in Jesus,
> was on the island called Patmos
>> because of the word of God and testimony from [of] Jesus.

10   I was (rapt) in the Spirit on the Lord's day
and I heard behind me a great voice like that of a trumpet,
11   saying:
> What you see write in a book
> and send (the book) to the(se) seven churches:
>> to Ephesus
>> and to Smyrna
>> and to Pergamum
>> and to Thyatira
>> and to Sardis
>> and to Philadelphia
>> and to Laodicea!

12   And I turned to see the voice that was speaking with me;
and, after turning, I saw
> seven golden lampstands
13   and in the midst of the lampstands one like a Son of Man, [quite like a man]

> clothed with an ankle-length robe
> and girded at the base of his chest with a golden band;
14   his head and hair (were) white as wool (is) white as snow,
> and his eyes like (the) blaze of fire,
15   and his feet like flashing bronze, as in a refining-furnace,
> and his voice as the voice of cascading [many] waters;
16   and (he was) holding in his right hand seven stars,
> and from his mouth (was) issuing a sharp, two-edged broadsword,

and his countenance (was) as the sun shines in its full
strength.

17   And when I saw him, I fell at his feet as one (who drops)
dead.
And he placed his right hand upon me, saying:

18   Do not be afraid!
I am the first and the last
and the living one;
and I was dead,
and behold I am living for ever and ever,
and I hold the keys of Death and of Hades [Burial/the
Grave].

19   Write, therefore,
the things you saw
and the things that are
and the things which will occur hereafter.

20   (As for) the mystery of the seven stars which you saw in
my right hand,
and the seven golden lampstands:
the seven stars are angels of the seven churches,
and the seven lampstands are the seven churches.

John writes in his own name. Unlike other apocalypses, Revelation is not pseudonymous—cast as the work of someone more
famous in the past. John of Patmos cannot be equated with any
of the Twelve (for they are a special group, belonging to the past;
18:20; 21:14), and he qualifies as a prophet (cf. 22:18), not an
Evangelist. Nor does he speak with the authority shown by John
(the Elder), the author of the Johannine epistles. He introduces
himself as a fellow Christian who has in common both the negative and positive aspects of his hearer's lives, namely, their trials
and a share in the kingdom, and who also works out this life in
"patient endurance," the day-to-day corollary of the virtue of
hope. He writes of his experiences on what was probably a place
of political exile, Patmos, although the island was not remote,
since it lay on a trade route between Ephesus and Rome.[40] He
suffered there for his preaching and his witness to Jesus, although

[40]Cf. Henry Barclay Swete, *The Apocalypse of St. John* (London:
Macmillan, ²1907) 12.

his later whereabouts are unknown. John underlines the liturgical circumstances of his vision (Sunday, the Lord's Day; cf. *Didachē* 14; Ign., *Magnesians,* 19), not the date. Where OT prophetic books were not infrequently dated according to the years of a reigning monarch, Revelation highlights the liturgical celebration of the Lord's resurrection. Jesus Christ is the ever-reigning monarch.

The mystical experience to which John refers ("rapt in the Spirit") will later be recalled and heightened at the beginning (4:1) of the major vision (— Second Main Part of Revelation) and again at the outset of the twin interpretation-scenes concerning the fall of Babylon (17:1) and the advent of the New Jerusalem (21:10). Accordingly, this inaugural experience opens out not only into the missives to the seven churches but also into the grand, general vision of Part Two and into interpretations of its climactic moments: the destruction of the godless city, Babylon the whore, and the manifestation of the city of God, Jerusalem, the bride of the Lamb. With a clarion call, a voice commands John to write each of seven churches, moving north from the metropolitan center, Ephesus, to Smyrna and to Pergamum, and thence south to Thyatira, Sardis, Philadelphia, and Laodicea. All seven communities will read all of these communications (for a concluding formula in each speaks of heeding what the Spirit says to the churches), though each missive proves to have special relevance to a particular community. There may well have been other, outlying communities, but the group of seven represents a fully adequate totality, and all the communications look directly to an urban environment.

John then recounts his vision of the one ("the voice") who was speaking to him (1:12). He does not see a menorah, but seven individual lampstands in the midst of which is a genuinely human image *(homoion . . .)* but appearing in an other-worldly, triumphant transfiguration as Son of Man, the heavenly judge. His clothing (v. 13), described in two lines, is both priestly and royal (cf. Exod 28:4, 27; Wis 18:24; Jos., *Antiquities* 3.15; 1 Macc 10:89). The seven descriptions of his body combine images both religious and secular which stress universal sovereignty and the power of displaying irresistible strength; in particular, they convey the impression that the one beheld is the sovereign judge of the world.

His head and hair are white (v. 14), like those of God depicted as the Ancient of Days who judges the world (Dan 7:13; *1 Enoch* 71:10); the amplification, "as wool is white as snow" stresses blinding brilliance rather than color. His eyes (v. 14b) shine like those of the angelic figure, Gabriel, responding to supplication (Dan 10:6) and, more appositely, like those of one exercising divine judgment (Rev 2:18; 19:11-12). His feet (v. 15a) appear like a blazing metal alloy of silver and gold *(chalkolibanon),* gleaming like molten brass—probably conveying a sense of stability in contrast to an image like that of the statue with reenforced feet of terra cotta (Dan 2:33-34). His voice (v. 15b) sounds like a mighty cataract or waterfall ("many waters," in John's limited, Semitic idiom), which recalls the ambience of the Almighty as Ezekiel described him (Ezek 1:24; 43:2). His right hand, like figures of the Roman Emperor on imperial coins,[41] grasps seven stars (v. 16a)—the seven heavenly "wanderers" or "planets" as reckoned in John's day—which are later (v. 20) identified as the directors in some sense of the Seven Churches. Thus, the Lord of the world is not Caesar but Jesus Christ, and his royal sovereignty is expressed particularly in terms of the heavenly (supernatural) character of the communities on earth to which John must write. From the Son of Man's mouth (v. 16b) issues the sword of judgment, which Isaiah had used of the messianic Servant (Isa 49:2; cf. 11:4). Lastly (v. 16c), John speaks of the Lord's countenance, like that which Jgs 5:31 uses of the friends of God: the sun in full strength—not just rising, however (Jgs 5:31), but continually and mightily shining, an image of the unconquerable, *sol invictus.*

The vision overwhelms the seer. With words and touch, however, reminiscent of Matthew's account of Jesus' reassurance to his disciples after the transfiguration (Mt 17:7), Christ the Redeemer, who is the first and the last (cf. Isa 44:6), enables John to overcome his fear and take up the writing task assigned to him with assurance. In his Christian perspective, John bases that assurance on Jesus' being the ever-living one who rose from the dead and thus has power over death and the grave. "Hades" (the pit / burial / the grave), paired with "death," expresses the dread

[41]Cf. G. R. Beasley-Murray, *Revelation* (Grand Rapids: Eerdmans, [2]1978) 69-70.

finality, from a human standpoint, of death itself. For pagans, as even for the ancient Hebrews, there was no hope of a real, fully human life after death; at best, one could hope for a shadowy spiritual existence which was more consoling than the fate of the wicked. Christ, however, has conquered death and its apparently inevitable result, the mouldering grave. Although John does not seem to develop the point in a Pauline sense, one may reflect that Christ conquered death not by avoiding it, but by going through it and passing beyond it to fully human, renewed existence. Hence, death can do no more than what it did to Jesus, nor can those in Christ remain entombed. Jesus Christ's power as the risen Lord supplies further assurance and insurance to the churches to which John is commanded to write.

Whether or not v. 20 is a gloss (that is, a marginal clarification which was later worked into the text of Revelation), it fits well with the scope of this vision, and provides a smooth transition to the seven missives which John is about to pen. In the scope of this vision, the "seven stars" suggest permanent, heavenly types (and guardian angels) of the seven corresponding (and perhaps very flickering or else steadily shining) lampstands on earth, the seven churches. The stars express the Lord's universal rule, whereas a given church may falter, in which case (as the most prominent church, Ephesus, is warned; 2:5), its lampstand will be removed; that is, it will disappear.

The Seven Proclamations (2:1–3:22)

The so-called "Seven Letters," which follow a very consistent format, are not actually letters, for they do not conform to any known "letter-pattern." They are a mixed genre created by John and combine features of a royal proclamation or edict, the prophetic judgment-salvation oracle,[42] and an element from wisdom

[42]According to a paper read by David Aune to the Seminar on the Apocalypse at the meeting of S.N.T.S. in Cambridge, 1988: "The Form and Function of the Proclamations to the Seven Churches (Rev 2–3)," *NTS* 36 (1990) 182–204.

Each of the seven missives contains an address and command to write (*adscriptio*), which is not part of the edict-form. The Lord's self-identification, however, together with the phrase "thus says" corresponds to the *praescriptio* of the edict. The next feature of the edict, the *proe-*

literature, the "hearing formula" *(Weckformel)*. All seven missives or proclamations follow basically the same order:

1. The address and command to write:

   John is instructed to write to an "angel" of a given church. The following contents of the message, however, envisage the whole community and/or particular groups or individuals within it. Accordingly, John is not actually writing "to" the angel, but rather "for" him. The "angel" is a messenger to the given church, perhaps in fact a human messenger, but designated in apocalyptic language as the Lord's own "heavenly" emissary, a kind of guardian angel.[43] These angels represent the Lord's universal authority (cf. 1:16a and 1:20) on the plane of heavenly guidance, just as the churches figure as lampstands, earthly lights, among which the risen Lord is present (1:12-13, 20).

2. The self-identification of the Lord, together with Christological predicates:

   The exalted Lord addresses the community through an appropriately "exalted" messenger, the angel. Many of the titles predicated of him repeat parts of John's vision of the

mium (the portion which is intended to create good will and arouse interest) is absent here—and unnecessary. The *promulgatio* (what is known or made known) and the *narratio* (an account of the state of affairs which occasions the enactment) are recognizable in the *oida* ("I know . . .") portion of each of the seven missives. A key element, the decision or *dispositio* is also in evidence, especially in the commands to repent, to hold fast, or not to fear. The end-clauses (*sanctio* or *corroboratio*), which are directed to bringing about obedience to the enactment are discernible in the closing pair of the promises to the victor and the command to heed what the Spirit says to the churches.

To simplify the exposition of the letters, this commentary reduces their structure to four points, combining *promulgatio, narratio* and *dispositio* under the third point as the "body" of the communication.

[43]In Jewish apocalyptic, angels were sometimes represented as guardians of certain nations; cf. Dan 10:12-13; 10:20–11:1; 12:1, esp. 10:21 and 12:1: "Michael, your prince."

Just as angels execute God's plan in Rev 8:2–16:21 (notably in the septenaries of the trumpets and of the libation-bowls), so here the mediators of the Lord's edicts to local churches are fittingly represented as angels.

risen Christ (1:13-18) or anticipate attributes which will appear elsewhere in Revelation. In every case, the address befits the sovereign, and states the authority by which the edict is pronounced. The introductory formula, *tade legei,* has the archaic flavor (though not pedantically conveyed by the translation) of "thus saith the Lord."

3. The body of the edict:
   This contains two distinct but closely interrelated parts. The first, introduced by "I know *(oida)*" reminds the addressees of the Lord's awareness of the precise situation in each particular church. The second, notably longer, contains detailed points of praise and/or blame. Only two churches (Smyrna and Philadelphia) do not receive a command to repent; only one (Laodicea) receives no words of praise. The judgment and/or salvation formula emerges unmistakably in this portion of the edict.

4. The paired, concluding elements of challenge and promise:
   The "hearing formula" ("Let one who has an ear heed what the Spirit says to the Churches") and the promise to the victor are distinct, but closely connected. In the last four letters (as one turns southeast from Pergamum towards Thyatira), the order of the hearing formula and of the promise to the victor is inverted.[44] Accordingly, emphasis falls on the need to heed what is said—not just to one church, but to all. The hearing (or "wake-up!") formula reminds one of wisdom literature, especially of the parabolic sayings of Jesus (Sir 6:33; Mark 4:9, 23; Matt 11:15). The challenge calls for proper, reflective interpretation of metaphorical language and personal response to its religious intent. To listen, and especially to heed, means much more than merely to hear. Even as the risen Lord speaks, it is the Spirit, too, as the source of prophetic inspiration, who addresses each and all of these churches. A lesson to one stands as a lesson to all who catch the message and implement it in their daily lives. Thus, the seven edicts take on the character of an encyclical communiqué. Thus, too, the

---

[44] The change of order also helps show that the promise is tied to the Lord's communication as a whole, not just to the last thing he said, and, indeed, that the promise is paired with the hearing-formula.

hearing formula covers everything said in the proclamation, not just the promise to the victor. The second element, the promise to the victor, is as distinctive as the first element is repetitious, and yet, combined with the hearing formula proves relevant to all who listen. The promise is couched, of course, in militant terms, as befits an apocalyptic document.[45] Nevertheless, the victory in question is won by moral renewal or fidelity, not by belligerent action against others. Most of the promises to the victor anticipate life in the New Jerusalem (the New Creation at the general resurrection, 21:9-22:6a). They designate gifts, not mere recompense.

The text of each of the seven proclamations, respecting the lineup of portions as indicated above, is provided below, followed by a modest but detailed commentary on each.

I. EPHESUS (2:1-7)

2:1-7

1   To the angel of the church in Ephesus write:
These things says
  he who holds the seven stars in his right hand,
  he who walks in (the) midst of the seven golden lamp-
    stands.
2   I know your works and toil
and your patient endurance
and that you are not able to bear evil men,
  and have tested those who call themselves apostles and
    are not,
  and have found them (to be) liars;
3   and you have patient endurance
and have borne (up) because of my name,
and have not grown weary with toil.
4   But I have against you (the fact)
  that you have set aside your first love.

___

[45]The notion of conflict arises from the context of *perceived* oppression. The pervasive thematic of the Holy War contributes significantly to John's designating the recipient of the reward as "the victor."

⁵ Remember, then, whence you have fallen,
  and repent,
  and do the works (you did) at first.
  Otherwise, I shall come to you and move your lampstand
    from its place—
    (that is,) unless you repent.
⁶ But you have (in your favor) this:
    that you hate the works of the Nicolaitans,
    which I, too, hate.
⁷ Let one who has an ear heed what the Spirit says to the
    churches!
  To the victor:
    I shall give him to eat from the tree of life,
    which is in the garden [the paradise] of God.

As he introduces himself to the church of Ephesus (a major metropolitan center and one of the four or five largest cities of the Roman Empire at that time) the Lord reminds the faithful that he governs and sustains all the churches and moves among them personally.

He commends them for their practical, discerning faith (cf. 1 Thess 1:3) shown in the day-by-day virtue of "patient endurance" *(hypomonē),* the "tails" of the coin of which the "head" is "hope" *(elpis).* The first three lines of the commendation (v. 2abc) are balanced by the last three (v. 3) and they set off, in the position of central importance (v. 2de), the specific point of the Lord's approval: the testing of those who pretended to be apostles. That test probably looked to their understanding of who Jesus uniquely is (for the Ephesians have been faithful to his "name") and to their moral character (for the Ephesians could not bear evil men). The "first love," which he then reproves them for setting aside, most likely refers to their concern for others, for the only practical way to love the Lord (and the issue here is "works," or practical love) is to show kindness to others and to offer them self-sacrificing help. Even an imposing Christian community like that of Ephesus must "repent" or lose its existence (removal of its lampstand, v. 5). Still, returning (v. 6; cp. vv. 2-3) to the theme of false teachers, Jesus commends the Ephesians for resisting the Nicolaitans. These seem to have been a libertine gnostic sect which pretended to be Christian. In their minds, the human body did not really matter; what counted was spiritual illumination. The resurrection was or would be no more than an enlightened transformation. Hence, sexual excesses were irrelevant.[46] The phenomenon of such guru-led communes has apparently not disappeared, even in the twentieth century.

The Lord couches his promise to the victor in banquet-imagery: eating from the tree of life. Ultimately, the tree of life is the cross as bearing the fruit of salvation, namely, the resurrection. Its placement in God's garden, paradise, symbolically includes both the abode of the just in the heavenly kingdom (cf. Luke 23:42-43) and the new creation at the final resurrection (cf. Rev 22:2). One should note that apparently disparate elements of this missive (the introduction of the speaker, the body—including here both commendation and reproof, and the closing promise to the victor) are linked by key words or themes. For instance, we find reference to the status of the Ephesian church in vv. 1b and 5 (the term "lampstand[s]"), and allusions to belief in the resurrection in v. 7b.

II. SMYRNA (2:8-11)

2:8-11

8   And to the angel of the church in Smyrna write:
    These things says
        the first and the last,
        he who was dead and has come to life.
9   I know your tribulation and poverty,
        but you are rich;
    and (I know) the blasphemy of those who call themselves
        Jews,
        and are not,
        but (are) Satan's synagogue.
10 Do not fear what you are going to suffer.
    Behold, the Devil is going to throw (some) of you into
        prison,

---

[46]Cf. Beasley-Murray, *Revelation,* 74. Concerning the Nicolaitans, cf. also E. Schüssler-Fiorenza, "Apocalyptic and Gnosis in the Book of Revelation and Paul," *JBL* 92 (1973) 565-581, 567-571, and A. Y. Collins, *Crisis and Catharsis,* 43-44.

> so that you will be tested,
> and you will have tribulation during ten days.
> Be faithful to death,
> and I shall give you the crown of life.
>
> 11 Let one who has an ear heed what the Spirit says to the churches!
> The victor will not be harmed by the second death.

In telling the Smyrnaeans that he is the first and the last (2:8), Christ equivalently appropriates the title Alpha and Omega, which is proper to God alone (cf. 1:8). For Jesus Christ is also the beginning and the end of the redemptive creation. He mentions, too, his death and resurrection (v. 8), which is to be re-lived in the Christian experience of the Smyrnaeans (v. 10). Accordingly, in the closing promise to the victor, he guarantees an eternal life (v. 11b), the millennial, heavenly kingdom (20:6), which entails freedom from the second death (hell; cf. 20:6, 14). Linked to the closing promise and to the introduction of the speaker, the "crown of life," mentioned in the body of this proclamation (v. 10b), suggests the same reward as Jesus' personal gift. John may have adapted the expression from the "crown of light" of the mystery religions. In his perspective, however, the reward amounts to a share in the life proper to those who participate in Jesus' royal status by their victory over death.

The Smyrnaeans' particular problem, hostility from the Jews, reemerged in following decades, and appeared most strikingly in the Jews' denunciation of Polycarp, bishop of Smyrna, who was martyred there in A.D. 155.[47] The ten-day tribulation (cf. Gen 24:55; Dan 1:12) which John has in mind stands for an indeterminate but relatively short period. Some aspects of the persecution must have included imprisonment and, for some, even death (v. 10). On the other hand, its general aspect (as the clarification of "tribulation" by the word "poverty" shows, v. 9) may have been economic repression. If one was not a member of a recognized religious group which had its own trade guilds and business connections, then one's economic opportunities were severely curtailed and one forfeited "social security." Significantly, it is the Christians who, in John's eyes, constitute the genuine Israel.

---

[47] *Martyrdom of Polycarp*, 12; 17–18.

As the inheritors of God's promises, they have become the real Jews. He does not view the self-styled "Jews" of Smyrna as a racial group, but as a hostile religious sect (a synagogue or gathering under Satan) which differs insignificantly from assemblies of pagans (cf. the reference to Satan's dwelling in the next missive, 2:13).

III. PERGAMUM (2:12-17)

2:12-17

[12]   And to the angel of the church in Pergamum write:
These things says
> he who holds the sharp two-edged broadsword.

[13]   I know where you dwell, where Satan's throne is,
> and (I know) that you hold fast to my name
> and did not deny faith in me
> even in the days of Antipas, my faithful witness,
> who was killed among you,

where Satan dwells.

[14]   But I have against you a few things:
> that you have there those holding fast to the teaching
> of Balaam,
>> who taught Balak to cast a stumbling-block
>> before the children of Israel,
>>> to eat food sacrificed to idols and to practice immorality;

[15]   thus, you indeed have (some) who hold fast to the teaching of the Nicolaitans
in the same manner.

[16]   Repent, then!
Otherwise,
> I shall come to you quickly
> and wage war on them (using) the broadsword from my mouth.

[17]   Let one who has an ear heed what the Spirit says to the churches!
To the victor:
> I shall give him (a portion) of the hidden manna,
> and I shall give him a white pebble
>> and on that pebble a new name written (down),
>> which no one knows except the one receiving (it).

To the church at Pergamum, the Lord presents himself as the messianic warrior-judge who will do battle with false prophets (v. 2; cp. v. 16).

The throne or dwelling-place of Satan (v. 3) well depicts the gigantic altar of Zeus which occupied a prominent place on the temple-filled acropolis of Pergamum. With its flanking columns on three sides, it looked like a huge throne. The martyred witness Antipas must certainly have been an individual Christian, and most likely a prophet, which would explain his being singled out. The word for witness, *martys,* had not as yet taken on the specific sense, "martyr," in contrast to prophets, confessors, and the like. In the light of Num 25:1 together with 21:6, John regards false prophets as those who try to corrupt Christians, the true Israel, by licentious teaching. The eating of food sacrificed to idols, at least if done within the precincts of a pagan temple (cf. 1 Cor 8:10-13) supposed acquiescence in a pagan way of life. Basically, the issue was not a given food, but compromise with idolatry. In turn, moral conduct cannot be separated from one's deep-seated, religious beliefs. The Nicolaitans seem to have exemplified a particularly virulent form of an ultra-liberal, paganizing tendency among some who considered themselves Christians.

Appropriately, the Lord's promise to the victor features religious banquet-imagery. Manna is the food which the Lord provided for his people during their journey to the promised land. Its "hiddenness" suggests that it will be restored in the manifestation of the messianic age (for the imagery, cp. Exod 16:32 and the story about Jeremiah's burial of the treasures of the ark, 2 Macc 2:1-8). For John, the hidden manna connotes the heavenly banquet shared with Christ as acknowledged Lord and Bread of Life (cf. John 6:30-58). The white pebble reflects a custom known from Asia Minor,[48] of sending on a small stone an engraved, royal invitation to a banquet. That no one knows the name except the one receiving it apocalyptically expresses a special, personal prerogative[49] and breathes an aura of mystery. The "newness" of the name further suggests (cp. Isa 62:2) a transfigured manifestation of who one really is in God's eyes. The victorious

[48]Heinrich Kraft, *Die Offenbarung des Johannes* (Tübingen: Mohr, 1974) 66–67.

[49]*See above,* note 35.

believer himself (not Christ) is the one whose "secret name" is
mentioned in this context.

IV. THYATIRA (2:18-29)

2:18-29

¹⁸   And to the angel of the church in Thyatira write:
      These things says
         the Son of God,
         he who has eyes as a flame of fire,
         and whose feet are like flashing bronze.
¹⁹   I know your works and love and faith and service,
         and your patient endurance,
         and (that) your latter works are more numerous than
            the former ones.
²⁰   But I have against you (the fact)
         that you tolerate the woman Jezebel,
            who calls herself a prophetess,
            and teaches and leads astray my servants (so that they)
            practice immorality and eat food sacrificed to idols.
²¹   I have given her time to repent,
         and she does not want to repent of her immorality
            [fornication].
²²   Behold, I shall cast her on a sickbed
         and those who commit adultery with her into great tribu-
            lation
         unless they repent of her works
²³   and I shall kill with pestilence all her children,
         and all the churches will know
         that I am he who searches minds and hearts;
      and I shall give to each of you according to your works.
²⁴   To the rest of you, though, in Thyatira, I say:
         Whoever do not hold this teaching,
         whoever have not known, as they say, "the deep things
            of Satan"—
         I shall not impose [cast] on you (any) other burden but
            (this):
²⁵   What you have, hold fast to until I come.
²⁶   And the victor, namely, [and] he who keeps my works to
            completion—

To him I shall give authority over the nations,
27   and he will shepherd them with an iron rod,
        as earthen pots are broken in pieces,
        as I myself have received authority from my Father;
        and I shall give him the star of dawn.
29   Let one who has an ear heed what the Spirit says to the
     churches!

Again, Jesus Christ addresses a church in language which suggests sovereign judgment: the eyes like flaming fire (v. 18; cf. 1:1), search minds and hearts (v. 23; Jer 17:9-10), and the feet of blazing metal (v. 18; cf. 1:15a) befit stable authority. The title "Son of God" prepares for the promise to the victor in vv. 26-28, which is based on a coronation psalm and ultimatum (Ps 2, esp. vv. 6-11). Jesus' assurance to the winner, the one who stands fast by works, keeping Jesus' words in constant practice to the end of one's completed life on earth, stresses a share in the Lord's kingly power. This does not imply cruel, heartless domination, but expresses in standard biblical imagery unquestioned authority over the world. John finds the imagery necessary, especially for his integrating theme of messianic war. This power of wielding the rod (or sceptre/staff, also connoted) is basically that of a shepherd protecting his flock. The power derives ultimately from the Father, not from a tyrant, and is exercised to save and preserve the flock as well as to destroy foes. An additional reward, the morning star, alludes to the bright planet Venus (an ancient symbol of brilliant rule and of victory over opposition). This symbol is later predicated of Jesus himself (22:16), so that the morning star here connotes a personal share in the power which he himself has by reason of who he is.

Although the basic virtues of the Thyatirans include the key ones of love, faith, and hope, especially in the practical dimensions of service and patient endurance, the community is faulted in large part. This time, a prominent prophetess, biblically labeled as a self-indulgent enemy of prophets, Jezebel (1 Kgs 18:13; 19:1-3; 21:5-26; 2 Kgs 19:21-37) is the villain. Her sins are those of the earlier-mentioned Nicolaitans and followers of Balaam. In particular, her teaching apparently supposed that initiated or perfect Christians must practice vice ("the deep things/mysteries of

Satan," v. 24) in order to overcome it.[50] Concretely, this entailed participation in pagan guilds. For even though Thyatira was largely a center for tradesmen and merchants, it was also another urban center or focal point of the cult of the Emperor and of major gods.[51] Various cult-practices were proper to these guilds. The Thyatirans are blamed for being indifferent towards elements within their community which conducted themselves in a way totally at odds with norms for Christian morality.

V. SARDIS (3:1-6)

3:1-6

[1] And to the angel of the church in Sardis write:
These things says

he who has the seven spirits of God and the seven stars.
I know your works,

that you have a reputation [name] that (in effect) you
are living,

and (yet) you are dead.

[2] Come awake,

and strengthen what is left and is about to die,
for I have not found your works fulfilled in the sight
of my God.

[3] Remember, then, how you have received and heard,
and observe (that) and repent.
If you will not awake,

I shall come as a thief,
and you will not know during what hour I shall come
to you.

[4] But you have (in your favor) a few persons [names] in
Sardis

who have not soiled their garments;
and they will walk with me in white (garments),
for they are worthy.

[50]Elisabeth Schüssler-Fiorenza, *Priester für Gott. Studien zum Herrschafts- und Priestermotiv in der Apokalypse* (Münster: Aschendorff, 1972) 374, and nn. 149, 151.

[51]E. Schüssler-Fiorenza, *The Book of Revelation—Justice and Judgment* (Philadelphia: Fortress, 1985) 193 [repr. in *Semeia* 36 (1986) 123–146, 136].

⁵   The victor shall be clad thus—in white garments—
     and I shall not blot out his name from the book of life,
     and I shall confess his name in the sight of my Father
     and in the sight of his angels.
⁶   Let one who has ear heed what the Spirit says to the
     churches!

Jesus introduces himself to the Sardians a bit proleptically. For "the one who has the seven spirits" refers ahead to 5:6 as well as back to 1:4. These spirits stand for the "angels of the presence," who symbolize God's all-knowing, instantaneous contact with creation. According to some commentators, they represent the Holy Spirit in his fulness. But the Holy Spirit's distinctive role is rather to channel God's word to the prophets, not to function as a plethora of spirits standing before the throne of God or held in control by Christ. The seven spirits are coupled with another seven, namely, the stars. Again, these are angelic figures, but they represent the seven churches.

The promise to the victor repeats the motif of the seven spirits by assuring the faithful of public proclamation of the victor "before my God and before his angels." The assurance to the victor also includes both the "interim" heavenly state of the blessed ("white garments," cf. 6:11) and its guaranteed sequel, the favorable final or general judgment in which the victor's name will be found in the book of life (cf. 20:12).

Repeatedly, in the rest of Revelation (as even earlier, cf. 2:7b), John sees a continuity in fully personal salvation for those who attain "heaven" and subsequently resurrection from the dead. He does not distinguish a state of "separated souls" in heaven before a bodily resurrection at the final judgment. Rather, he views the heavenly state as a real *anticipation* of the same but universally *manifested* state of the resurrection to come. The clearest exposition of this perspective will have to await John's scenario of those enjoying the "first resurrection," secure from "the second death" (cf. 20:6).

The problem with the church of Sardis, put bluntly, is that it is dead, though not altogether (vv. 1-2). The faithful are called to awake, both to come to life now and to be alert to the future, or the Lord's visitation, like that of a thief, will catch them unawares. The Lord does not hesitate to present himself as the great fooler of those too dulled to deal with their own need for security (cf. Matt 24:43; Luke 12:39; 1 Thess 5:12; 2 Pet 3:10; Rev 16:15). To avoid such a trap for the unwary, they must remember how (namely, by the Spirit; i.e., by God's grace) they have received and heard Jesus' message and thus fulfill their deficient works, the proof of their faith. Such "repentance" involves not just sorrow for past infidelity, but rather "a change of mind and heart" *(metanoia),* which will set them on a renewed course of how one should live in the sight of God. A curious feature of this missive to the Sardians plays on the comparison between the industry for which the city was noted (woolen products and the dyeing of wool) and the present and future status of the faithful, walking with Jesus in white garments (v. 4; cp. v. 5a).

VI. PHILADELPHIA (3:7-13)

3:7-13

⁷   And to the angel of the church in Philadelphia write:
These things says
  the Holy One,
  the True One,
  he who has the key of David,
    he who opens and no one (then) shuts,
    and who shuts and no one (then) opens.
⁸   I know your works.
Behold, I have given before you an opened door
  which no one is able to shut,
    because you (yourself) have little power,
    and (yet) you have kept my word,
    and you have not denied my name.
⁹   Behold, I give (you deliverance) from the synagogue of
    Satan,
    from those who call themselves Jews and are not (such)
    but lie.
Behold, I shall make them come and prostrate themselves
    at your feet,
    and they will know that I have loved you,
¹⁰   because you have kept the word [lesson] of my patient
    endurance;

and I shall keep you from the hour of trial [testing, temptation]
about to come upon the whole inhabited world
to try [test, tempt] those dwelling on the earth.

11 I am coming quickly;
hold fast what you have, so that no one will take your crown.

12 The victor—
I shall make him a pillar in the sanctuary of my God
and he will no longer go outside;
and I shall write on him the name of my God
and the name of the city of my God, the new Jerusalem,
which descends from heaven from my God,
and my own new name.

13 Let one who has an ear heed what the Spirit says to the churches!

As elsewhere (cf. 2:8; 3:1), the risen Jesus introduces himself with titles elsewhere used of God the Father ("the holy and true" one, 6:10), whose word is just and will surely be effective. Furthermore, he is head of the royal household, with kingly authority (the key of David, cf. Isa 22:22) to dispose of its riches. The particular scope of this title finds an echo in the body of the proclamation, where the Lord has opened for the community a door (here, not a missionary opportunity, as in 1 Cor 16:9; 2 Cor 2:12, but rather the passageway to everlasting life), just as he had the keys to unlock death and the grave (1:18). Jesus' promise to the victor may also recall the text of Isaiah 22:22-23 in assuring him a place as a pillar in God's temple. In any event, the temple mentioned here represents the heavenly abode of the saints, not its final transformation as the New Jerusalem come to earth (for in that city there is no temple; cf. 21:22). According to the imagery of the time, pillars, like statues, had inscriptions celebrating those to whom they were dedicated or family members whom they had honored by their lives. The "names" involved show that the one made permanent in a heavenly state as a pillar belongs to and honors God the Father, God's forthcoming new creation, and the Lord Jesus himself. Thus, those with little power, apparently impotent before their adversaries, can rely on the stability and power which the Lord will guarantee them.

The nettlesome problem faced at Philadelphia was not universal, but was indeed shared with the church at Smyrna: Jewish persecutors. These persons no longer represented God's people as "genuine Jews," but were equivalently a gathering headed by Satan, a figure who is God's archenemy as well as that of the Philadelphians. In biblical language, these adversaries will be overcome (v. 9) as Isaiah 60:14 predicts Israel's victory over the Gentiles (pagans). As in the case of Smyrna, a test is in the offing, but this time a much more general one—on the whole inhabited world (3:18; cp. 2:10)—from which, however, the Philadelphians will be protected. Thus, with this sixth letter (somewhat as with the sixth element in subsequent groups of seven: unsealings, trumpet-blasts, and libation-bowls) John alerts the reader to a universal, world-wide test to come. This universal perspective, as distinguished from the particular scope of the series of seven proclamations, will be developed in Part Two (chs. 4–22) of John's apocalypse. Lastly, only to the Philadelphians, as to the Smyrneans, does the Lord omit a command to repent. To the Smyrnaeans, he had offered freedom from fear; to the Philadelphians, he gives an exhortation to hold fast. Both are assured of the crown of life for their fidelity (2:10; 3:11).

VII. LAODICEA (3:14-22)

3:14-22

14   And to the angel of the church in Laodicea write:
      These things says
         the Amen,
         the Witness Faithful and True,
         the Beginning of God's creation.
15   I know your works, that you are neither cold nor hot.
16   Would that you were cold or hot!
         Thus, because you are tepid, and neither hot nor cold,
         I am about to spew you from my mouth.
17   Because you say:
         I am rich,
         and I have become wealthy,

and I have no need (of anything),
and you do not know
that you are lowly and pitiful and poor
and blind
and naked,

18 I shall counsel you to buy from me
gold refined by fire so that you may become rich,
and white garments so that you may be clothed,
and the shame of your nakedness not be seen,
and salve to anoint your eyes so that they may see.

19 Those whom I love I reprove and chasten;
be zealous, then, and repent!

20 Behold, I stand at the door and knock.
If anyone listens to my voice and opens the door
I shall come inside to him
and shall dine with him and he with me.

21 The victor—
I shall grant him to sit with me on my throne,
as I myself am victorious,
and sat down with my Father on his throne.

22 Let one who has an ear heed what the Spirit says to the
churches!

"Laodicean" later became a byword for half-hearted, spiritually "sloppy" Christians—those not really worthy of the name "Christian." For this final, seventh edict contains not a word of praise or approval. The Smyrnaeans and Philadelphians were doing well, despite their plight in the face of religious persecution; the four other churches, partly reproved and partly commended, were called to repentance. Brusquely, the Lord jolts the Laodiceans to an awareness of their need for renewed spiritual concern (zeal) and change of heart and mind (*metanoia,* repentance). Jesus uses the jarring image of vomiting them from his mouth. Like the lukewarm water which flowed over a cliff facing Laodicea—from hot springs in Hierapolis some six miles away—and nauseated anyone who drank it, the Laodiceans are neither hot nor cold, equivalently "good for nothing." It looks almost as though the Lord will simply reject or replace them, as, in the first proclamation, he warned the Ephesians he might do to them (cf. 2:5). One tends to feel depressed upon reading this last and climactic communiqué to the seven churches.

On the other hand, one should recognize that the risen Jesus is using the language of unrequited but intense love,[52] which merits repentance on the part of the offending partner. In many ways, the proclamation to the Laodiceans, for all its necessary formality, at least in the opening and closing, "frame" passages, breathes more heartfelt emotion than any other in this set of seven. Alluding to the profitable enterprises of the city,[53] John mentions their banking industry, their medical profession, famed for its eye ointments, and their linen and wool products. They do not know how spiritually poor and blind and naked they are (v. 17). The Lord advises them to look to him in each case as their demanding but sympathetic supplier (v. 18). His spiritual commodities have a price, which is renewed spiritual interest and repentance. But the Lord speaks also as a father, reproving and disciplining those he loves (v. 19; cf. Prov 3:12). He offers to be the self-invited dinner guest, depending on their response to his request for hospitality. He will not force his way in, but will take the initiative to establish personal, friendly, even familial contacts. In Canticles 5:2 (LXX) it is the beloved whose voice is heard when he knocks on the door and asks to be admitted; the closing part of the body of the proclamation seems to allude to this heartwarming passage from the Song of Songs.

This familial aspect of Jesus' contacts is borne out both by the opening address and especially by the closing promise to the victor, albeit in the necessarily "imperial" language required by the edict-form. Thus, Jesus refers to himself as the "Amen," the Hebrew equivalent of "the God of *truth*" in Isaiah 65:16 and, clarifying this title, as the faithful and true witness. Moreover, in Christian perspective, Jesus Christ is the prime source of all creation, the wisdom by which the world was created (cf. Col 1:15-20, developing in a Christian way the imagery of Prov 8:22-30). This perspective of the "first" creation apparently extends to its ful-

---

[52]Cf. Vanni, *L'Apocalisse,* 148; Beasley-Murray, *Revelation,* 103, 106.

[53]W. M. Ramsay, *The Letters to the Seven Churches of Asia* (London: Hodder and Stoughton, 1904, repr., 1963) contains helpful observations concerning the geographical and economic conditions of the seven churches.

fillment, the redemptive "second" creation as well, as John later indicates in the promise to the victor. Fully exercised sovereignty supposes the completion of one's earthly struggle, as it proved to be in the free choice of the Son himself (cf. Phil 2:1-11).

THE SECOND MAJOR PART OF REVELATION: THE PRINCIPAL, UNIVERSAL VISION OF THINGS TO COME HEREAFTER

§*I. Heavenly Acclaim of God and of the Divine Redeemer (4:1–5:14)*

The first major section (chs. 4–5) of the second part of Revelation begins with John's vision of a door opened in heaven (v. 1a) and his ecstatic response (v. 2a)[54] when the voice of Christ (4:1b; cp. 1:10, 12) commands him to ascend. The opened door is meant to be passed through, not just looked through. It serves as the

---

[54]John's state is "ecstatic" not as though he has an "out-of-the-body experience," but inasmuch as he keenly perceives the Spirit of prophecy. He senses he is inspired. Admittedly, the phrase "in the spirit" serves also as a sign of the topical structure of John's compostion, as its placement suggests (scil., in 1:10 and 4:2, and with clearly conventional, spatial modifications, in 17:3 and 21:10); cf. R. L. Jeske, "Spirit and Community in the Johannine Apocalypse," *NTS* 31 (1985) 452–466, 464. Moreover, the phrase attests, as Jeske also argues, John's participation in the community of the spirit; it is not individualistic (ibid., 460–463). Mystical experiences, however, are not uncommon among the saints, especially prophetic saints, and it seems gratuitous to reduce John's affirmations (especially his liturgically-dated one, 1:10) to a merely literary device or to a conventional expression of community discernment.

opening into the dome of heaven. On ascending, John will find out the things which must take place in the future. This "necessity" looks primarily, as the course of the narrative will unfold, to the cosmic triumph of God over every conceivable form of evil in order to fulfill his redemptive creation for the faithful.

After this brief introduction, chs. 4–5 contain three main divisions. First (4:2b-11), John describes the throne-room of the heavenly court (equivalently, a temple) together with the worship of the almighty creator by the four living beings (representing, in modified astrological terms, the creation) and by the twenty-four elders (standing for the royal court and endowed with priestly as well as royal functions). Second (5:1-5), John sees at the right hand of the Enthroned a mysterious, sealed scroll. An angel poses the question about who is qualified by his accomplishments ("worthy") to open it. John reacts with acute grief because no one can apparently be found to do so. He receives a consoling interpretation from one of the elders, who says in effect that the Davidic Messiah, because of his victory, is entitled to open the book and thus disclose its contents. Third, the foregoing interpretation-scene, which focuses the central issue of these two chapters and prepares for the seven unsealings (see below, §II. 6:1–8:6) is followed by the vision of the Lamb, with acclamation of the Lamb and of the Enthroned (5:6-14). The acclamations come to a universal, world-wide crescendo when the angels and every living creature join their voices to those of the four living beings and the elders.

A. THE ENTHRONED IN THE HEAVENLY TEMPLE (4:2b-11)

4:1-11

1   After these things, I looked—
        and lo, a door (lay) opened in heaven,
        and the former voice, as of a trumpet, which I had
            heard speaking to me, (was) saying:
            Come up hither, and I shall show you what must
            take place after these things.
2   At once I was in the Spirit.

    And lo, a throne was set (there) in heaven

and upon the throne one seated,
3 and the one seated like jasper and carnelian in appearance,
and a nimbus round the throne like emerald in appearance;

4 and around the throne twenty-four thrones,
and on the thrones twenty-four elders seated, clothed in
white garments
and on their heads golden crowns;
5 and from the throne came forth lightnings and voices and
peals of thunder;

and seven torches of fire burning before the throne
which are the seven spirits of God;
6 and before the throne, as it were, a glass sea like crystal;

and in the throne-setting [in (the) midst of the throne]
and encircling the throne, four living beings,
full of eyes in front and in back,
7 and the living being, the first one, like a lion,
and the second living being like a young bull [calf]
and the third living being having the face, as it were, of
a man,
and the fourth living being like an eagle flying.
8 And the four living beings, each of them having seven
wings,
around about and inside are full of eyes,
and they have no rest by day and by night saying:
Holy, Holy, Holy Lord, God the Almighty,
who was and who is [who being] and who is coming!

9 And when the living beings were to [would/should] give
glory and honor and thanksgiving
to the one seated on the throne,
the one living forever and ever,
10 the twenty-four elders would fall down
before the one seated on the throne,
and they would worship
the one living forever and ever,
and they would cast their crowns before the throne, saying:
11 You are worthy, Lord and our God,
to receive glory and honor and power
because you have created everything

and on account of your will they were,
and they were created!

John limns four features of the Enthroned (vv. 2b-3): the throne itself, one seated on it, his appearance, and a nimbus proper to the throne. John deliberately modifies the more anthropomorphic vision of Ezekiel (Ezek 1:26-28). The Enthroned is like precious, luminescent stones (reddish-white in appearance). The nimbus is not the rainbow, a sign of reconciliation (Ezek 1:28; Gen 9:12), but a greenish arch or halo. John, of course, had never beheld the aurora borealis, but the reader may be helped to visualize the nimbus either as that phenomenon or as the pre-dawn glow in the sky.

In describing the twenty-four elders of the court (4:4-5a), John follows the same, fourfold format, though the closing phenomenon links the court to the Enthroned rather than describes something proper to the elders. There are twenty-four thrones encircling the principal one. The number is the superlative of twelve. It seems unnecessary to attempt further to determine the identity of these elders (for example, as representing personages or functions proper to the OT and/or to the NT). The elders later function as a kind of heavenly counterpart of the faithful, the true Israel, but are consistently distinguished from them, as well as from the angels and the four living symbols of creation. The elders, too, are seated (at this point), and their appearance (white robes and golden crowns—together with later references to their activity) prompts one to construe them as a kind of heavenly model or type of the priestly kingdom. Accompanying features, the fourth aspect mentioned, do not highlight their own glory, but rather the motif of power which emanates from the throne of God: lightnings, voices, and thunders. This motif will recur often as the thematic of Yahweh's war unfolds in the rest of Revelation, taking on other features of might (namely, earthquake, hailstones; cp. Rev 4:5; 8:5; 11:19; 16:18) which would, of course, be unsuitable in this depiction of heaven. Here, John alerts us to the ultimate font of these awesome portents.

John then (vv. 5b-6) enlarges the picture of the dais of the throne. In front of the throne (cf. *2 Baruch* 21:6) are seven torches, representing the seven "angels of the presence" and God's spiritual might in communicating his will to the whole world. Even-

tually, these angels of the presence (cp. 1:4; 3:1) will appear as
the angels with trumpets (8:2) who herald the aspects of the climactic conflict. The dais itself, in front of the throne, is a "heavenly
sea" of crystal, representing the classically biblical "firmament,"
or solid but invisible distinction between earth below and God's
heavenly, serene abode on high.

The puzzling phrase in v. 6b, literally: "and in the midst of
the throne and encircling the throne" may represent the whole
throne itself in a wider sense, as heaven, or, more likely, may be
a Hebraic way of saying "in the throne-setting, completely encircling the throne." In either case, the phrase seems to situate
the four living beings as though they were constellation-like chandeliers in the domed vault of heaven. It may, on the other hand,
describe constituent elements of the throne itself (like its encircling corner-posts).[54a] The description of each of these beings
begins (v. 6c) and ends (v. 8b) with emphasis on their eyes (cf.
Ezek 1:18; 10:12), which probably alludes to the stars as the eyes
of God. Although traits of the four living beings recall the inaugural visions of Ezekiel (Ezek 1:1–2:7) and of Isaiah (Isa 6:1–13)
they differ on a number of points. In Ezekiel, each beast has four
faces; here, each has only one; in Ezekiel, each has four wings;
here, each has six (like the seraphim in Isa 6:2); in Ezekiel, they
do not speak but they do move; here, they sing but do not move.
Their function here is to acclaim the Almighty (much like the seraphim in Isa 6:3), but in the distinctively eschatological language
of John's revelation as "he who was, and is, and is coming." Similarly, John seems to have modified the imagery from four of the
Babylonian symbols of the zodiac, representing spring (the lion,
a fire-sign), summer (the bull, an earth-sign), fall (the scorpion,
a water-sign, later represented as one with the face of a man),
and winter (the water-carrier, later represented as an eagle, an
air sign).[55]

[54a]So Robert G. Hall, "Living Creatures in the Midst of the Throne:
Another Look at Revelation 4.6," *NTS* 36 (1990) 609–613, 610–612. This
most promising interpretation (published when this book was in the press)
would present God as enthroned at the center of his creation—indeed,
"in it"—and help one avoid considering the throne as a kind of separate
piece of "furniture."

[55]Cf. Kraft, *Offenbarung,* 99. The application of these images to the

The illuminating scope of this scene begins to emerge from John's composite, modified presentation of all the images proper to the ambit of God's throne. Zodiacal imagery serves only to show created powers holding a fixed place in heaven and symbolizing God's control over times and seasons, as well as over the four elements (fire, earth, water, air). This interpretation squares with their adoration of him as the Almighty, past, present, and to come. Biblical imagery, which dominates John's borrowings from current astrology, highlights these symbolic figures' homage to God. The scene as a whole is not that of a prophetic, inaugural vision (as in Ezekiel or in Isaiah). John receives no call; his own inaugural vision was Christological (1:9-20). Nor does it depict the Lord enthroned in a heavenly war-chariot, ready to move where his people are (as in Ezekiel), or as the sovereign about to pronounce chastisement on a disobedient people (as in Isaiah). Similarly, the scene is not one of judgment against the nations (as in the throne-vision of Dan 7:9-10), although the "attendant thrones" of the elders reflect an allusion to that Danielic image of a royal court. Rather, the scenario celebrates the heavenly, almighty and eternal creator, awesome in power (v. 5a), yet serene.

The concluding portion (vv. 9-11) of this scene bears out the scope of the previous inferences. The twenty-four elders respond to the four beings' superlative adoration of God (the *trisagion* or "thrice holy" of v. 8b) in worshipful reverence and song.[56] Repetition ("the one living for ever and ever," vv. 9, 10) of the elders in concert with the four living beings focuses these worshipful declarations on the eternal one who is enthroned (v. 10a). By casting their crowns before the throne, the elders acknowledge that all power, even their own special share in God's sovereignty, derives from him. Where the living beings, as representatives of creation, gave glory and honor and *thanksgiving* (v. 9, which is reserved for the Godhead, and is echoed again only in Rev 7:12 and 11:17, where the elders are again mentioned), the elders here speak of glory and honor and *power* (v. 11a). They

four Evangelists, representing the fourfold gospel to the world, goes back to Irenaeus, *Adv. Haer.* 3, 11, 8.

[56]K.-P. Jörns seems to be somewhat over-precise in distinguishing between adoration hymns and proclamation hymns, rejecting the term "acclamations"; *Das hymnische Evangelium,* 18-19, 62-63.

then articulate what that power has achieved: God's creation of everything. The added explanation, "and because of your will they were and they were created," does not suppose a fashioning of primeval matter or coming to grips with chaos, but indicates that the very existence of things, as well as their fashioned form, depends on God's will.

Another, hitherto unmentioned detail of the throne-vision, namely the sealed scroll at the right hand of the Enthroned, now emerges (5:1) and dominates the intervening interpretation-scene (5:1-5), in which acclamations of God (or, subsequently, of the Lamb as well) do not appear. In this way, the seer limelights the key issue in this celebration of creation (4:1-11) as realized in the redemption (5:6-14). By itself, the "throne-vision" of 4:1-11 lacks adequate definition of purpose. What it really means will be disclosed through what immediately follows, particularly through the posing of the key issue, the mysterious, sealed book (5:1-5).

B. THE SEALED SCROLL: AN INTERPRETATION-SCENE (5:1-5)

5:1-5

1. And I saw at the right of the one seated upon the throne
   a book [papyrus roll]
   written on the inside and on the back,
   sealed with seven seals.

2. And I saw a mighty angel heralding with a great voice:
   Who is worthy to open the book and to break its seals?

3. And no one in heaven or on earth or under the earth was able
   to open the book or to look (into) it.

4. And I wept much,
   because no one was found worthy
   to open the book or to look (into) it.

5. And one of the elders said to me:
   Do not weep:
   Lo, the lion has conquered,
   the one from the tribe of Judah,
   the root of David,
   (so as) to open the book and its seven seals.

The scroll, written in such a way (front and back) as to be "packed" with information, is so sealed that its contents cannot fully be disclosed until all seven seals will have been opened. The final unsealing puts the decrees of the scroll into effect. The unsealings themselves, as the forthcoming narrative will suppose, provide "previews" of the thematic contents of the scroll. Background for such a mysterious scroll in the context of a heavenly assembly and a decree proper to God himself (since it is at the right hand of the Enthroned) is multiple. As often in Revelation, John combines, with his own modifications, both mythological imagery and biblical imagery. Thus, the context suggests the "book of destinies," the secrets of kingly rule bestowed on the human king at his accession to executive power to govern his people.[57] As written on the front and on the back, it is also reminiscent of God's covenant with his people (Exod 32:15) and of a prophetic message (Ezek 2:10). This book, however, will prove to contain not just words of lamentation and woe (as in Ezek 2:10), but also conditions under which fidelity to God's commands merits a blessing (as in Exod 32:15).

After describing the book, John immediately subjoins a characteristically apocalyptic scene of puzzlement and its resolution. A "herald angel's" question (v. 2) challenges to come forth anyone who is qualified to open the scroll. Next (vv. 3-4), noting the impotence of created beings, John feels keenly that the challenge will rest unanswered and the mystery undisclosed. The vision of the sublime, heavenly throne-room has reached a crisis. What is the point of the vision if there lies ahead no possible opening of the mysterious, sealed book at God's right hand? Lastly (v. 5),

---

[57]Cf. A. Y. Collins, *The Combat Myth,* 23-25. Normally, a scroll could not be read until all the seals had been opened. In Revelation, however, the book is not read. Collins further says that John is given to understand its contents and scope by the series of visions at its unsealing; cf. Collins, ibid., 25. I think that the contents are *sounded* out and *acted* out in the next septenaries: *see below,* note 74.

Contra Collins (ibid., 26), it is not only the seven trumpets which are connected with the final unsealing, but also, as latching onto the trumpet-septenary, the seven libation-bowls. There is no "break" in 11:19—as allegedly based on the introduction of the little scroll (Revelation 10) in the enlargement of the sixth trumpet.

the crisis is resolved by a spokesman from the heavenly court (an unnamed elder of the royal and priestly attendants). The victorious, Davidic Messiah is entitled by his victory to open the sealed document. In effect, with reference back to v. 4, the Davidic Messiah is not considered to be a mere creature—in heaven, on earth, or under the earth—but, implicitly, the Lord of creation. The third and last scene of this section will clarify his role and his unique status as the divine redeemer, the one who achieves God's creation through redeeming for God a universal people.

C. THE REDEEMING LAMB ACCLAIMED WITH THE ENTHRONED (5:6-14)

5:6-14

⁶   And I saw in a central position
         in the setting of the throne and the four living beings
         and the elders
      a Lamb standing,
         slain, as it were,
         having seven horns
            and seven eyes,
               which are the spirits of God sent to the whole earth;
⁷   and he came
      and he took (the book)
         from the right of the one seated upon the throne.

⁸   And when he had taken the book,
      the four living beings and the twenty-four elders
         fell down before the Lamb,
            each one (of the elders) having a harp
               and golden bowls filled with incense,
                  which are the prayers of the saints,
⁹   and they sang [sing] a new song, saying:
         Worthy are you to take the book and to open its seals,
            for you were slain,
               and you redeemed for God in your blood (persons)
                  from every tribe and tongue and people and nation,
¹⁰   and for our God you made them a kingdom and [=
               namely] priests,
                  and they will rule over the earth!

11 And I looked,
and I heard a voice of many angels encircling the throne
and of the living beings
and of the elders—
and their number: myriads of myriads and thousands
of thousands—
saying in a great voice:
12 Worthy is the Lamb,
the one slain,
to receive power and wealth and wisdom and might
and honor and glory and praise!
13 And every creature in heaven
and on earth and under the earth
and on the sea,
and all the things in them,
I heard saying:
To the one seated on the throne and to the Lamb,
praise and honor and glory and sovereignty
for ever and ever!
14 and the four living beings were saying:
Amen!
and the elders fell down and worshiped.

This final division of the first major section proceeds in three principal stages. John beholds the Lamb and his action (vv. 6-7), and then (vv. 8-10) the adoring acknowledgment of the elders, who represent "the saints," the redeemed faithful, and are joined by the four living beings in celebrating the redemption. His vision then enlarges (vv. 11-14) to encompass the sight and sound of the whole heavenly assembly and of every creature anywhere, concluding with the Amen by the four living beings and the adoration of the elders. In the latter two stages, the court hails the redemption by the Lamb; in the last stage, the doxology includes both the Enthroned and the Lamb. Thus, the final division of the first major section reveals the links between creation and redemption.

The Lamb's position is indicated by an awkward Semitic phrase (literally: "in [the] midst of the throne and of the four living beings and in [the] midst of the elders") that seems to stress his central position without detracting from the prominence of the

Enthroned. The Lamb should be visualized on the dais of the throne, with the "astral chandeliers," the four living beings, round about, but much closer to the throne than the encircling heavenly court, the elders (v. 6). The Lamb, previously introduced as the royal, Davidic Messiah (5:5) is "standing, slain as it were." In short, the triumphant Messiah is a sacrificial Lamb who has risen. His victory consists in his sacrificial death and his resurrection. Accordingly, he possesses fulness of power ("having seven horns") and world-encompassing wisdom together with universal power ("seven eyes . . . ;" cp. Zech 4:10) identical with the powers attendant on the Enthroned ("the seven spirits," cp. 4:5), but this time described as effectively *sent* anywhere on earth. In the limelight of the dais, by God's throne, he takes up the scroll (v. 7).

His right to take the scroll has been explained both by the foregoing interpretation-scene (esp. v. 5) and by the description in v. 6. Apocalyptic clarification, however, requires others' actions and words as well as narrative description. Accordingly, the response (vv. 8b-10) is presented forthwith: adoration of the Lamb by the four living beings and the elders. That there is only one God, creator of everything that exists, has been proclaimed by the adoration of these same figures in 4:1-11, especially in vv. 8-11. They now equally acknowledge the Lamb, though with appropriate distinctions. The elders offer libation-bowls filled with the prayers of the redeemed and, with harps, as a heavenly orchestra joined by the representatives of creation, chant a song of victory (a "new song," cf. Pss 33:3; 96:1; 144:9). The victory which they celebrate (vv. 9-10) is that the Davidic Messiah, Jesus Christ dead and risen, has by his death acquired ("redeemed/ purchased") for God a universal people, no longer restricted to one race or nation much less to one tribe or tongue. Repeatedly, John's vision will stress the actual or prospective redemption of any human being regardless of such apparent barriers.[58] Further-

---

[58]The fourfold grouping (tribe [*phylē*], tongue [*glōssa*], people [*laos*], race or nation [*ethnos*]) comes up five times but always in a different order: 5:9; 7:9; 11:9; 13:7; 14:6. In the remaining two of seven instances all-told, "tribes" (*phylai*) is replaced by "crowds / mobs" (*ochloi*) in 17:15 (disparagingly), and by "many . . . kings" (*basileis polloi*) in 10:11 (probably with prophetic reference to 13:1, which is explained in 17:9-14, 16-17).

more, the results of this victory, the fulfillment of the promissory covenant of Exodus 19:3-6, cover both the present and the future. For this universal kingdom is composed of people sharing Christ's rule (a kingdom) over the hostile world and consecrated to him (priests—not ministerially, but as sanctified by baptism in his death) who will eventually inherit the earth and control it.

A universal chorus (vv. 11-14) now even more closely links adoration of the Lamb to adoration of God, the enthroned creator. Billions of angels around the throne—an innumerable number for the ancients—join the living beings and the elders in giving the Lamb a sevenfold (that is, fully complete) recognition of his accomplishment (v. 12). The distinguishable realm below the throne, namely, the created world in which human beings live out their days: sky, land, and water, join in (v. 13) to give fitting, fourfold recognition ("four" being the appropriate "number" of creation): praise, honor, glory, and sovereignty for ever and ever. The inclusion of "sovereignty" *(kratos)* aligns the Lamb with the Enthroned as the Almighty *(pantokratōr)*. The living beings conclude with an Amen (v. 14) and the act of worship on the part of the elders similarly equates reverence for the almighty creator with reverence for the redeeming Lamb.

As yet, nothing has actually begun to happen for the faithful on earth, apart from the all-important fact of their redemption by the Lamb. Only in the course of subsequent sections will their earthly and heavenly lot be spelled out. The first septenary (or sevenfold lineup of events and/or motifs), the unsealings (§II), will provide an overview of the apocalyptic struggle through which the Lamb's redemptive sovereignty will be demonstrated. The second, expanded septenary of the trumpets (§III) will herald and inaugurate the climactic contest. The third and last—and relatively short—septenary, that of the libation-bowls containing the last plagues (§IV) will bring to a decisive climax the end of evil. Subsequently, three sections of Revelation will develop that climax: an interpretation-scene concerning the end of Babylon (§V); a narration treating the end of the remaining eschatological adversaries (the Beasts, Satan, and Death and the Grave), together with the advent of the new creation (§VI); and an interpretation-scene concerning the New Jerusalem (§VII). In this highly orchestrated work, one must try to keep one's bearings.

Immediately ahead lie the unsealings (§II), which provide a kind of oracular preview of what is contained in the sealed scroll, the book of the messianic destiny shared by the faithful.[59]

§II. The Seven Unsealings (6:1–8:5)

A certain rhythm characterizes the unsealings and, with further adjustments, the subsequent two septenaries. The first four are rather alike in structure; the fifth draws more attention to itself, the sixth even still more, especially since it contains an expansion (wrongly called an "interlude"[60]) which anticipates subsequent key events; lastly, an emphatic seventh occurs and regularly "latches on to" or dovetails with the following section of Revelation. Thus, diagrammatically: 1, 2, 3, 4, 5, 6, 7. The first four unsealings (6:1–8) entail commands from each of the four beasts and the appearance of different horses and riders. The fifth unsealing (6:9–11) discloses the souls of the martyrs, their prayer of complaint, and their interim, heavenly reward. Two key features of the climactic Day of the Lord dominate the sixth unsealing (6:12–7:17). First (6:12–17), universal panic breaks out at the signs of the Day of the Lord. Second (7:1–17), a prospective expansion including an interpretation-scene discloses that the faithful will be preserved from such terror and will acknowledge God's salvation after a period of earthly trial. The climactic, seventh unsealing (8:1–5) comprises a short silence (8:1), the introduction of the trumpet-angels (8:2, dovetailing the unsealings with the subsequent trumpet-blasts [8:6ff.]), and an image of the efficacious prayers of the saints (8:3–4; an angel's offering the incense of their prayers and then casting fire upon the earth).

The text given below will be divided according to the over-all rhythmic progression of the unsealings.

---

[59]*See above,* note 57. The messianic destiny is a triumph through death and resurrection, like Christ's own messianic mystery (as attested, for instance, in the passion predictions of the Gospels), and is "previewed" in the enlargement of the sixth unsealing (Revelation 7).

[60]Cf. C. H. Giblin, "Revelation 11. 1–13," *NTS* 30 (1984) 433–459, 434–436 and n. 9.

A. THE FIRST FOUR UNSEALINGS (6:1-8)

6:1-8

1   And I looked when the Lamb opened the first of the seven
seals,
and I heard the first of the four living beings saying
as (in) a voice of thunder: Come!

2   And I looked,
and lo, a white horse,
and the one seated on it holding a bow,
and a crown was given to him,
and, victorious, he went out to win (again) a victory.

3   And when he opened the second seal,
I heard the second living being saying:
Come!

4   And there came out another horse, a red one,
and to the one seated on it
was given (power) to take away peace from the earth,
so that men would kill one another,
and there was given to him a great sword.

5   And when he opened the third seal,
I heard the third living being saying:
Come!
And I looked,
and lo, a black horse,
and the one seated on it holding in his hand a pair of
scales.

6   And I heard a voice, as it were, in the midst of the four
living beings saying:
(Charge) a day's pay [denarius] for a quart of wheat
and a day's pay [denarius] for three quarts of barley,
and (yet) do not harm [cheat on, by overcharging for]
the oil and the wine!

7   And when he opened the fourth seal,
I heard (the) voice of the fourth living being saying:
Come!

8   And I looked,
and lo, a green(ish) horse,
and the one seated upon it (was) named Death,

and Hades [Burial, the Grave] followed along with
him,
and there was given to them power over a fourth
of the earth,
to kill
by the broadsword
and by famine
and by pestilence [death],
and by the wild beasts of the earth.

The first of the four living beings (the lion, perhaps alluded
to by the "voice of thunder,") calls forth the first portent. The
white horse[61] presages victory, a theme underscored by the description of its rider, a crowned warrior, already victorious, but going forth to conquer anew. On the basis of a set of four horsemen,
most commentators group all four as representing dire plagues,[62]
albeit under God's control, since they are summoned by beings
representing his power over creation. Nonetheless, warlike imagery, especially at the beginning of this septenary, where it probably anticipates the motif of the horseman (the Word of God)
in 19:11-16, fits well as introducing passages which will repeat
the motif of the Day of the Lord, his Holy War against evildoers.

[61]The motif of victory was already announced with reference to the
Lamb in 5:5 and is developed throughout Revelation, with the King of
Kings as the ultimate victor. Cf. Vanni, *La Struttura letteraria,* 227-233.
The victor in 6:2 need not refer specifically to Jesus Christ, but first
manifests in the course of the apocalyptic action upon the earth a theme
which will eminently be realized only in him.

J. M. Court, *Myth and History in the Book of Revelation* (London:
SPCK, 1979) 61–62, following Gunkel, accepts the likely allusion to the
warrior Mithras as the "unconquered sun" (*sol invictus*).

Of the four horsemen, only the fourth, Death (significantly paired with
Hades, 6:8) can be considered an "anti-God" figure, scil., as an eschatological adversary (cf. 20:14).

[62]The four plagues of Ezekiel 14:12-21 (sword [*rhomphaia*], famine,
evil beasts, and pestilence) are *not* distributed among each of the four
horsemen of the Apocalypse. All four plagues are linked specifically with
the fourth horseman (6:8). A short sword (*machaira*) is given to the second horseman, but with a different scope, namely, to cause internecine
strife among mankind.

John adapts the motif of four horsemen from Zech 1:8 and 6:6, adjusting the colors to suit not the winds (as in Zechariah) but the effects or moods of the passage. White, appropriate to victory, will be balanced by black (the color of the third horse), befitting mourning or gloomy oppression; the red of war (the color of the second horse) will be balanced by the green of a decomposing corpse (the fourth horse). In taking the first horseman as standing for victory in war, one need not assume that John wants his reader at this point to identify him as Jesus Christ. It suffices to take him as a non-Roman figure, since he is armed with a bow, and to construe him thematically, as one must do in the case of the other horsemen. Triumphant victory, not the grim aspects of bloody war itself (which appears as the characteristic of the next horseman), is proclaimed by the first unsealing.

At the second unsealing, the second beast (the young bull) summons forth a horseman who takes peace from the earth and incites murderous strife. Since the living beings are numbered, they apparently have some significance with regard to each of the first four unsealings, though it is difficult to determine this consistently and, perhaps, without some caricaturing of their heavenly aspect. Thus, the lion, proverbially the king of beasts, summons forth the victor (the first horseman). The young bull, which can be a violent animal, summons forth war (the second horseman). The living being with the face of a man summons forth one who deals with daily human affairs—with the market place, although under the aspect of social oppression (the third horseman).[63] Lastly, the fourth living being, the eagle (or, equivalently, according to context, a vulture) summons forth Death and the Grave (the fourth horseman and his companion).

The third unsealing discloses a rider carrying a pair of scales. In this connection, John significantly varies the format of the first four unsealings. After noting as usual the unsealings, the voice of command, and then seeing the horse, its rider, and his equipment, John returns once more to something he *heard*. This time, the command emanates from "the midst" of the four living beings, which suggests that it conveys a stronger note of divine command. This insistence would also explain why the third figure is not described by the phrase used of the other horsemen, namely:

[63]Cf. Vanni, *L'Apocalisse,* 192–213.

". . . was given to him" (6:2), or "he/they were given (power)" (6:4, 8). What is more, the command interprets the meaning of the pair of scales. In effect, this horseman is to charge economically oppressive amounts of money for basic commodities like wheat or barley without "harming" wine and oil. For a day's wage, a man would scarcely have enough to feed his family. At the same time, more optional items like oil and wine—not seldom associated with a life of luxury (cf. Prov 21:17)—would not be touched.[64] Later, John clearly targets social injustice prompted by a love of luxury (18:11-13). Social injustice would fit quite well here as a preview of the sins for which Babylon is condemned.[65] Usually, interpreters suggest famine as the thematic point featured by the third horseman. Famine, however, is expressly mentioned as part of the effects of the next figure (the fourth horseman, 6:8).

The fourth unsealing contains a double sign: Death and Hades (equivalently, Burial, the Grave) riding together with Death. The method of their destruction is patterned on Ezekiel 14:21, but looks beyond Jerusalem to the whole world. Thus, its effective extent is a quarter of the earth. Proportions of destruction increase as Revelation progresses. The septenary of trumpet-blasts, for instance, will feature the larger fraction of "one-third," and the septenary of the libation-bowls will cover everything. This liter-

---

[64]Vanni, ibid., 199–200. The third element in each septenary deals with aspects of closely similar human sustenance: food, both solid and liquid (third unsealing), fresh water (third trumpet, 8:10-11, and third libation-bowl, 16:4-7). Significantly, however, the third unsealing does not figure specifically as part of God's wrath, which is always tied to the events of the Day of the Lord (sixth unsealing, 6:12 ff.). The first four unsealings announce ongoing and ultimate victory (6:1-2) and then "preliminary signs" of three evils to be endured and/or overcome: discord, causing wars (6:3-4); social injustice (6:5-6); and death in various, painful forms (6:7-8).

[65]Vanni, *L'Apocalisse* 210–212. Similarly, the preliminary character of the third unsealing (6:5-7) nevertheless prepares for the sanctions in events of the Day of the Lord as borne out by the third trumpet (8:10-11; "Absinthe [wormwood]" imagery, cp. Jer 23:14-15) and by the third of the last plagues (16:4-7), where specific evil deeds are being punished. Conversely, in retrospect from 8:10-11 and 16:4-7, the third unsealing makes much better sense when taken as Vanni understands it, viz., as referring to an evil, socially unjust *policy,* not to crop-failures.

ary device of ever-increasing proportions must not be taken literally, if only because, mathematically, it does not add up. By expressing devastation in terms of successive fractions or, later, totalities, John orchestrates his visions to a crescendo.

Beginning with the motif of victory, the first four unsealings go on to cover war, social injustice, and painful forms of death. This paradoxical but mainly grim forecast of events to transpire hereafter is not final, however, as the next three unsealings will make clear.

B. THE FIFTH UNSEALING (6:9-11)

6:9-11

9   And when he opened the fifth seal,
  I saw underneath the altar
    the souls of those slaughtered
      because of the word of God
      and the witness which they had (given to it).
10 And they shouted in a loud [great] voice saying:
  How long,
  Master holy and true,
    will you not judge and avenge our blood
      at (the expense of) those dwelling on the earth?
11 And there was given to each of them a white garment,
  and they were instructed [it was said to them]
    that they should rest for yet a little while,
  until (the count) would be completed
    both (of) their co-servants and their brethren
      who were going to be slain as they themselves (had
      been slain).

The sufferings of God's servants seem to be supposed in the foregoing, fourfold series, at least in the last three. With the fifth unsealing, however, John perceives a reward for God's witnesses in the past.[66] The perspective here is most likely that of all the

---

[66]The complaint, "How long . . . ?" is well-placed under the *fifth* unsealing. For the next, the sixth, proceeds in response to announce the *end* of it all, the imminent Day of the Lord, his wrath upon sinners, whereas the preceding four unsealings disclosed only "ongoing" (or "everyday") earthly events, mainly tribulations.

just since Abel whose blood cries out for God's vindication.[67] The language is surprisingly free of distinctively Christian phraseology. "The witness which they had" (v. 9), may simply be that which they possessed in view of their knowledge of the word of God. If that witness was also given, as it surely was in the case of prophets (Mt 23:29-36), John has avoided mentioning that it was given to Jesus.[68] John sees these souls beneath the altar. In Revelation, the altar (always situated in heaven) has a "generic" function. That is, it does not stand for an altar on which animals were immolated (the altar of holocausts). Such sacrifices are not described in Revelation; whenever the altar is specified, it is the altar of incense, associated with the prayers of the saints and/or with portents regarding those on the earth (e.g., 8:3-5). Nonetheless, alluding to Leviticus 17:11, where "life is blood," the souls of those who gave up their lives because of God's word are appropriately located underneath the altar (Lev 4:7).

These martyrs voice a prayer of complaint to the Lord (patterned remotely on Ps 79:5) for speedy vindication of their deaths, unjustly inflicted by the godless on earth. Hence, they address God as a holy (righteous) and true (faithful) Master. Throughout the body of Revelation, prayers are always voiced or depicted on the heavenly plane—within the ambit of God's throne—and are correlated with the subsequent course of events upon the earth. Here, accordingly, though the prayers of the martyrs are somewhat rewarded with interim bliss (white robes and rest) a further development must occur—more fellow martyrs yet to come.[69] Unlike a somewhat similar scene in the Jewish apocalyptic work, *2*

[67]A. Feuillet, "Les martyrs de l'humanité et de l'Agneau égorgé," *NRT* 99 (1977) 189-207, 195-196.

[68]Feuillet, ibid., 191-195.

[69]Beasley-Murray, *Revelation,* 135-136, notes the rabbinical view that the souls of the righteous are in a position of honor, "buried beneath the throne of glory" (R. Eliezer, *Shabbath,* 152b). John indicates a further transformation, from the state of being souls (located, moreover, in a rather "confined" place) to an implicitly bodily state, each one being given a white robe and rest. Cp. the transformation supposed in 20:4 (the millennial kingdom) between "(seated) souls" and their coming to (scil., risen) life. On the theme of continual "rest," cp. the beatitude in 14:13.

Esdras 4:33-37, those who here await the fulfillment of their number from brothers and co-servants of the Christian era do receive an important change of status. They are clothed with white robes (associated in Rev 3:5 with a heavenly reward suggesting the first resurrection) and are intended to have rest (6:11; cp. 14:13). Repeatedly in the course of Revelation 4–22, John picks up the theme of a state of blessedness in a "vertical" dimension. Before the advent of the New Jerusalem at the final, manifest judgment, which will complete the "horizontal" progression of events, there exists a heavenly state of happiness for each of those who will have proved faithful through earthly trials. This state, as graphically sketched here, includes a "bodily" presence in heaven which goes beyond the existence of "separated souls."

The first four unsealings featured ongoing aspects of creation as it affected humankind. The fifth unsealing focuses this worldwide picture in terms of the plea of God's servants from ages past: How long will this continue and defer a fitting reckoning? The sixth unsealing will provide the *answer:* God's response is the Holy War waged by the Enthroned and the Lamb. Thus, there is a kind of narrative sequence and logical coherence to these unsealings.

C. THE SIXTH UNSEALING AND ITS ENLARGEMENT (6:12–7:17)

6:12–7:17

12 And I looked when he opened the sixth seal,
   and a great earthquake occurred,
   and the sun became black as sackcloth,
   and the whole moon became like blood,
13 and the stars of heaven fell to the earth,
      as a fig tree shaken [set quaking] by a great wind
      casts its summer-figs,
14 and the sky [heaven] was furled up like a rolled scroll,
   and every mountain and island was dislodged.

15 And the kings of the earth,
   and the potentates,
   and the generals,
   and the rich,

and the mighty,
and every slave and (every) free man
hid themselves in the caves and in the rocks of the
mountains;
16 and they said to the mountains and to the rocks:
Fall upon us,
and hide us
from the face of the one seated on the throne
and from the wrath of the Lamb.
17 For the great Day of their Wrath has come,
and who is able to stand (upright before it)?

7 1 After this,
I saw four angels standing at the four corners of the earth,
controlling the four winds of the earth,
lest a wind blow on earth or sea or any tree.
2 I saw another angel ascending from the rising of the sun,
carrying the seal of the living God,
and it shouted in a loud [great] voice to the four angels
to whom it was given to harm earth and sea,
3 saying:
Do not harm earth or sea or trees
until we shall have sealed on their foreheads
the servants of our God.
4 And I heard the number of those sealed,
a hundred and forty-four thousand (were) sealed,
from every tribe of the sons of Israel:
5 From the tribe of Judah, twelve thousand sealed;
from the tribe of Reuben, twelve thousand;
from the tribe of Gad, twelve thousand;
6 from the tribe of Asher, twelve thousand;
from the tribe of Naphtali, twelve thousand;
from the tribe of Manasseh, twelve thousand;
7 from the tribe of Simeon, twelve thousand;
from the tribe of Levi, twelve thousand;
from the tribe of Issachar, twelve thousand;
8 from the tribe of Zebulon, twelve thousand;
from the tribe of Joseph, twelve thousand;
from the tribe of Benjamin, twelve thousand (were)
sealed.

⁹ After these things,
   I looked,
        and lo, a huge crowd, which no one could number,
        from every race and tribe and people and tongue:
        (they were) standing before the throne and before the
            Lamb,
            clothed in white garments,
            and (there were) palm branches in their hands.
¹⁰ And they shout(ed) with a loud [great] voice, saying:
        Salvation (is owed) to our God, seated on the throne,
        and to the Lamb!
¹¹ And all the angels stood in a circle (about) the throne
        and the elders and the four living beings,
   and fell on their faces before the throne
   and worshiped God saying:
¹²   Amen!
        Blessing and glory and wisdom and thanksgiving
            and honor and power and might
        (belong) to our God for ever and ever.
        Amen!
¹³ And one of the elders responded, asking [saying to] me:
        These clothed in white garments—
   who are they and whence have they come?
¹⁴ And I replied to him:
        Sir [my lord], (that is something) you know.
   And he said to me:
        These are they who have come from the great trial
            [tribulation],
        and have washed their garments,
        and have made them white in the blood of the Lamb.
¹⁵   Therefore, they are before the throne of God
        and worship him night and day in his sanctuary.
        And the one seated on the throne will dwell with them
            [spread his tent over them].
¹⁶   They shall not hunger again or thirst any more
        nor shall the sun scorch [fall upon] them nor any fire,
¹⁷   for the Lamb at the center of the throne will shepherd
            them,
        and will lead them to the fountains of the waters of life,
        and God will wipe every tear from their eyes.

The sixth unsealing expressly pictures catastrophic events as a preview of the Day of the Lord, "the Great Day of His Wrath," which is the prophetic equivalent of God's Holy War. First, both earth and heavenly bodies are shaken (6:12-13; cp. Joel 2:10). The sky is rolled up like a scroll (cp. Isa 34:4), and both mountains and islands are dislodged (v. 14). Second, all mankind, sketched in seven classes, from rulers through all social types or classes are thrown into panic. Their cry echoes that of sinners in Hos 10:8. It shows no trace of repentance but voices only fear of divine punishment from God and the Lamb on the forthcoming Day of Wrath (judgment) against which they are defenseless.

At this point, however, John takes care to adjust the picture in order to distinguish the lot of the faithful both before the coming Day of Wrath and following upon it. This long passage (7:1-17), like one occurring in conjunction with the sixth trumpet-blast (10:1-11:14, following hard upon 9:13-21) has mistakenly been labeled an "interlude." It does not interrupt or retard, however, the main course of the action. Rather, as an *enlargement* of the perspective in question (here, of the sixth unsealing; later, of the second woe, tied to the sixth trumpet-blast) it expands the scope of events, particularly with a proleptic description of the future.[70]

The enlargement itself contains two main portions. The first (7:2-8) covers the protective sealing of God's people, Israel, prefaced (v. 1) by a period of quiet (like a calm before the cosmic storm of 6:12-14). The second (7:9-17) depicts the same group under a different aspect, as an innumerable multitude composed of all kinds of people, and concludes with an interpretation-scene (vv. 13-17) specifying their final reward from God and the Lamb.

A universal calm, symbolized by the control of four angels representing the "corners" of the world (cp. Jer 49:36), unexpectedly prevails (v. 1). John finds its explanation (vv. 2-3) in the corresponding vision of the angel rising from the east with the protective seal of the living God. The four "wind angels" have power to damage earth and sea, but are commanded by the angel ascending from the rising of the sun not to do so before the pro-

---

[70]This proleptic enlargement occurs again, though briefly, with the sudden introduction of the Lord's unannounced word under the sixth libation-bowl (= the enlargement, 16:15, in the context of 16:12-16).

tective sealing will have been completed. This sealing will protect them (according to the context, especially the contrast between the images of trees before the wind, 6:13 and 7:1-3) from the terror to come upon sinners.

The "sealing" develops the imagery of Ezekiel 9:4, but is extended to the whole people of God. John's visual experience (7:1, 2-31) finds its counterpart in the auditory vision (vv. 4-8), where he hears the number of the 144,000 sealed. This symbolic number (a thousand times twelve-squared) represents the complete and multitudinous Israel of God. As earlier in Revelation, the "true Jews" are Christians. Perhaps to help indicate this, John does not follow any of the OT listings of the twelve tribes. Significantly, he begins the list with Judah, not the first born, but the patriarch from whose line came the Messiah. Also, he omits Dan, substituting for it Manasseh, a part of the tribe of Joseph. Dan had acquired a "bad name" in Jewish tradition, being associated with idolatry.[71] John does not describe the form of the seal. Later views, building on the letter tau of Ezekiel's vision (which was once written as an X and could be converted into the sign of the cross) developed the imagery in terms of baptismal sealing (2 Cor 1:22; Eph 1:13; 4:30), the sealing with the Spirit in view of Christ's death. What John does stress is that the seal marks out those who belong to the living God and who are not by their alienation from God subjected to the final cosmic storm as a frightening judgment. The sealing does not mean protection from all tribulation, as the sequel will show. Rather, it represents the marshalling of the Lord's own as not subject to the despair felt by pagans. A corresponding instance of the same theme will be found later, under the fifth trumpet (9:1-12).

The second portion of the enlargement takes up once more visual imagery, and interprets a group which, though innumerable and from all peoples, must be taken as corresponding to the 144,000 sealed from the tribes of Israel. Apocalyptic writing makes much of *series of visions (Visionsreihen),* one member of the series helping to explain another. In this way, apocalyptic becomes profoundly theological, presenting mysteries linked one with another, so that the hearer's knowledge is progressively enriched even though the mystery in question remains elusive and can never fully

[71]Beasley-Murray, *Revelation,* 143-149.

be grasped or precisely decoded (as if it were a mere problem). Thus, what John *sees* (v. 9) must be conjoined with what he has *heard* (v. 4; cp. the pattern in 1:10-11 and 1:12-20, which occurs within John's inaugural vision), so that the numbered Israel must be equated with an innumerable group from every nation, tribe, people, and tongue.

The white robes of this immense throng fit their heavenly status (before the throne and the Lamb) as one of the elders will further explain. Their palm branches stand for their victory and joy (2 Macc 10:7; 1 Macc 13:51; cp. John 12:13) and they proclaim their victory (Ps 3:8) as salvation attributable both to the Enthroned and to the Lamb. A chorus of the whole heavenly court (introduced and closed with an "Amen") seconds their worship of God and articulates sevenfold praise, perhaps highlighting as its central and most important element "thanksgiving."

Concluding the enlargement, John recounts a pointed identification of the triumphant throng he has seen (vv. 13-17). An elder makes clear the fact that these are those who have shared through tribulation Christ's redemptive sacrifice. The "washing" stands for a "making holy" demanded by the presence of God (Exod 19:10, 14; 29:4).[72] Their adoration of God in his temple, which is heaven, anticipates their status in the new creation, still to be beheld on earth. For the language here, indebted as it is to prophetic motifs from Isaiah 49:10; 25:8; Psalm 23:1-2; Jeremiah 31:16 evokes in advance the imagery John will employ apropos of the New Jerusalem (cf. Rev 21:4; 22:1-5). The major distinction between this interim, "vertically oriented" reward in heaven and the state of the blessed after the general or "second" resurrection consists in reference here to the sanctuary (*naos,* the central feature of the "temple").[73] For John, the New Jerusalem

---

[72]E. Schüssler-Fiorenza, *Priester für Gott,* 394. Here, it is clearly the Lamb who has purified these who have triumphed through the Holy War. In 14:1-5, their own pure, blameless testimony further accounts for their victory. The victory, however, supposes the scenario in which their testimony was given (scil., Rev 13). John's clarifications are *progressive.*

[73]John never uses the word "temple" (*hieron*). Suggestively, he speaks of the "forecourt" (*aulē*. . . .) which amounts to the part of the *hieron* distinct from the immediate area of the sanctuary (*naos*), and he equates it with the profane world-city (11:2, 7-10).

contains no sanctuary (21:22). Before the New Jerusalem appears, the sole sanctuary is God's heavenly abode.

D. THE SEVENTH UNSEALING (8:1-5)

8:1-5

1 And when he opened the seventh seal
there was silence in heaven for about half an hour.
2 And I saw the seven angels who stand before God,
and seven trumpets were given them.
3 And another angel, holding a golden censer,
came and stood by the altar.
And a large amount of incense was given him,
that he might offer (it) for the prayers of all the saints
upon the golden altar which (is) before the throne;
4 and the smoke of the incense for the prayers of the saints
went up from the hand of the angel before God.
5 And the angel grasped the censer
and he filled it (with hot coals) from the fire of the altar
and cast (the contents) to the earth,
and there occurred thunders, voices, lightning, and an
earthquake.

Dramatically, the seventh unsealing first announces a half-hour silence in heaven (8:1). This striking pause appositely prepares for the solemn heralding of the Day of the Lord by the angelic trumpeters. In the OT, silence is enjoined as awe of the Lord (Hab 2:20), especially at his forthcoming judgment (Zech 2:12) on the Day of the Lord (Zeph 1:7). The pause here further serves (v. 2) to reintroduce the angels of the presence (Rev 4:5 and 5:6)[74] as

[74]The only "pure spirit" in Revelation is one who is never depicted and who speaks without his voice's being predicated of any symbolic but corporeally functional image—the Spirit: cf. 11:1 (*legōn*); 14:13b (an unannounced affirmation of a voice from heaven). Like angels, and, indeed, compared with them as being mere creatures (19:10; 22:9), the spirits who are angels are regarded as having physical contours or "bodies" (albeit non-human ones, made of a different kind of matter; cf. 1 Cor 15:40-41). Only with the development of ontological theology, as in scholastic, Thomistic theology of the thirteenth century, could one arrive at the sophisticated understanding of angels as pure spirits who

those who usher in the climactic conflict culminating in God's final judgment. As serving both the Enthroned and the power of the Lamb, they attest the execution of divine commands with a greater degree of "immediacy" than did, say, the four living beings.[75] Moreover, their appearance at this point, before they sound their trumpets (as they will do beginning with v. 6) helps lock together the septenary of unsealings with the septenary of the trumpets.[76]

Before they sound the calls that begin and progressively mark the stages of God's war against the forces of evil, another angel offers the prayers of God's holy ones (the saints) and performs a significant action. In the format of the Holy War, oracles of the future, based on God's past accomplishments, were followed

were not God (v.g., by each one's being a pure nature or essence—a form without matter—endowed with faculties of intellect and will, but having a really distinct act of existence, and therefore unlike God, whose spiritual essence is his unique, unlimited, underived act of existence).

How the "angels (spirits) of the divine presence" are "sent to all the earth" (5:6) becomes evident in the visual representation of the trumpet angels. That they are initially (4:5) called "lampstands" (stationary, brightly-burning figures) creates no conflict in apocalyptic imagery. Cf. the earlier equation of "stars" with "angels" (1:20). When referred to for the second time (5:6) as the "eyes" of the Lamb, these spirits (scil., "lampstands" / "eyes") are "sent" to the whole world! Unless we are to suppose that John then simply forgets about them, these are the same spirits reintroduced as "*the* seven angels who stand before God" and who *sound out* what the Lamb has unsealed.

[75]The four-living beings, which represented the created world, summoned forth the four horsemen, which were baneful figures of ongoing human events that evoked the prayerful complaint for the need of an "*end*-time" (6:10). The four horsemen, then, did not announce specifically the nearness of the "Day of the Lord," or even the fact of such a time of judgment. Even the first horseman announced—vaguely at that—"ongoing victory." A sense of "immediacy" begins with the events enacted during the dramatic half-hour silence of the seventh unsealing. John will later note that the expected climax does not come without *apparent delay* (the seven thunders as dovetailed with the trumpet-series, 10:1-4); the genuine climax comes at the end of the trumpet-series, and in a "moment" which proves to be a protracted unity: ". . . but *in the days* of the voice of the seventh angel. . . ." (10:6b-7).

[76]U. Vanni, *La Struttura letteraria,* 124–125.

by sacrifices, then by trumpet-blasts leading into the conflict proper, then by the utter destruction of the godless enemy (and allied figures) by God's own might, and lastly by the possession of his land as an untroubled people. The earlier unsealings provided the equivalent of oracles for the future. The trumpet-blasts and their sequel will appear in subsequent sections of Revelation.

At this juncture, however, the angel at the altar dramatizes the sacrifice (in the strict sense of "making holy" by presenting something to the Lord and by symbolically showing his power over life) and its import for the world. This "incense angel" first takes his golden censer and offers at the golden altar the prayers of the saints (those made holy by God's power). From his hand (holding the censer), the prayers ascend to God. Then he enacts the counterpart—indeed, the response—to these prayers. He fills his censer (the same implement supposed in his offering up the prayers of the saints) with fire (burning coals) from the same altar and casts it down upon the earth. With an escalation of Rev 4:5, there occur thunders, shouts (voices), lightning, and *an earthquake*. This portent will be further escalated at the seventh trumpet blast (11:15, 19b, where hail is added to the list) and at the climactic, seventh plague (16:17-21, with insistence on the "great" earthquake and the tremendous hailstorm). Thus, the seventh unsealing constitutes both the end of the oracular previews which attend the opening of the scroll and the beginning of the following scenario entailing the septenary of the trumpets. The engagement heralded and inaugurated by the trumpets, especially as effected with the seventh trumpet, will in turn reach a climax with the seventh plague of the angels with the libation-bowls of God's wrath.

§III. The Seven Trumpet-Blasts (8:6–15:8)

The seven trumpet-blasts encompass the longest and most highly orchestrated section (8:6–15:8) of the major vision (4–22). Most commentators view these chapters not as a unified continuum, but as a collection or concatenation of distinct parts. Some, indeed,[77] would divide the whole of Revelation with the so-called

[77]For example, A. Y. Collins, *The Combat Myth*, 25–28, 32; *The Apocalypse* (Wilmington: Glazier, 1979) 79. For a critical discussion of structural outlines proposed between 1970 and 1980, especially Collins's, cf. Vanni, *La Struttura letteraria* ([2]1980) 255–297.

"interlude" (actually, an enlargement) in Rev 10–11, truncating what is clearly a series of three woes beginning in Revelation 8:13 (with the fifth trumpet-blast) and running until at least 12:12. A patient, perceptive reader, however, should appreciate the remarkable unity and coherence of this septenary of trumpet-blasts, which amounts to about thirty-eight per cent of the major vision (4–22). The trumpet-blasts begin with a brief series of four (8:6-12). The fourth is followed by a special announcement (8:13) of three woes connected with each of the next three trumpet-blasts and, indeed, articulated by them. Each of these woes contains a newly-introduced factor, namely, demonic action, which is only partially successful but becomes progressively escalated as the fifth, sixth, and seventh trumpets are sounded. The fifth trumpet-blast (9:1-12) discloses the first demonic attack (on the "unsealed"). The sixth (9:13-11:4) contains a plague entailing the theme of non-repentance on the part of pagans (9:13-21) and an enlargement (10:1-11:14) stating that the climax is to occur with the seventh trumpet's sound and with a depiction of demonic opposition to Christian prophets after John. The seventh trumpet-blast (11:15) introduces a magnificent panorama, framed by heavenly hymns and signs (11:15-15:8), of the final conflict with demonic forces both in its vertical (heaven–earth) and horizontal (earthwide) dimensions. The conclusion of this section latches on, once more, to the following, rather short septenary of the angels with the libation-bowls of God's wrath poured on the unrepentant (16:1-21). This wrath occurs only after the last appeal and opportunity for repentance—enunciated in the course of the disclosures at the sound of the seventh trumpet and insistently expected earlier in the septenary of the trumpet-blasts.

The unity of this section will remain a paramount concern in this commentary. At the same time, easily readable portions of John's vision require that the text be taken in certain installments. Accordingly, we shall treat at the outset the grouping of the first four trumpets and the added notice of the three forthcoming woes. We shall next take up in turn the fifth trumpet (enunciating the first woe), and then the sixth (with its enlargement and designation as the second woe). In dealing with the seventh trumpet-blast, which comprises twenty-five per cent of the major vision in Revelation, it will prove necessary conveniently to subdivide the text into its seven concentrically-structured portions for easier reading and relevant commentary.

THE FIRST FOUR TRUMPETS AND THE ANNOUNCEMENT OF THE THREE WOES (8:6-13)

8:6-13

9 And the seven angels holding the seven trumpets prepared
themselves
to blow (their) trumpets.

7 And the first blew (his) trumpet,
and there was hail and fire mixed with blood
and it was cast upon the earth,
and a third of the earth was burned up,
and a third of the trees was burned up,
and all the green grass was burned up.

8 And the second angel blew (his) trumpet,
and (something) like a great mountain blazing with fire
was cast into the sea,
and a third of the sea became blood
9 and a third of the living creatures in the sea died,
and a third of the ships foundered.

10 And the third angel blew (his) trumpet,
and there fell from heaven a great star blazing like a
torch
and it fell on a third of the rivers
and on the sources of (fresh) waters;
11 and the name of the star: Wormwood,
and a third of the waters turned into wormwood,
and many human beings died from the waters,
because they had been poisoned [made sour].

12 And the fourth angel blew (his) trumpet,
and a third of the sun was smitten,
and a third of the moon,
and a third of the stars,
so that a third of their light [a third of them] became
darkness,

and the day did not shine for a third of it,
and the night likewise.

13   And I looked,
and I heard a (single) eagle [or: vulture]
    flying in mid-heaven,
    saying with a loud [great] voice:
        Woe, woe, woe
        (upon) those dwelling on the earth—
        from the remaining sounds of the trumpet(s)
            of the three angels
            who are about to sound (their) trumpets.

In sequence, the first four trumpet-blasts herald the striking of the earth with its vegetation (v. 7), of the sea and what is in or upon it (vv. 8-9), of the fresh waters and human beings dependent on them (vv. 10-11), and of the heavenly bodies (v. 12). In the first three, a fiery element is thrown to earth or falls from heaven—probably to help tie these three, opening portents (and, implicitly, the whole series of trumpet-blasts) to the immediately foregoing, dramatic action of the incense-angel (8:5). In the fourth of this series, the heavenly lights are dimmed. In the repeated chronicle of devastation, John favors the more ominous fraction, "one-third" (cp. "one-fourth" earlier, 6:8). At the same time, the fraction draws attention to the fact that destruction is not complete—as it will be later, in the series of the seven libation-bowls (16:1-21). The motif of "one-third" also serves to highlight the third trumpet-blast and, at the end of the opening group of four, the three woes.

The third trumpet-blast heralds the falling of a torch-like star (a comet or meteor) labeled wormwood (absinthe), a bitter and often fatal herb. In the OT, wormwood serves as a metaphor for the perversion of justice (Amos 5:7; 6:12), the bitter fruits of idolatry (Deut 29:16-19), and divine chastisement (Jer 9:12-16). Appropriately, then, multitudes die for the sins which poison their source of life (the fresh waters).

Immediately after the cosmic dimming of the lights of heaven (v. 12), an eagle (or vulture[78]) abruptly appears at the sun's ze-

---

[78]Cf. Beasley-Murray, *Revelation,* 159. In Luke 17:37 and Matthew 24:28, where the "eagles" (*aetoi*) are equivalently vultures, the notion

nith ("mid-heaven") proclaiming three woes to come upon the earthdwellers. Most of these woes will not exclude the faithful, but they afflict mainly the huge majority of human beings at the time of John's writing, namely, the pagans. From the first woe, which is despair, Christians will be exempted. In the second woe, Christian prophetic testimony after John will be hatefully attacked, but will ultimately bring about the conversion of most of those who will have been opposed to it. During the third woe, all earthdwellers will suffer, though the faithful will receive their heavenly reward. As the woes develop, their specific character becomes evident: they introduce for the first time the element of satanic attacks, which are always at least partially successful, and are more virulent than natural catastrophes or merely human strife. The deliberate escalation of catastrophe to the demonic level helps demonstrate by its frustrated outcome that God can overcome evil in its conceivably most powerful and dangerous forms. The announcement of three woes enables John to amplify coherently the visions introduced by the last three trumpet-blasts. Again, as in the case of the seven unsealings, the series of trumpet-blasts follows the progressively emphatic schema: 1, 2, 3, 4, 5, 6, 7.

THE FIFTH TRUMPET (= THE FIRST WOE) (9:1-12)

9:1-12

1   And the fifth angel blew (his) trumpet,
and I saw a star fallen from heaven to earth,
    and there was given to it the key to the shaft of the Abyss,
2   and it opened the shaft of the Abyss,
    and smoke went up from the Abyss like smoke from a huge furnace,
    and the sun and air became darkness from the smoke from the shaft.

3   And from the smoke locusts came forth over the earth,
    and they were given power as scorpions of earth have power;
4   and they were told not to harm

the grass of the earth
or any green thing
or any tree,
but (were told to harm) only
the human beings
who do not have on their foreheads the seal
of God;

5   and they were given (power) not to kill them,
but to torment them for five months,
and their torment is like the torment of scorpions
when they strike a human being.

6   And in those days,
human beings will seek death and not find it,
and desire to die—and death will flee from them.

7   And the appearance of the locusts (is) like that of
horses ready for war,
and on their heads crowns like gold,
and their faces like faces of human beings,

8   and they have hair like women's hair,
and their teeth (are) like those of lions,

9   and they had breastplates like iron breastplates,
and the sound of their wings (was) like the sound
of chariots (drawn by) many horses rushing to
battle [war],

10   and they have tails and stings like those of
scorpions,
and in their tails is their power to harm human
beings
for five months.

11   And they have over them a king, the angel of the Abyss;
his name in Hebrew: Abaddon;
and in Greek: Apollyon [Destroyer].

12   The first woe has passed;
lo, there are still two woes after (all) this.

of slaughter is evident. The Greek word *(aetoi)* is ambiguous. Perhaps the ancients did not distinguish, as we tend to do, "noble" birds of prey from those which live on carrion. One may remind oneself that even "the noble American bald eagle" sometimes feeds on (fresh) carrion.

At the sound of the fifth trumpet, John sees a fallen star, perhaps an allusion to Lucifer. John's main interest, however, lies not in describing Lucifer's fall, but in representing Satan or a satanic figure as the Destroyer *(Apollyōn,* v. 11), probably a pun on the pagan god, Apollo.[79] This demonic power opens the Abyss, not to illuminate, but to becloud the earth with smoke, and then serves as the king of the Abyss, the leader of the plague of locusts which he led forth.

In order to discern and appreciate the main points of this woe, one must take note of its carefully wrought literary structure. The passage is arranged concentrically, in fivefold *(A, B, C, B', A')*[80] format. One can observe this from following the placement of key words. The key term in *A* and *A'* is *Abyss* (vv. 1 and 2, v. 11). In *B* and *B'*, which develop the image of the plague, five key terms appear, almost always in exactly the same order, thus:

B (vv. 3-5)	*B'* (vv. 7-10)
locusts	*locusts*
power	*scorpion*-like tails
of *scorpions*	with *power*
to harm	*to harm*
for five months	*for five months*
torment of *scorpions*	

Within *B* (vv. 3-5) a subordinate concentric structure appears:

a (v. 3) *They were given* power of *scorpions*

    b (v. 4) *They were told* not to harm . . . but (to harm) only
    . . .

a' (v. 5) *They were given* . . . torment of *scorpions.* . . .

The particularly important, central portion, C (v. 6) describes the plight of human beings (apart, of course, from Christians, those "sealed," v. 4). Where the plague itself excluded death (v. 5), humans seek to escape it by death, but death flees from them. Their despair in desiring to die becomes frustrated (cf. Job 3:21; Jer 8:3). The central portion *(C)* sums up the five-month period

---

[79]In Hellenistic times, Apollo *(Apollōn)* was considered to be a sungod; *Oxford Classical Dictionary,* ²1970, 82. To the Greeks, Apollo was the revelatory god *par excellence.*

[80]Cf. Giblin, "Revelation 11. 1–13," *NTS* 30 (1984) 433–459, 446–448.

of torment *(B* and *B'*) with an apt, opening, "end-time" phrase: "In those days." It is further linked to *B* and to *B'* by the term *human beings* (v. 6; vv. 4 and 5; vv. 7 and 10).

The imagery of the plague derives from Joel 2:1-11. Much as in Joel,[81] the opening, agricultural imagery of the plague *(A, B)* yields to that of military might, an other-worldly, royal cavalry *(B', A')*. Significantly, however, John's locusts do not do the one thing for which locusts are notorious, namely, devouring grass, trees, and any green thing, nor are they merely a metaphor for an attacking army; they constitute the demonic enemy of mankind. The locusts' torment is defined as the sting of scorpions, one of the classic punishments inflicted on idolaters and other sinners (Sir 39:27-35; Deut 32:21-24). The duration of the plague, five months, covers not just the few days or weeks of a plague of real locusts, but the full life-span of locusts. Their assault is unremitting for as long as they are allowed to exist on earth. Symbolically, five months also stands for a relatively lengthy, but eventually terminated devastation (as in Gen 7:24, apropos of the waters of the deluge).[82] Perhaps the temporal factor supposes a divinely-intended change of human conduct after world-wide chastisement of the ungodly. The text is silent, however, about whether or not such a change actually takes place.

John does not intend to delimit the plague to a set of historical circumstances (for example, to a given emperor's reign or to a particular empire). The intended points of this episode can be de-

[81]Ibid., n. 54.

[82]The period of five months may therefore stand quite precisely for a period after which God expects human beings will no longer conduct themselves as they did in the past. Thus, after the "hopelessness" experienced for "five months," mankind may be converted. Under the fifth trumpet (= first woe), only an experience of pain is articulated (cf. the fifth unsealing, 6:10); no consequence emerges. The sixth trumpet and its enlargement (= second woe) encompasses disparate reactions (non-repentance, 9:20-21; conversion, 11:13b). Under the fifth libation-bowl, the element of "pain" is again noted (*bis*, 16:10-11); at that time, however, the prospect of repentance is obdurately rejected. Much is suggestively disclosed if one follows the *progressions* of John's sedulously articulated septenaries and sequences of visions (*Visionsreihen*). Repentance is constantly urged, but not forced; for pagans, matters pass from bad to worse, though not necessarily so. The mystery of evil lies in human obstinacy.

tected in its very structure. Thus, the concentrically-shaped content of *B* (vv. 3-5) defines at its central point, *b* (v. 4) the precise focus of the plague: all human beings who have not been "sealed" by God, that is, who do not belong to him as his very own people. What is more, the scope of the plague, despair and the frustration of even a perverse desire for death, is defined by the central portion, *C,* of the whole concentrically-structured passage. The diabolical character of the plague can be determined not only by the phantasmagorical imagery of *B* and *B'*, but especially by *A* and *A'* which speak of the one who unleashes the locusts, the angel of the Abyss who is their king.

THE SIXTH TRUMPET AND ITS ENLARGEMENT (= THE SECOND WOE) (9:13–11:14)

9:13–11:14

9[13] And the sixth angel blew (his) trumpet,
and I heard a (single) voice from the (four) horns
of the golden altar (which is) before God
[14] saying to the sixth angel, who (was) holding the trumpet:
Set loose the four angels bound at the Euphrates,
the great river!

[15] The four angels were set loose,
(they had been kept) ready
for the hour and the day and the month and the year
to kill a third of mankind.

[16] And the number of the cavalry was two hundred million—
I heard the number.

[17] And thus did I see in the vision
the horses and those seated upon them:
(They) had breastplates fire-red, deep blue, and sulphur-yellow;
the horses' heads like lions' heads.
And from their mouths came forth fire and smoke and sulphur.

[18] From these three plagues a third of mankind died,
from the fire and the smoke and the sulphur coming from their mouths.

¹⁹   For the power of the horses (lies) in their mouths and
              in their tails
       for their tails are like serpents, (since) they have heads,
       and with these they (do their) harm.

²⁰   And the rest of mankind, those not killed by these plagues,
       did not repent their handiwork [the work of their hands],
           so as not to worship the demons and the idols [demonic
              images]
           (made of) gold and silver and bronze and stone and
              wood,
           which are able neither to hear or to see or to walk;
²¹   and they did not repent
              their murders,
              or their incantations [sorcery]
              or their fornication
              or their thefts.

10¹   And I saw another mighty angel coming down from
              heaven,
              wrapped [clothed] in a cloud,
              on his head (was) the rainbow,
              and his face (was) like the sun,
              and his feet like pillars of fire;
²   and he (was) holding in his hand an opened booklet
                 [small scroll].
           And he placed his right foot upon the sea
                 and his left on the earth.
³   And he shouted with a loud [great] voice, as a lion roars,
           and when he shouted, seven thunders uttered their own
                 voices;
⁴   and when the seven thunders (made their) utterance,
           I was about to write (what they had spoken).
       And I heard a voice from heaven saying:
           Seal (up) the things the seven thunders uttered
           and do not write them (down)!

⁵   And the angel,
              whom I saw standing on the sea and on the earth,
              lifted up to heaven his right hand
⁶   and swore by the one living for ever and ever,
                 who created heaven and the things in it,

and the earth and the things in it,
and the sea and the things in it:
There is no longer (ongoing) time;

7   instead, in the days of the sound [voice] of the seventh angel,
when he is about to blow (his) trumpet,
God's mystery will indeed be brought to fulfillment [completion],
as he announced (that) good news to [evangelized] his servants, the prophets.

8   And the voice which I (had) heard from heaven
was again speaking with me, and (now) saying:
Go, take the book which is opened in the hand of the angel
who is standing on the sea and on the earth.

9   And I went to the angel telling him to give me the booklet.
And he said to me:
Take (it) and eat it;
it will indeed make your stomach sour,
but in your mouth it will be sweet as honey.

10   And I took the book from the hand of the angel
and I ate it,
and it was in my mouth sweet as honey,
but when I had eaten it,
my stomach soured.

11   And they said to me:
You must again prophesy
to many peoples, nations, tongues, and kings.

11¹   And there was given to me a reed like a rod,
(as a voice was) saying:
Rise, and measure God's sanctuary, including [and] the altar and those worshiping in it.

2   And exclude [cast out] the courtyard outside the sanctuary,
and do not measure it,
because it has been given to the nations [Gentiles]
and they shall trample on the holy city for forty-two months.

3   And I shall grant (authority) to my two witnesses
      and they shall prophesy, clothed in sackcloth,
      for one thousand two hundred and sixty days.

4   These (two) are the two olive trees and the two lampstands
      which (are) standing before the Lord of the earth.

5   And if anyone wants to harm them,
            fire comes forth from their mouth(s)
            and devours their enemies;
        and if anyone shall want to do them harm,
            thus must he himself be slain.

6   These (two) have the power to shut up heaven [the sky]
        so that no rain will fall during the days of their
            prophecy;
      and they have power over the waters, to turn them into
          blood,
          and to strike the earth with every plague,
          as often as they wish.

7   And when they will have completed their testimony,
        the beast coming up from the Abyss
          will wage war on them and conquer them and kill
              them;

8   and their bodies (will lie) in the square of the Great
              City,
            which is called prophetically [spiritually] Sodom
                and Egypt,
            where also their Lord was crucified.

9   And (those) from the peoples and tribes and tongues and
        nations
        will look upon their bodies for three-and-a-half days,
        and will not allow their bodies to be placed in a tomb.

10 And those who dwell on the earth will rejoice over them,
        and congratulate themselves,
        and send gifts to one another,
          for these two prophets tormented those dwelling on
              the earth.

11 And after the three-and-a-half days,
        a spirit of life from God entered into them,
            and they stood on their feet,
                and great fear fell upon those beholding them;

¹² and they heard a loud [great] voice from heaven saying
to them: Come up here!
and they went up to heaven on the cloud,
and their enemies beheld them.

¹³ And at that (very) hour,
a great earthquake occurred,
and a tenth of the city collapsed [fell]
and there were killed in the earthquake seven thousand persons [names];
and the rest became overawed [quite fearful]
and gave glory to the God of heaven.

¹⁴ The second woe has passed;
lo, the third woe is coming soon [quickly].

At the sound of the sixth angel's trumpet, a voice from the four
corners (that is, from the four "horns" or power-symbols) of the
golden altar of incense calls for the unleashing of the four "time-
angels" at the Euphrates. In the light of previous passages which
represent prayers of the saints answered in conjunction with a sign
of their victory (6:9-11) or of judgment on the world (8:3-5), the
voice evokes God's governance in accord with the petitions of the
saints. This governance he exercises either directly or, as in the
case of the angel from the altar who has power over fire (14:8),
through the mediation of a heavenly messenger. The Euphrates
formed the eastern boundary of the Roman Empire, beyond which
lay hordes of belligerent Parthians. Jewish apocalyptic (*1 Enoch*
56:5-57:3) viewed them in biblical terms (cf. Ezek 38:1-39:8).
Through the onset of this horde, Jewish apocalyptists thought that
God would see to it that sinners would be punished and Israel
be made secure. John, however, recasts even the basic biblical
theme. The horde is not destroyed, but devastates the Empire (as
the civilized region he knew and dwelt in). Its purpose is not ultimately the destruction of sinners, but rather so to chastize mankind as to prompt repentance. Even this vision of "hell on the
march," however, does not move them. What may save many
will emerge in the latter portion (11:1-13) of the enlargement. But
"terrifying people into repentance" even by this hellish plague
does not work.

John hears the opening command, and notes the intended effect, to kill one-third of mankind (vv. 3-15). He also hears the

incredible number of the cavalry, two hundred million—a world to itself (v. 16). Complementing this auditory experience is the visionary one (vv. 17-19). Artfully, the riders and especially their steeds are described in a concentric fashion: *A*, v. 17b.; *B*, v. 17c; *C*, v. 18a; *B'*, v. 18b; *A'*, v. 19. The centrally placed element, *C* (v. 18a), pinpoints the chastisement: the death of a third of mankind from three hellish plagues. The adjoining passages, *B* and *B'*, describe the plagues as fire and smoke and sulphur issuing from the mouths of the horses. The opening and closing elements, *A* and *A'*, are linked especially by mention of "heads." The heads of the horses resemble lions' heads, but their power is not just in their mouths; it also lies in their tails, which have the heads of serpents. The breastplates of the horsemen *(A)*, with the colors of fire-red, bluish-black, and sulphurous yellow alert the reader to the three specific plagues.

The closing portion (vv. 20-21) of the whole scenario discloses its purpose: to prompt repentance. The rest of men, however, refuse to change their hearts either in what they worship (v. 20) or in what they do (v. 21). Cult and morality are closely bound together, especially in this biblically-inspired, polemic caricature of false worship. In particular, superstitious practices ("sorceries"), with attendant immorality, follow from the worship of "demons," represented as gods who are basically impotent.[83]

As in the case of the sixth unsealing, the vision after the sixth trumpet-blast leads into an enlargement (*not* an "interlude") which prepares the reader for still further disclosures, notably as affecting the faithful. This amplification comprises two main divisions. The first (10:1-11) deals with John's own prophetic experience and the completion of his written composition. The second (11:1-13) communicates to him a message concerning Christian prophetic testimony during the days following his own, and its salutary effect on the world-city.[84]

Three figures dominate the first division (10:1-11): the mighty angel, the heavenly voice, and John's own reaction to the course

---

[83]Paul's attack on idolatry contains a similar, but theologically more profound attack on false worship and attendant moral vice (Rom 1:18-32); for example, human beings' worshipping the very image of corruptible man(kind) (Rom 1:23).

[84]Giblin, "Revelation 11. 1-13," 443-444.

of events which they occasion or determine. The whole scene gravitates towards v. 11, where both the heavenly voice and the angel ("they") interpret John's bittersweet experience of consuming the book as his task of prophesying to many peoples, nations, tongues, and kings. Three portions of the scene, each ending with a divine word directed to John (vv. 4b, 8, and 11) help articulate its progression. First (vv. 1-4), God declares a further, stormily preparatory septenary (the thunders) to be irrelevant to John's communication. Second (vv. 5-8), God commands John to take the scroll which the angel proclaimed (scil., the decree of imminent fulfillment of the mystery of the gospel). Third (vv. 9-11), on the basis of his having assimilated this bittersweet decree, John has been nourished to renew (and bring to completion) his prophetic task, and both God and the angel declare it.

The phrase "another mighty angel" (10:1) suggests an angelic agent functioning as the voice from the altar (9:13), but perhaps also the only foregoing reference to a "mighty" angel—the one connected with the book of destiny (5:5), which only the Lamb proved worthy to open. In any event, he is a much more formidable figure than either the angel in 9:13 or that in 5:5. Though not identified with the Enthroned or the risen Jesus, he seems to be a stand-in for the Lord, with his face like the sun and his feet like pillars of fire (v. 1b; cp. 1:16). An outstanding feature, developed in the rest of the whole first division, is his *holding* a small scroll (*bibliaridion*—not, therefore, the *biblion*, the scroll with seven seals) which has already been opened, and needs only to be proclaimed (v. 2). Descending from heaven and wrapped with a cloud, like that which symbolized God's directing the route of Israel (Exod 14:21), he takes his stand firmly on land and sea and cries out in the commanding tones of a lion. In response, another septenary, that of seven thunders, commences. John promptly begins to write down what these disclose, but a heavenly voice (God's own command) aborts further "preliminaries." This abrupt, negative termination of disclosures leaves open the question of what the opened scroll proclaims.[85]

[85]God's silencing (10:4) the noisy thunders, which replied to the angel's roar (10:3), enables the angel articulately to proclaim (10:6-7) the document which he holds (10:2). This entire scene then places the remaining two woes in a new perspective: *the triumph of the prophetic gospel* in spite of coming hazards to God's prophetic witnesses.

Immediately (vv. 5-7), John hears from the angel he has seen an *articulate* cry, not a lion's roar, but a clearly formulated oath on the word of the creator of heaven, earth, and sea and all that they contain. In this cosmic perspective, the angel swears, proclaiming the *contents* of the scroll (as, later, an eagle holding a proclamation—the eternal Gospel—announces its contents, with, moreover, reference to the creator of heaven, earth, sea, and the fresh waters, 14:6-7). The mighty angel declares that time has reached its end-point (eschatologically speaking, the last phase of the end-time). That time, of course, is the ultimate crisis not in terms of clock-and-calendar time but within the aeon of prophetic fulfillment: the end of the "last days." No further preliminaries heralding its advent (the squelched seven thunders) are necessary. All fixes on the sounding of the seventh trumpet. That sound will mark the realization of the divine mystery, an evangelical, (i.e., gospel) proclamation fulfilling God's words to the prophets (scl., concerning his judgment of the world). The message given by the angel, and restated in the course of the events ushered in by the seventh trumpet blast (the eagle's proclamation in 14:6-7) restates in apocalyptic imagery the initial and decisive proclamation by Jesus himself, as recounted especially in Mark 1:14-15: ". . . preaching the Gospel of God and saying: The time is fulfilled and the kingly rule of God is at hand; repent and believe in the Gospel (that is, in this good news which I am preaching to you)."

Thus far, the message of the opened scroll has been delivered. The following verses (10:8-11) of this first division (10:1-11) of the enlargement (10:1-11:13) treats the further issue of what is to be *done* with the scroll—in short, with the way its contents are to be assimilated by the seer and implemented through his prophetic task. What follows in vv. 8-11 is not a distinct "inaugural experience" introducing a new, major portion of Revelation. Rather, it is a dramatized interpretation-scene, not unlike John's personal anguish before the opening of the sealed scroll (5:1-5). Here, however, the contents of the open scroll are already known, at least in general terms, and the prophet's discomfort looks both to the future and to the fulfillment of his mission. The voice of God commands him anew (here, positively, not as before [v. 4], negatively) to take the scroll, which he does; then, in response to the angel, he consumes it. Its message is difficult to stomach.

Recalling the imagery of Ezekiel 2:8–3:3, with a sharp difference, John finds that the scroll is honey-sweet (as did Ezekiel, for it is the Lord's word, cp. Ps 19:9-10), and yet it sours his stomach. He does not thoroughly relish the experience, but such is the lot of prophets.

In conclusion, focusing the issue by mentioning both voices together, though hitherto God's voice and that of the angel have been distinguished, John says that he was told the meaning of this sweet but bitter experience: He must speak out to (*epi* plus dat.), not necessarily against many peoples, nations, tongues, and kings.[86] The standard fourth element in this grouping, namely, "tribes," is here deliberately replaced by characterizing *rulers* of peoples, nations, tongues, or tribes. The subsequent division (11:1-13) of this enlargement does not deal with kings, much less with "many kings." John's experience here looks ahead to the kind of thing he will write after the sounding of the seventh trumpet, especially what he depicts in Revelation 13-14, but also, indeed, to the end of his prophecy (cp. 21:24-26).

The second division (11:1-13) of the enlargement of the sixth trumpet-blast contains strikingly the specific element of each of the three "woes": partially successful diabolical activity. One can sense diabolical activity in the hellish plague from the Euphrates, just after the sixth trumpet has been sounded, especially since it so strikingly resembles in structure and tone the locust plague heralded by the fifth trumpet, which is the first woe. One might also find a note of woe in the bitter aspect of John's prophetic task, the souring of his stomach at the prospect of continuing to do what the Lord has required of him in recounting a victory which supposes many trials and much destruction. Be that as it may,

---

[86]The adjective "many" (*polloi*), which occurs at the end of the series, may modify only the word "kings." Obviously, however, the other terms are also plural here and, elsewhere, "every" (*pas*) often occurs before the first word of the whole series (5:9; 7:9; 13:7; 14:6). "Many," therefore, should be taken with all four terms.

E. Corsini, *Apocalisse prima e dopo* (Turin: Società Editrice Internazionale, 1980) 277-278, points out that John's task, unlike Ezekiel's (Ezek 3:1-4) is universal in scope. One may add that it looks particularly to leaders ("kings," here substituted for the usual "tribes") as well as to the masses.

the precise, diabolical aspect of the three woes appears clearly within the ambit of the sixth trumpet only in this second division of the enlargement, where the beast from the Abyss slays God's prophets.

At the outset (11:1-2), John is to perform a symbolic action, the measuring of God's sanctuary. The mysterious, commanding voice is that of the Spirit.[87] The area measured stands for the protected, immune sanctuary of heaven, with its altar (of incense) and worshippers. Excluded is the forecourt, as an area profaned by the nations for the "classic" period of anti-God activity, three-and-a-half years (cf. Dan 8:25; 12:7), here defined in terms of thirty-day lunar months. This excluded, indeed "alienated" area stands for the profaned earth, the forecourt of heaven, the world at large.[88]

Three major sub-sections follow the foregoing introduction (11:1-2). First (vv. 3-6), the Spirit speaks of two Christian witnesses, his spokesmen, who are *theologically identical twins* exemplifying the power of at least six OT figures, who were paired not only as distinct, but as different. Here, they are identical twins ("these are the two . . . ; these have"), since identical powers are predicated of them precisely as a pair. Second (vv. 7-10), John describes their martyrdom in what has become the "worldly city," the same which crucified their Lord, and the shame they must endure even in death. Third (vv. 11-13), John depicts their resurrection by God's power, their ascension, and the paradoxical success of their earthly suffering and disgrace. A devastating earthquake tithes the godless city and kills seven thousand persons. Amazingly, this is "remnant imagery," but here delimits the destruction to a relatively small portion so that the rest, the hitherto unconverted pagans, as the surviving majority, acknowledge the true God in an act of conversion.

Verse 14 concludes the second woe (identified with everything from 9:13 to 11:13) and alerts the reader to the climactic, third woe. This, in turn, has been heralded (10:7) as identified with the events introduced by the voice of the seventh trumpet.

[87]Giblin, "Revelation 11. 1-13," nn. 24, 58. *See above,* note 74.
[88]Ibid., 438–440. For John, the earth has been "corrupted" (*phtheirein, diaphtheirein*) especially by pagan Babylon (11:18; 19:2).

In the introduction, John is given a measuring-rod with which to distinguish two areas of activity on the part of others. One, encompassing God's sanctuary, the altar, and worshippers, represents the place immune from assault, the heavenly sphere. The other area, "cast out (or aside)" comprises the temple court lying beyond the sanctuary and expanded in this context to include an area merged with the Holy City, of which the forecourt was, in effect, the central square or forum. This portion will be trodden down by the nations for a time which signifies harrowing but basically frustrated persecution—here, forty-two months.[89] As the scenario soon develops (v. 8) the Holy City is not the actual Jerusalem of A.D. 70 or of any period thereafter. It is typed as a "World(ly) City," equivalently the pagan world biblically characterized as immoral Sodom and idolatrous Egypt, in which genuine Christian prophets will be slain, as their Lord was crucified in it. Symbolically, the unmeasured, unprotected temple court / Holy City is the profaned forecourt of God's abode. His final abode with mankind, the New Jerusalem, will be secure from any even intended assault, and contain no division between heavenly sanctuary and earthly forecourt. That vision, however, awaits the realization of the Gospel mystery to be proclaimed by the seventh trumpet.

John has received this command from a heavenly voice. Clearly, the voice must be divine, since it goes on to refer to giving authority to "my two witnesses" (v. 3). At the same time, it cannot be the voice of Christ, who is referred to in the third person as "their Lord" (v. 8), or of God (the Father), again referred to in the third person in vv. 1, 11, and 13. Accordingly, the voice must be that of God's Holy Spirit, who inspires the prophets and speaks for the Lord (2:7, 11, 17, 29; 3:6, 13, 22; 14:13).

The first *(A,* vv. 3-6) of three sub-sections bearing out John's symbolic action identifies the two witnesses as prophetic figures

---

[89]Ultimately, the number derives from the three and a half years (half a "week of years") of the desolation of the temple under the persecutor Antiochus IV Epiphanes: "a time, two times, and half a time" (Dan 7:25 and 12:7). In turn, this period is based on an angelic interpretation in terms of *weeks* of years of Jeremiah's prediction of seventy years before the end of Jerusalem's desolation (Dan 9:1-2, 24-27) as half a week (that is, three and a half years, Dan 9:27).

calling for repentance or recognition of God's demands (cp. the "sackcloth and ashes" motif of v. 3; cp. Isa 20:2).[90] The period of their activity coincides with the period of persecution or tribulation, expressed this time in terms of 1260 days. More important, it helps identify them, specifically Christian prophets though they be (cf. v. 8), as two identically-twinned prophets who fulfill OT images of God's witnesses, chosen spokesmen. John describes *each* and *both* in imagery recalling the royal figure Zerubbabel and the high priest Joshua (v. 4; Zech 4:3, 11, 14), both of whom he places in the context of a prophetic function represented especially by Elijah and by Moses (vv. 3, 5, 6).

Typologically, these theologically identical twins are more alike than Tweedledum and Tweedledee. Contrary to almost every commentary, one is not to be thought of as a given type (for example, as Joshua or as Elijah) and the other as a paired, but different type (that is, as Zerubbabel or as Moses) nor are both to be taken in sequence as paired types (Joshua-Zerubbabel; Elijah-Moses). John's insistence on the identity of the two (in terms of function) stresses their *duality as witnesses.* According to a commonplace biblical adage, Deut 19:17, the testimony of *two* witnesses is essential to sustain an accusation. Although these prophetic witnesses have power to smite the earth, to shut up the sky, and to control the waters, they are not said to do so. What they do, indeed, is "torment" the earth-dwellers (v. 10) by their speaking out against corruption.

In the next sub-section (*B,* vv. 7-10), their prophetic testimony is completed. The witnesses do not speak for a given local community or set of such communities; their theater of operations is the worldwide pagan audience for Christian prophetic testimony to the Gospel, to the fulfillment of the law and the prophets. This becomes clear from the place of their martyrdom, the Great (World) City—though not yet called Babylon—made up of humans from all peoples, tribes, tongues and nations (ethnic groups). Their martyrdom comes about through diabolical activity, a mystery of evil corporately symbolized by the beast from the chaotic Abyss. This beast is not further defined, but, in this

[90]Note also the failed expectation of repentance in the plague allowed under the sixth trumpet (9:20-21), with which 11:1-3 is bound as part of the prospective enlargement.

second woe, recalls especially the angel of the Abyss of the fifth trumpet (9:1-11) and points ahead to the beast of 13:1 and 17:8, a mutant of Satan. Here, however, it suffices to represent it as the apparent victor over God's prophets and as the cause of what others perceive as the martyrs' complete disgrace. The earth-dwellers rejoice in the silencing of the "unbearable accusations" ("torments") of Christian prophecy.

The last sub-section (*C*, vv. 11-13) begins (v. 11a) by noting the end of the witnesses' unburied state, again using (here in a short compass of three days and a half) the symbolically timed period of trial or tribulation. Then John describes first, in two sets of three, coordinated lines, their resurrection-ascension (vv. 11b-12) and second, at that moment, its amazing effectiveness (v. 13). Their death and being dishonored in death has not converted their enemies; what does so is their resurrection-ascension, their heavenly triumph by God's gracious command. Looking at the correspondences in vv. 11-12: when the spirit of life from God enters them, they hear his command to "ascend hither"; they stand on their feet ("standing up" is resurrection) and ascend to heaven by God's power ("on the cloud"). Terror lays hold of their enemies (the onlookers) as they gaze upon them in awe. Their being borne up to heaven despite the expectations of their enemies (that death and disgrace were final) precipitates another awesome and surprisingly encouraging scene (v. 13). At that very moment, an earthquake occurs and a "remnant" of the earth-dwellers (that is, the tenth part of the city and seven thousand inhabitants) perishes, but the rest, the majority, experience awe and voice their conversion. The phrase "give glory to the God of heaven" stands for the very opposite of the non-repentance of idolaters (16:11) and implies conversion to the one, invisible God (Dan 2:19) in contrast to the false worship of pagans.[91]

The "numbers destroyed" cannot consistently be interpreted by the sequence employed in the septenaries (one-fourth; one-third; all). Nor does John belittle or downplay an awesome event by his "tithing" of the city and mentioning the number, relatively small in apocalyptic characterization of disasters, of seven thousand. The numbers he uses express a Christian paradox by em-

---

[91]Giblin, "Revelation 11. 1-13," 445 and n. 46.

ploying standard OT imagery for destruction, according to which a small fraction survives as a remnant (in answer to the prophetic challenge) in order to rebuild their past association with God (Isa 6:13; Amos 5:3; 1 Kgs 19:18; cf. Rom 11:4-5). In Christian perspective, it is not a remnant that survives; rather, the great majority, however hostile, can be and, with prophetic hope, shall be converted.

This passage serves as a vivid, perhaps needed corrective to the pessimistic results of the first woe, in which the rest of mankind was not shocked into repentance, but despaired of life, and to the hellish host introduced by the sixth trumpet, where, expressly, the two-thirds left remained unconverted. Likewise, it prepares for further disclosures which imperatively announce the possibilities of a positive response to the Gospel up to the very moment of the final judgment on obdurate wrongdoers. John's Revelation is not a cynically vindictive book. It reaffirms, to be sure, God's vindication of the right way of thinking and acting and his punitive power, though not at all as hate-inspired or without a persistent appeal for conversion as well as for fidelity. Strategically-placed, power-laden moments in the elaborate structure of this narrated vision, like 11:1-13, speak louder and more tellingly than merely repeated offers. The way God answers the prayers of his martyrs (6:9-11; 8:2-5) may find fulfillment by mercifully going beyond their conception of perfect justice, as 11:1-13 attests—if only by the Christian, paradoxical reversal of OT remnant-imagery.

John leaves no doubt that the second woe comprises the enlargement as well as what immediately follows the blast of the sixth trumpet (v. 14; cp. 8:13). In the course of the first two woes, diabolical attack against pagan mankind in general (9:1-12; 9:13-21) has been partially successful, even largely so. Against Christians, this attack cannot trigger despair; the worst that it can do is slay the prophets and degrade them. Thus, the worst possible adversary one can conceive, namely, a devilish, super-human force, will not conquer. God's control of the situation is absolute, and his commands, based on the achieved triumph over death through the resurrection and an ascension to new physical life, prevail. The third woe will elaborate similar triumphs in the climactic conflict. In the fulfillment-time perspective of this apocalypse, that imminent moment is at hand; it comes quickly.

As announced (10:7), the decisive phase of the end-time events is expressed by the voice of the seventh angel as sounded in his trumpet-blast. The forthcoming passage contains many ramifications, but is carefully, clearly articulated by its literary structure. Furthermore, it coheres well both by its opening and by its concluding passages—the latter of which will introduce the seven angels with the seven last plagues. To comment on the range of the seventh trumpet-blast, however, requires an over-all perception of its seven (albeit unnumbered) major components, followed by attention to each in turn.

THE SEVENTH TRUMPET AND ITS RAMIFICATIONS (= THE THIRD WOE) (11:15–15:8)

With the sound of the seventh trumpet, a sevenfold series of events unfolds. They are not numbered, but specially significant events ("signs") near the beginning and end of the sequence enable one to delimit and examine the components of the whole. This sevenfold series or set of events strikes one as a kind of operatic *septet:* not a septenary or series of successive events so much as seven ways of dealing with aspects of the same climactic "moment," that is, "the great tribulation (woe)." Note the following outline (pp. 118–119), which provides an overview of the sevenfold concentric structure *(A, B, C, D, C', B', A')*. The focal, major point of the structure lies at the very center, *D* (14:1-5), the Lamb on Mt. Zion with the redeemed. This is the picture of victory, which fittingly forms a substantive *part* of the third woe (much as the resurrection-ascension of the prophets formed an essential part of the second woe). The opening section, *A* (11:15b-19) and the closing section, *A'* (15:2-8) present canticles celebrating the realization of the messianic kingdom *(A)* or also of final deliverance *(A')*. Furthermore, they each contain striking *openings of God's heavenly sanctuary,* accompanied by awesome portents. The next corresponding sections, *B* (12:1-18) and *B'* (15:1) specifically mention (a total of three) *signs in heaven,* of which the first, contrastingly paired signs *(B)* herald the inauguration of the conflict, which moves from heaven to earth (and states the third woe, 12:12), while the last *(B')* looks to heavenly figures whose action will again move from heaven to earth, resolving the conflict. The third corresponding series, *C* (13:1-18) and *C'* (14:6-20) highlights the conflict on earth: *C,* the tyranny of the beasts; *C'* the coming of judgment. Sections *C* and *C'* have two complementary portions each, and are closely linked by reference to false or genuine worship and by refrains concerning the patient endurance and fidelity of the saints (*C* and *C'*).

11:15a		*Sounding of the Seventh Trumpet*
11:15b-19	*A*	Canticle celebrating the messianic kingdom; opening of heavenly sanctuary (ark of covenant appears).
12:1-18	*B*	A great sign in heaven (the pregnant woman) and another sign in heaven (the dragon threatening her messianic child). Angelic conflict in heaven (the dragon cast down). A canticle of victory. The dragon *versus* the woman on earth.
13:1-18	*C*	The beast from the sea (false worship). Refrain: the patient endurance and fidelity of the saints (13:10). The beast from the earth (false worship). Call for wisdom (13:18): the beast's number.
14:1-5	*D*	The Lamb on Mt. Zion with the redeemed; mention of their (uncited) canticle.
14:6-20	*C'*	Three angelic figures in heaven: One, with an everlasting Gospel (for true worship); a second, announcing Babylon's fall; a third, threatening judgment (for false worship). Refrain: the patient endurance and fidelity of the saints (14:12-13). Two pairs of angelic figures: two (one, Son of Man) engaged in

the wheat harvest (gathering the just);

two engaged in the grape harvest (gathering the wicked)—for the winepress of God's anger.

15:1   *B'* Another great and wondrous sign in heaven (seven angels with the final plagues)

15:2-8   *A'* Canticle of Moses and the Lamb celebrating deliverance; opening of heavenly sanctuary (of the tent of testimony) and description of the angels with the final plagues.

16:1   *Activation of the last septenary upon a command to the seven angels with the last plagues.*

John has carefully marked by key words and rhythmic repetitions his line of thought in these four and a half chapters. He has provided marker-buoys, as it were, to guide the reader through this long channel. A special instance of this technique is *B'*, the mention of another great and wondrous sign in heaven. Although only a single verse long, the main function of *B'* (15:1) is to balance the relatively lengthy *B* (12:1-18) and to hint mysteriously at the decisive end to the end-time conflict. This short passage also serves to introduce the figures of the last septenary, latching it on to the end of the trumpet series.[92] The salient section of the whole sevenfold arrangement, however, describes not the conflict as such, but its salutary resolution: the Lamb on Mt. Zion with the redeemed. Christians, symbolically represented as the 144,000 sealed, who have proved themselves faithful, have been rescued from the earth (from perverse mankind) for God and the Lamb and now exult in heaven.

John's concentric structure also contains a progression on various counts. For instance, he moves from heavenly signs of primal conflict (the dragon's attack on the woman) to a great and marvelous sign of God's deliverance (the angels with the libation-

---

[92]U. Vanni, *La Struttura,* 125–130. A distinction obtains, however, between the "announcement" and the "activation" of a septenary (cp. 5:1-14 and 6:1 ff.; 8:2 and 8:6 ff.; 15:1, 8 and 16:1 ff.).

bowls, which express the prayers of the saints). He proceeds from a celebration of God's dominance in heaven to his dominance on earth as well. Lastly, his refrains progress from the plight of the faithful on earth under the oppression of the beasts from sea and earth to their reward at the fall of Babylon, the institutionalization of beastly success.

Section A (11:15b-19) Under the Seventh Trumpet

11:15-19

[15]   And the seventh angel blew (his) trumpet.

[15]   And there were [occurred] loud voices in heaven:
   The cosmic kingdom of our Lord and of his Anointed
   [Christ]
      has taken place [occurred],
   and he shall reign for ever and ever.

[16]   And the twenty-four elders,
      those seated on their thrones before God,
   fell on their faces and worshiped God, saying:

[17]   We thank you, Lord God,
      the Almighty,
      who are [is] and who were [was],
   because you have taken your great power
      and (started to exercise your) rule.

[18]   And the nations were enraged [wrathful]
   and (then) came your (own) wrath,
      and the time for the dead to be judged,
      and to give your reward to your servants the prophets
         and to the saints and to those who fear your name—
         the small and the great—
      and to destroy those destroying [corrupting] the earth.

[19]   And God's sanctuary in heaven was opened,
      and the ark of his covenant was made visible in his
      sanctuary,
      and there occurred lightnings and voices and thunders
      and an earthquake and a huge [great] hail(storm).

When the seventh angel sounds his trumpet (11:15a) a pair of events occurs (to be balanced by a similar pair at the close of the trumpet series, *A'*, 15:2-8): voices in heaven speak of God's victory, and God's sanctuary in heaven opens to disclose an element of the Holy War motif. Within the first (11:15b-18) of the pair, loud voices, apparently those of a heavenly multitude composed of angels and the blessed, declare that the world-rule of their Lord and his Anointed (the Messiah) has come to pass, so that he will rule forever (v. 15b). Both the Lord God and Christ (the Messiah), though distinguished, are indivisibly one in exercising their rule over the world. Thus, John expresses his monotheism in functional terms. Next (vv. 16-18), echoing this proclamation of God's royal supremacy, the elders, members of the heavenly court, worshipfully offer thanksgiving for the third, climactic time (cp. 4:9; 7:12). They pointedly omit from the hitherto repeated title "who is, who was, and who is coming" (v. 17; cp. 1:4, 8; 4:8) the third element, namely, "and who is coming." For they are celebrating that "coming" in kingly power; it had not taken place and is now taking place in the whole panorama opened up by the seventh trumpet. The passage goes on to explain how God's royal power is manifested in his rightful wrath against the raging of the nations (Pss 99:1; 46:7): he judges the dead, rewards his servants, and destroys those who have destroyed the earth by their corruption. The latter act is reminiscent of God's treatment of Babylon, Revelation 19:2 (cp. Jer 51:25).

What we have in vv. 15-18 does not determine a point in clock-and-calendar time, but rather denotes a decisive, momentous period in the manifestation of God's kingly rule. The "time" in question is the opportune period *(kairos)* for judgment. Its purview, as indicated by what is said in v. 18, goes even beyond the events taken in by the seventh trumpet and the seven last plagues, and must extend at least to the moment of judgment depicted in 21:1-8. The end-time scenario of apocalyptic is not that of a historian or a canonist. John does not attempt to depict the *kairos* by noting merely a single event. He announces in this canticle the whole panoply of images in chs. 12-15, brought to their climax against Babylon in ch. 16, and subsequently including God's termination of other eschatological adversaries (the beasts; Satan; Death and the Grave) in 19:11-21:8. In short, the hymn programmatically announces God's total victory, which has come and at the same time is being worked out fully, in all its ramifications.

The second, paired scene (11:19), in which God's heavenly sanctuary is opened, reveals the palladium carried into battle in the

Holy War to represent God's effective presence with his people: the ark of his covenant. Here, it does not budge from the heavenly sanctuary (where it is visualized as placed in the holy of holies), much less is it carried by humans into battle. Nonetheless, it symbolizes God's militant presence in forming his own people by delivering them from their enemies.[93] Accompanying and clarifying portents recall those of the casting of fire to earth from the altar of incense (8:5), with the significant addition of huge hailstones (11:19)—a motif which will reappear, quite escalated, at the climactic moment of the destruction of Babylon (16:18-21). The Holy War, understood as God's executing his own wrath against wrongdoers, particularly those who have tormented his own people, the faithful, has reached the moment of truth. Foregoing unsealings (6:1–8:5), equivalently oracles of the future, concluding with efficacious prayers (8:3-5) and with trumpets leading to the final engagement (8:6–11:15a), have now opened out into the awesome panorama of the final, decisive conflict.

Section B (12:1-18) Under the Seventh Trumpet

First, two counter-signs appear in heaven: that of the woman in labor and that of the dragon (12:1-2, 3-4a), with the woman's successful parturition and her escape (vv. 4b-6) for the symbolic period of persecution (1260 days). Second, a war in heaven, with Michael as its hero, casts the dragon and his angels to earth (12:7-9), and a victory-shout (vv. 10-12) explains the dragon's defeat. Third, returning to the theme of the conflict between the woman and the dragon (vv. 13-17), John describes the dragon's unsuccessful pursuit of the woman on earth, and she subsequently remains immune from him for the period of persecution (a time, two times, and half a time). Frustrated, the dragon goes off to

---

[93]The ark signified the militant presence of God among the people *as a whole* (scil., as involving all of the tribes); cf. G. von Rad, *Der Heilige Krieg,* 12–13, 27–28.

In the period close to the NT, the ark was expected to appear as a sign of God's mercy to his people (2 Macc 2:4-8) and of his deliverance of them from those who intended their destruction; cf. *Life of the Prophet Jeremiah,* 14–15, [1st C.], in D.R.A. Hare, "The Lives of the Prophets," J. A. Charlesworth, *The Old Testament Pseudepigrapha,* II (Garden City: Doubleday, 1985) 379–399, 388.

wage war with the rest of her children. In an ominous conclusion (preparing for his link with the beasts shortly to be described), he stands at the shore of the sea (v. 18), a symbol of the chaotic abyss.

12:1-18

1   And a great sign appeared in heaven:
>a woman wrapped [clothed] with the sun,
>and the moon beneath her feet,
>and on her head a crown of twelve stars,

2   and she was pregnant;
>and she cried out in labor and anguish to give birth.

3   And another sign appeared in heaven:
>and lo, a great, fiery-red dragon
>having seven heads and ten horns,
>and on his heads seven diadems;

4   and his tail swept (up) a third of the stars of heaven
>and cast them to the earth.

And the dragon stood before the woman
>who was about to give birth,
>in order that when she would give birth to her child
>he might devour (it).

5   And she gave birth to a son, a male (child),
>who was going to rule [shepherd] the nations with an
> iron rod;
>and her child was carried off to God and to his throne,

6   and the woman fled to the desert,
>wherein she had a place prepared by God,
>so that there they will feed her for 1260 days.

7   And war broke out [occurred] in heaven:
>Michael and his angels (started) to wage war against the
> dragon,
>and the dragon waged war and (so did) his angels,

8   and they were not mighty (enough),
>nor was a place found for them any longer in heaven,

9   and he was cast down—the great dragon,
>>the primeval snake [the ancient serpent],
>>the one called the Devil and Satan [the Adversary],
>>the one deceiving the whole inhabited world—

he was cast down to earth,
and his angels were cast down with him.

10   And I heard a loud [great] voice in heaven:
Now has salvation occurred,
and the power and the kingdom [kingly rule] of our
God
and the authority of his Anointed [Messiah, Christ],
for cast down is the accuser of our brothers,
the one accusing them before our God day and night.

11   And (indeed) they themselves have conquered him
on account of the blood of the Lamb
and on account of their (own) witness,
for indeed they did not love their lives (selfishly) up to
death.

12   Therefore, congratulate yourselves, O heavens,
and you who dwell [tent] within them;
(but) woe upon the earth and the sea,
for the Devil has come down to you,
having (in his heart) great anger,
knowing that he has little time.

13   And when the dragon saw that he was cast down to the
earth,
he pursued the woman who had borne the male child.

14   And there were given to the woman the two wings of the
great eagle,
so that she might fly to the desert
to her place (there)
where she will be [is] fed for a time, two times, and
half a time,
away from the (threatening) face of the snake.

15   And the snake sent out [cast] from his mouth,
(following) in back of the woman,
water like a river,
so as to have her carried off in the flood.

16   And the earth came to the aid of the woman,
and the earth opened its mouth and drank up the river
which the dragon had sent out [cast] from his mouth.

17   And the dragon was enraged [wroth] with the woman,
and he went off to wage war with the rest of her offspring,

those who observe the commands of God
and hold (fast) the(ir) witness from [of] Jesus.
18 And he stood on the sandy shore of the sea.

The spectacular, threefold sequence of scenes which John produces results from his careful composition and expansion of source-material. The following commentary will explain the sequence as it stands, however, and not from the standpoint of a technical examination of the process of composition. Nevertheless, some attention to John's use of source-material serves to show the modern reader (who cannot be expected as readily to recognize its motifs as did John's original hearers) how John produces a distinctively Christian perspective both from biblical and from pagan mythological language. Christianity reworks its biblical heritage and transforms pagan thinking in line with its own aim of communicating the truth in its cultural context. Its tendency to inculturate the Gospel without adulterating it is as old as the NT itself.

As Adela Yarbro Collins has argued,[94] John has adapted two Jewish sources: first, a narrative of conflict between a woman with child and a dragon—a story also similar to the Greek myth of Leto, the mother of Apollo, opposed by the dragon Python; second, the depiction of a heavenly battle. This commentary must prescind from giving further details. Suffice it to say that this passage, like others in Revelation, becomes a Christian synthesis of primeval conflict situations so as to televise, as it were, the cosmic victory of God's exercise of his kingly power, as heralded in §A.

Opening the first portion of the threefold sequence, two countersigns appear (12:1-4a), although they are not yet said to be in conflict one with the other. The woman appears, robed with the sun, the moon beneath her feet, and with a crown of twelve stars on her head. She represents God's people, the Israel of old[95] to

---

[94]A. Y. Collins, *The Combat Myth,* 83, 101-155.

[95]Kraft, *Offenbarung,* 164. Sun, moon, and stars are attributes of celestial divinities. John, of course, does not represent the woman, the "Queen of Heaven," as a goddess. For him, the twelve stars no doubt recall the twelve tribes and suggest the woman's role as a representative of God's people. Sun and moon highlight the excellence of the royal and

be sure, but she must subsequently be interpreted as the mother of Christians as well. Obviously, she is on both scores a heavenly type, not a given individual person, much less a given historical institution. For John, the genuine Israel and the faithful are fused as one and the same. The image of the heavenly woman was later applied to Mary, the mother of the divine Messiah, the Son of God, and the mother of Christians. This application, almost certainly not intended by John of Patmos, does not falsify the sense of the text, but appositely represents the theological continuity between Israel and the Church in terms of unique motherhood.[96] Accordingly, it may serve as a poetic or homiletic *application* of the text, even though it does not serve as an explanation (exegesis) of it. The woman's agony, glorious and triumphant though she is in the context of heavenly bodies (the sun, the moon, and the stars), expresses the traditional "birth-pangs (bringing forth) of the Messiah." In short, her bringing the Messiah into the world entails pain, not just glory, and only through this pain is her mission accomplished and God's messianic reign achieved. The countersign which appears is that of the fiery monster, depicted in the combined imagery of chaos and of the worst anti-God beast, with seven heads and ten horns.[97] He sweeps to earth a third of heaven's angels (the stars; cp. v. 9), a fraction which rivals God's own power (cp. the stressed one-third of the trumpet series).

The rest of the opening portion helps establish a chiastic, *a, b, a'* pattern for 12:1-18 as a whole. Components *a* (specifically, vv. 4b-6) and *a'* (vv. 13-17) deal, respectively, with *(a)* the dra-

---

priestly tribes (Judah and Levi) in the important *Testament of Naphtali,* 5, and may connote here the royal and priestly dignity of God's people, a theme frequently expressed elsewhere in Revelation.

[96]On the non-Marian literal sense of the passage, cf. R. E. Brown *et al, Mary in the New Testament* (Philadelphia: Fortress, 1978), "The Woman in Revelation 12," 219–239.

[97]For an illustration, cf. J. B. Pritchard, *The Ancient Near East in Pictures Relating to the Old Testament* (Princeton: University Press, [2]1969) illustration # 691, p. 121; the "seven-headed fiery dragon" (attacked by two gods) appears on a cylinder-seal. John derives the ten horns from the climactically awful beast in Dan 7:7 (where the beast, a war-elephant representing the empire of Alexander, has "ten" successors as potent offspring, the most notable of which is the Syrian tyrant Antiochus IV Epiphanes).

gon's unsuccessful design to devour the woman's child, the Messiah, and *(a')* the dragon's unsuccessful assault against the woman herself, and his turning to wage war against the rest of her children. The central, key component, *b* (vv. 7–12) describes first the dragon's defeat in heaven at Michael's hand and his being cast to earth, and, second, the victory-shout explaining this event and noting expressly the "third-woe," affliction for those on earth, including the faithful. These two elements within *b* are linked as event and interpretation, especially apropos of the Devil's being "cast down."

The dragon's opening confrontation with the woman (vv. 4b–6) deals with the dragon's attempt to kill the woman's child at birth. The tale creatively varies the myth of the birth of Apollo. Python (the dragon) had learned that he would be slain by the as yet unborn son of Leto. Consequently, he pursued her to destroy her. He stirred up the sea into such an uproar that Leto could not bear Apollo until earth came to her aid and raised up the island of Delos. Apollo attained full strength at birth, went to Mt. Parnassus, and slew the dragon.[98] John, of course, recasts the imagery in terms of his Christian, biblical perspective. The woman is not a goddess (Leto), but the personified image of Israel, God's people (cf. v. 1). At issue is not the birth of the god Apollo, but the birth of the Messiah, who will firmly rule all nations (v. 5; cp. Ps 2:9). Her son is not delivered by the aid of earth, but is taken up (by divine power, telescopically focusing on Jesus' resurrection-ascension, not his earthly birth) to God's throne. It is God himself who gives her a place, the desert, a traditional, biblical refuge of the persecuted,[99] secured from assault, but also provided with an oasis to nourish her for the classic, biblical period of persecution (1260 days). Her refuge will be recalled in equivalent form in the closing confrontation (v. 14, three-and-a-half years). What happens during that symbolic period of perse-

[98]Beasley-Murray provides a convenient summary, *Revelation*, 192–193; for detailed treatment, cf. A. Y. Collins, *The Combat Myth*, 65 ff., 245–261.

[99]Cf. Exodus 2:15; 1 Kings 17:2 ff.; 19:3 ff; 1 Maccabees 2:27-30. The Essene community at Qumran settled where it did for much the same reason: the desert location befitted those harassed by the Jewish "establishment" at the time.

cution, while the woman herself remains immune from it? The answer will be found in §*C,* which develops the assault against her other children. The Israel of God, the mother of the faithful, remains untouched, unhurt, as does her son the Messiah, though her other children, the faithful, may have to endure much from the bestial mutants of the dragon.

The central confrontation, *b* (vv. 7-12) begins by noting the victory of the archangel Michael, whose name itself ("*Who is like God?")* challenges any who would question the Lord's sovereignty. The great dragon receives multiple identifications. He is the ancient, primeval serpent (who misled the parents of humanity, Gen 3:1-15), the devil (Greek for "the adversary," as "Satan" is in Hebrew), and, newly, the one who misleads the inhabited world. Three times in v. 9 John stresses the "casting down" of this arch-adversary, and of his cohorts as well. On the heavenly plane, then, victory is complete and unquestionable. Further conflicts will occur on the earthly plane.

A heavenly voice interprets the meaning of this victory. Salvation has been determined from above in the defeat of the one who would accuse (condemn) "our brothers," that is, the faithful elsewhere, on earth, for the latter are also part of what was later called "the communion of saints." Even the faithful on earth share in this heavenly victory, for they are witnesses to the Lamb who has redeemed them. This theological bond obviously transcends temporal sequence. It may be illuminated somewhat by Jesus' remark to the seventy-two disciples (representing the universal mission of the Church founded by Jesus, but functioning after his ascension) when they returned successfully from their mission: "I saw Satan fallen [Satan's fall] like lightning from heaven" (Lk 10:18). In Revelation, the mission of the faithful is fidelity to death, shown by not "loving their lives to death," that is, by not placing first of all their own physical well-being. In retrospect, Michael is an archangel representing not himself as an independent angelic agent, but the faithful who will not compromise their allegiance to God. This "heavenly" victory does not entirely "pre-date" the militant testimony of the faithful on earth, the militant wing of the communion of saints, but only stages it in apocalyptic terms.

Nevertheless, the heavenly victory is not yet fully complemented by complete victory on earth. Consequently, this central scene *(b)* closes (v. 12) with a twofold proclamation of weal and of woe. The heavens and the faithful sheltered there (literally, those "tenting" in heaven) are to rejoice. Woe, however, to earth and sea because of Satan's presence in this albeit limited area! He has little time in the perspective of God's everlasting rule, but can still wreak on this earthly plane havoc against the inhabited world, including God's faithful here below.

The third woe consists "specifically" in what occurs according to the express warning given in 12:12, namely, satanic activity on the earthly plane. There is no need, however, to try to disengage from the well-integrated whole (11:15–15:8) the portion(s) (e.g., *C,* 13:1-18) that correspond most precisely to the statement of the heavenly voice. The announcement of the woe at hand (12:12) is itself embedded in a well-integrated canticle stressing salvation through conflict. Furthermore, even the portion of the sixth trumpet-blast which qualified most clearly as the *second* woe (scil., 11:1-13) featured as well the moment of the heavenly triumph of the two witnesses and, indeed, featured it climactically (11:11-13). Hence, one should regard the whole sweep of events given in the period covered by the seventh trumpet (11:15–15:8) as "the third woe." The "woe" paradoxically looks to salvation and even to victorious glorification as well as to suffering, as did Jesus Christ's own crucifixion.

The closing confrontation, *a'* (vv. 13-18) picks up the first, and develops the foregoing proclamation, especially its last verses (vv. 10-12), by defining the scope of the dragon's plans. Cast down to earth, he first (vv. 13-16) pursues the woman herself by an intensified, twofold attack, which is frustrated by his lack of *control* both of the air or the sky (supposed for the woman's flight with the wings of the great eagle) and of the earth itself. Turbulent waters are his only destructive means, but even these fail him—at least as symbolized by a river, which is fresh water. The ominous sea will be his only remaining resource (v. 18). The huge eagle probably alludes to God's protective power (cp. *Test. Moses,* 10:8). In frustrated fury, the dragon then (v. 17) turns to assault the rest of her children, Christians who remain faithful to God in their moral conduct and adhere to Jesus by the witness of their very lives. The major message of this final confrontation is that the people of God, represented by the woman and the rest of her children, remain at one and the same time immune to destruction, being providentially preserved during the whole period of tribulation, and yet vulnerable to diabolical attack.

SECTION C (13:1-18) UNDER THE SEVENTH TRUMPET

Fortunately, this lengthy section falls into two major portions (vv. 1-10 and vv. 11-18). Each deals with one of two beasts and each closes with a wisdom-utterance that alerts the Christian reader to consider the import of these scenes of false worship.

13:1-18

1   And I saw rising up from the sea a beast
         having ten horns and seven heads,
         and on its horns ten diadems
         and on its heads blasphemous titles [names].
2   And the beast which I saw
         was like a leopard,
         and its feet like a bear's,
         and its mouth like a lion's,
         and the dragon gave it his power and his throne
             and great authority.
3   and one of its heads (had been) slaughtered mortally,
         and (yet) its mortal wound had been healed.

     And the whole earth was wonder-struck (following) after
         the beast;
4   and they worshiped the dragon,
             because he gave authority to the beast;
         and they worshiped the beast, saying:
         Who is like the beast,
         and who can wage war with it?
5   And it was given a mouth to speak arrogantly [great
             things]
             and blasphemously,
         and it was given power to operate for forty-two months.
6   And it opened its mouth for blasphemies against God,
             to blaspheme his name and his dwelling [his tent],
                 those dwelling [tenting] in heaven.
7   And it was given (power) to wage war with the saints
             and to conquer them,

and it was given power over every tribe and people and
tongue and nation.

8 And all those dwelling on the earth will worship him,
all whose names are not written in the book of life
belonging to [of] the Lamb slain from the beginning of
the world.

9 If anyone has an ear, let him heed (this):
10 If anyone (is to go) into captivity,
he is to go into captivity;
if anyone (must) be killed by the sword,
he (must be) killed by the sword.
This is the way the patient endurance and fidelity of the
saints (works out).

11 And I saw another beast rising up from the earth,
and it had two horns like a lamb,
and it spoke like a dragon.

12 And it exercises all the authority of the first beast
in his presence [before him],
and makes the earth and those dwelling upon it worship
the first beast
whose mortal wound was healed.

13 And it does spectacular [great] signs,
so as even to make fire come down from heaven to earth
in the presence of human beings [before men];

14 and it deceives those dwelling upon the earth
through the signs it is given to do
in the presence of the beast [before the beast],
telling those dwelling upon the earth to make an image
for the beast
who has the sword-wound and came (back) to life.

15 And it was given (authority) to give breath to the image
of the beast
so that the image of the beast could even speak,
and could bring it about
that whoever did not worship the image of the beast
would be killed;

16 and he makes all,
the small and the great,
and the rich and the poor,

and the free and the enslaved,
give themselves a mark on their right hand(s)
or on their forehead(s)
17   and (does so) lest anyone be able to sell or buy
except one having the mark of the beast
or the number of his name.

18   This is the way wisdom (discerns):
One who has an intellect should decode [calculate]
the number of the beast, for it is a human's number:
and his number is 666.

The first portion (13:1-10) of §*C* (13:1-18) is straightforward.
It introduces the beast from the sea (vv. 1-3a), then, in a fivefold
concentric pattern, *a, b, c, b', a'* (vv. 3b-8), depicts false worship of the blasphemous monster, and, lastly (vv. 9-10) enunciates words of wisdom.

The beast rises from "the sea," a standard image of chaos (Dan
7:3). With its seven heads it mirrors the primeval monster of
chaos. The beast is intent on blasphemy, that is, injury and in-
sult directed at God himself. However one may opt to locate them,
the "ten crowned horns," updating the worst of the four beasts
in Dan 7:1-8, allude to kings or, rather, to Roman satellite kings.[100]
John fuses Daniel's cinematic vision of four world empires, a suc-
cession of hostile powers representing (as "four") worldwide
domination, into a single beast. He does so by including as well
characteristics of the leopard, the bear, and the lion (v. 3; cp. Dan
7:4-8). John does so to convey the image of an all-encompassing,

___

[100]*See above,* note 97. Cf. also *1 Enoch* 60:9; *2 Esdras* 6:49-52; *2 Baruch*
29:4. This beast is identical with the one in Revelation 17, notwithstanding the apparent diversity of origin (the sea, Revelation 13; the abyss,
Revelation 17), which is basically the same, namely, "chaos"; cf. A. Y.
Collins, *The Combat Myth,* 171.
If one counts the three imperial generals of A. D. 69, Galba, Otho,
and Vitellius, one may opt to take the kings as ten Roman emperors.
But this supposes needless reduplication. The kings seem to be symbolically a set ("ten") of Rome's allies or client-states (as, earlier, the Herods
were among "kings" controlled by Rome); cf. Revelation 16:13-14:16;
17:8-14, 16-17; 19:19-21. Gog and Magog stand for a different host, a
mythical one from beyond the sway of the Roman empire (20:7-10) and,
indeed, "cosmic" in nature (since the horde rises from the abyss).

bestial empire which is the agent of the dragon (v. 2). For John, of course, this agent is the imperial power of pagan Rome.

The figurative language John employs holds just as well for any godless world-empire, and is not to be delimited to coincide with a given, historical empire, even that of Rome. Rather, the image has a metahistorical quality. As a man of his own times, the prophet had to update and reorient the classical imagery of Daniel and allude to the current anti-God power he himself knew, namely, Rome. Concluding his sketch of this beast, John alludes to a specific emperor, Nero, as the slaughtered but healed head. According to a popular legend, which John's readers would have known, Nero was to have reappeared (after his suicide) to vindicate his policies.[101] More importantly, however, the "slaughtered but healed" aspect of this particular head grotesquely and blasphemously apes the death and resurrection of the real Lord of the world. Thus, this anti-God figure becomes also an anti-Christ image.

The concentrically-structured, dramatized scene of false worship (vv. 3b-8) emerges quite clearly when one first examines its central element, then its paired components. At the very center, *c* (v. 6), the beast blasphemously targets God, whose "name" stands for who he uniquely is, and also God's dwelling-place, the heavenly assembly of the saints. Both these objects prove to be out of the beast's reach. The opening and closing, paired components, *a* (vv. 3b-4) and *a'* (v. 8), which are next in importance in this kind of geometrically-designed literary composition, describe false worship by the earthlings. Key terms correlating these components (and appearing nowhere else in this tightly-woven composition) are "earth" and "worship." In *a*, the worship is ultimately satanic, directed toward the dragon, but proximately toward the apparently unconquerable beast, who enjoys the dragon's power. In *a'*, the earthdwellers are narrowed down to pagans, those whose lives to come are not guaranteed by association with the slain (slaughtered) Lamb of God. That the Lamb was slain "from the beginning of the world" (cf. 1 Pet 1:18-21) indi-

---

[101]A. Y. Collins, *the Combat Myth,* 176–183. Cf. John J. Collins, *The Sibylline Oracles* (Missoula: Scholars, 1974) 80–87; Tacitus, *Histories,* 1, 78; 2, 8.

cates God's providential governance[102] from the creation to the fulfillment of the redemption. Lastly, the intervening components, *b* (v. 5) and *b'* (v. 7), find a common bond in the repeated terms "it was given," especially with the added designation, "authority." Nevertheless, as in *a* and *a'* the concentric pattern does not remain static; it progresses. Thus, in *b,* the beast's activity appears as *vocal blasphemies* and as *temporally delimited* (namely, for the classical period of persecution, here expressed in terms of forty-two months). In *b'*, on the other hand, the beast's *physical activity* emerges (war against the saints), together with its *spatial reach* (every tribe, people, tongue, and ethnic group). The beast is frustrated in assaulting his primary targets (as was the dragon) but he succeeds partially against Christians on earth, and receives universal acclaim from the majority of the earthdwellers.

Concluding the first portion of §*B,* John makes use of parabolic language (vv. 9-10) derived largely from Jeremiah 15:2. He imparts a message to his reader which sums up the relevance of the foregoing bestial activity. What is to be heeded is the message of severely trying times ahead. The Christian may be subjugated, like a captive in war, and must endure it, or he may be martyred by the sword, and, again, must endure it. The spirit breathing these words is not punitive, however, as it is in Jeremiah 15:1-4, nor does the passage mark divine retribution for belligerent resistance (as in Matt 26:52, where both the context and the phraseology differ). The correlated saying in v. 10b explains that such is the way in which the patient endurance and the hope of the saints will have to be realized. Only through sharing the mystery of their crucified but risen Lord will they realize their destiny.

The second portion (13:11-18) of §*C* elaborates the theme of the false worship of a worldwide, imperial power at odds with God's power. More precisely, it features political and economic oppression as well as religious deception.

The beast from the earth parodies not only God and Christ but also the Spirit who directs genuine prophets. With horns like a

---

[102]"Predestination," as in St. Thomas Aquinas's commentary on Romans 8-9, can best be understood as providential governance, and certainly not as "predetermination." John surely considers Jesus Christ's sacrifice to have been offered freely, since it was an act of love (1:5).

lamb, and in the service of a prior figure, it parodies Christ. Speaking like a dragon, and able to brand (in a grotesque carica- ture of "sealing") those under its power, it mocks God the Fa- ther. Most strikingly, as the source of signs and a kind of breath of life, serving especially the intentions of the foregoing figure, it stands for an anti-Spirit or also, concretely, a false prophet. Insistently, John spells out what this other beast *does (poiei)* and makes others *do,* notably in the service of the first beast. Its power or authority is "given" it, ultimately, by God himself, who per- mits all this to happen. Nothing, however frightful or dangerous, escapes God's control. This false prophet probably represents pa- gan priests and wonder-workers who operate according to dia- bolical power or merely charlatan techniques, whether "magic" or ventriloquism.[103]

In closing this second portion of §*C,* John adds another word of wisdom. The name of the beast (not this beast from the earth, but the beast from the sea, to whom the second toadies) is to be construed by the intelligent reader. The "number of the beast" is a way of decoding its name, since letters were also used as num- bers (both in Greek and in Aramaic/Hebrew script).[104] It seems almost certain, particularly in the light of the Nero-motif apro- pos of the beast's healed wound (13:3a, 12), that the name is "Nero Caesar." Whenever John's work reached its final form— certainly not before A.D. 70 and probably as late as A.D. 100—Nero's persecution of Christians in A.D. 67, albeit not world- wide, served as a new but instantly classic image of what the faith- ful could expect from imperial Rome. Once more, John is not dating a specific clock-and-calendar period of oppression, but is providing a metahistorical symbol of it which the knowledgeable

---

[103]David Aune adduces solid evidence to suggest an "anti-magical po- lemic" pervades Revelation, notably in Jesus' own self-predications (e.g., as having the keys to Death and Hades, as being Alpha and Omega, as the one who comes quickly, and as the one who dines with those who acknowledge him); "The Apocalypse of John and Graeco-Roman Revela- tory Magic," *NTS* 33 (1987) 481–501, 493–494. *See below,* note 121 (con- cerning the magical notion of *ogdoas*).

[104]On a wall in Pompeii, a graffito reads: "I love her whose name is 545" (*philō hēs arithmos phi-mu-epsilon'*); cf. A. Deismann, *Light from the Ancient Near East* (London, rev. ed., 1927; repr., Grand Rapids: Eerdmans, 1978) 277.

reader should be able to grasp. The recurrent cult of the self-deifying State, here depicted in terms of a notorious Roman emperor, must be faced by every wise Christian of every generation.

Section D (14:1-5) Under the Seventh Trumpet

At the critical center, §D (14:1-5), of the cosmic panorama opened up by the seventh trumpet-blast lies a brief but heartening vision of the triumph of the saints. At least on the heavenly plane, this is already effected. The visual element (v. 1) consists of the Lamb on Mt. Zion (here, the symbolic, extra-terrestrial mount of God's sanctuary). The corresponding, audio element (vv. 2-5) describes the heavenly victory-song and concludes (vv. 4-5) with John's own identification of the victors.

14:1-5

1   And I looked,
      and lo, the Lamb (was) standing on Mount Zion,
      and with him a hundred and forty-four thousand
         having his name and the name of his father
         written on their foreheads.

2   And I heard a voice from heaven,
      like the sound [voice] of cascading [many] waters,
      and like the voice of great thunder;
   and the voice which I heard
      was like that of harpists playing on their harps.

3   And they sing a new song
      before the throne
      and before the four living beings and the elders.
   And no one has been able to learn the song
      except the hundred and forty-four thousand,
      those redeemed from the earth.

4   These are they who have not been defiled with women,
         for they are celibates [virgins];
      these are those following the Lamb wherever he goes;
      these were redeemed from mankind
         as (the) firstfruit for God and the Lamb,

5   and in their mouth(s) no lie has been found—
      they are blameless [unblemished].

That Mt. Zion here designates a metahistorical, supra-terrestrial place equivalent to heaven itself becomes evident from appended details. The Lamb, always hitherto situated in heaven, is accompanied by 144,000, the army of the Israel of God, sealed with his name (scl., "the Lord"[105] and his Father's name ("the Almighty," the *Pantokratōr).* This marshalled throng does not stand as sealed protectively *before* the Day of the Lord, as it did in 7:1-8, but as bearing the Lamb's name and that of his Father—accounting for their victory—*after* their triumph. For they sing a "new song," that is, a victory-hymn (v. 3; cp. Pss 98:5; 144:9) in God's court and have been redeemed from earthly trials (v. 3). In effect, they enjoy a risen life in heaven, that previewed in the latter portion of the enlargement after the sixth unsealing (7:9-17).

At this point, accordingly, there arises no need for an "interpretation-scene" given by a heavenly personage (as was the case in 7:9-17). John himself identifies them trenchantly in three clauses (vv. 4a, 4b, 4c-5). They are "virgins," that is, celibates. In apocalyptic imagery, this means that they are those who have not yielded to false worship and its attendant immorality, implied by fornication with women. The imagery is no more sexist than that of the beast and the false prophet, who were typed as male figures. Admittedly, this idealization (male celibacy) could hardly have been employed unless moral virginity, notably among males, was an accepted ideal of conduct in Johannine circles. At the same time, the validity of the image must extend to all the faithful (as implied by the collective, complete Israel of the 144,000) who have avoided the contamination of pagan worship and immoral conduct. The second clause defines them positively in terms of their constant following of the Lamb, the victorious Jesus who sacrificially died but has risen. The third, amplified clause tells us that these followers of Jesus have been redeemed not as the fully-completed, innumerable multitude, but as the "firstfruit," that is, God's guarantee of an abundant, final harvest. As the portent of the whole crop, they belong to God and to the Lamb. They

---

[105]The title of Jesus Christ in 19:16, "King of Kings, Lord of Lords" (= 777 in Hebrew or Aramaic letters: *see below,* note 129) stands opposed to that of the beast in 13:18 (whose number is 666) much as the divine "seal" (*sphragis*) on the faithful stands in contrast with the "brand" (*charagma*) of the beast.

are uncorrupted (blameless), again alluding to their symbolic celibacy, for they had not uttered the great lie, a false confession of evil as good (cp. Zeph 3:11-13).

This pivotal, central section does much to fashion the perspective of all the sections under the seventh trumpet. For it draws attention to the heavenly reward for those who will have remained faithful throughout their earthly struggle. Furthermore, it binds the "framing sections" (namely, §A and §A'), which are second only to this central section, D, in over-all importance, into an integrated panorama. For instance, the canticle of the redeemed is noted here, but not cited. Essentially, it remains a mystery, the personal prerogative of those who follow the Lamb in heaven, and therefore must remain uncited. Nevertheless, its quality as a victory-hymn recalls that in 11:18, which spoke of the reward for the saints, and prepares for the canticle of deliverance (the canticle of Moses and of the Lamb) in 15:2-4. Moreover, §D is situated on Mt. Zion, a heavenly spot in this context and by the same token the locale of God's heavenly sanctuary, mentioned in 11:19 (§A) and again in 15:5-8 (§A'). This Zion is a place of repose, of final respite and reward, disengaged from the belligerent imagery in §§A and A', not to mention that of all the other sections under the seventh trumpet. Appropriately, however, this very difference places the battle-imagery in proper perspective, as culminated in lasting, rewarded companionship with the slain and risen Lamb of God. The same subordination of battle-imagery to the vision of peace marks the progression of the entire major vision of Revelation (4–22), which concludes with the new creation and the discourse explaining the New Jerusalem.

SECTION C' (14:6-20) UNDER THE SEVENTH TRUMPET

Balancing §C (13:1-8), while at the same time moving ahead towards the moment of divine retribution, this passage provides God's answer to false worship. Two major components, with an intervening refrain (balancing a similar one in §C) stand out. At the outset (14:6-11), three angels make proclamations, announcing in turn the Gospel requiring repentance and true worship, the fall of immoral Babylon, and the penalty for false worship (of the beast from the earth and its idol, the beast from the sea). A refrain (vv. 12-13) concerning the patient endurance of the saints (soldering §C' with §C, cp. 13:9-10) is endorsed by a declaration of heavenly reward, affirmed by the Spirit. This time, the refrain features the reward, not the harsh reality of testimony under persecution. Lastly (vv. 14-20), two pairs of angelic figures reap the harvest. The first pair harvests the wheat (those ripe for salvation); the second pair, the grapes (those ripe for God's wrath, to be trampled). In all, a suggestively complete group of seven angelic figures appears in 14:6-20: three in a series, then two pairs, with the Spirit's affirmation of a heavenly reward for the faithful in between. Motifs both of the coming, final judgment and of the current, heavenly reward of the faithful are combined.

14:6-20

6   And I saw another angel flying in mid-heaven,
        holding an everlasting gospel to proclaim (as good news)
          to those dwelling on the earth
          and to every nation and tribe and tongue and people,

7   saying in a loud [great] voice:
        Fear God and give him glory,
        beause the hour for his judgment has come!
        Worship the one who has made
          the heaven and the earth and sea and sources of
          (fresh) water!

8   And another angel, a second, followed, saying:
        Great Babylon has fallen, fallen,
        she who has made all nations drink the wine of
        (God's) anger at her fornication.

9   And another angel, a third, followed them
        saying in a loud [great] voice:
        If anyone worships the beast and its image
        and takes (its) mark on his forehead or on his hand,

10   he himself will drink of the wine of God's anger
        poured out straight in the cup of his wrath,
        and will be tormented with fire and sulphur
        before the holy angels and before the Lamb.

11   And the smoke of their torment goes up for ever
        and ever,
        and they have no rest day and night,
        (those) who (are) worshiping the beast and its image,
        and [indeed if] anyone takes the mark of its name.

¹²   This is the way the patient endurance of the saints (works
        out),
            those keeping [observing] the commands of God
                and the(ir) fidelity to Jesus [the fidelity of Jesus].
¹³   And I heard a voice from heaven saying:
            Write:
            Blessed (are) the dead,
                those who die in the Lord from this point on.
            Yes (indeed), says the Spirit:
            They shall rest from their labors [toil],
                for their works follow along with them.

¹⁴   And I looked,
            and lo, a white cloud,
            and on the cloud one seated like a Son of Man [quite
                like a man],
            having on his head a golden crown,
            and in his hand a sharp scythe.
¹⁵   And another angel came out of the sanctuary
            shouting in a loud [great] voice to the one seated on the
                cloud:
            Send your scythe and harvest,
            because the hour for harvesting has come,
            because the harvest of the earth is dry
                [withered/ripened].
¹⁶   And he who sat on the cloud sent [cast] (forth) his scythe
            to the earth,
            and the earth was harvested.
¹⁷   And another angel came from the sanctuary in heaven,
            having himself a sharp scythe.
¹⁸   And another angel (came forth) from the altar,
            (the one) having authority over the fire,
            and he called in a loud [great] voice to the one having the
                sharp scythe, saying:
                Send your sharp scythe and gather the grapes
                    of the vine of the earth,
                for its bunches are ripe.
¹⁹   And the angel sent [cast] (forth) his scythe to the earth,
            and he gathered the vine of the earth
            and he cast (it) into the great winepress of God's anger.

20   The winepress was trampled outside the city,
        and there went forth from the winepress blood,
        as high as horses' bridles,
        for 1600 stadia [two hundred miles].

At the beginning of §*C* we find three abruptly-introduced angelic proclamations (14:6-7; 14:8; 14:9-11). The first, in particular, comes as a surprise, uttered by "another" angel when no other individual angel has been mentioned since Michael (§*B*). Why is he called "another"? Perhaps this angel synthesizes previous figures and their functions. Revelation 8:13 featured an eagle *flying in mid-heaven* (as does the angel in 14:6-7, although the eagle of 8:13, is not *said* to be an angel) and proclaiming the advent of three woes. In working out the woes, John introduced the note of expected repentance (9:20-21) or of actual conversion (11:13). Revelation 10:2-7 presented an angel who swore by the creator of heaven, earth, and sea, and who held in his hand a small scroll which he proclaimed as "gospel," the completion of God's mystery promised as good news *(hōs euēggelisen)* to his servants the prophets. Here, in Revelation 14:6-7, we find an angel flying in mid-heaven who proclaims the everlasting gospel to the world and calls attention to the creator of heaven, earth, and sea—adding "and fresh waters." It seems reasonable to assume that this angel figures in the context of the third woe (the seventh trumpet) as showing that, notwithstanding imminent judgment for false worship, there remains sufficient time in this period of woe for repentance according to the terms of the Gospel.

Again, a given element in a series of visions finds clarification in what follows. For a second angel (v. 8) proleptically proclaims the fall of Babylon for intoxicating the nations with immorality, thus incurring God's wrath.

A third angel complements the preceding two with a condemnation of false worship. The first angel (vv. 6-7) offered opportunity for repentance. The third spells out the consequences of non-repentance. The second, of course, has briefly stated the decisive moment, especially for the non-repentant. The third angel states the penalty conditionally, again allowing time for repentance (as in the proclamation of the first angel). His message is chiastically structured *(a, b, b', a')*. The outside portions, *a* (v. 9b) and *a'* (v. 11b), give the qualifying conditions, themselves stated in repeated order: worship . . . take the mark . . .). The inside, more weighty portions, *b* (v. 10) and *b'* (v. 11a), spell out the penalty (the key term being "torment"). The dire consequences threatened are no less than eternal damnation, not imposed by believers, however, but by God himself before the Lamb and the angels. Hell is a "good thing" for those who deserve it. God does not wish it (cf. vv. 6-7), and certainly the faithful do not gloat over their passive contribution to it. In this, the theology of Revelation differs markedly from some Jewish apocalyptic, which definitely contains a bitterly vindictive streak.[106] Still, salvation would be a rather vague ideal if there were no self-incurred catastrophe from which humankind should be saved. Recognition of eternal torment as the *alternative* to heeding the Gospel and enjoying forever God's kingdom helps authenticate a realistic religion.

Before proceeding to the second group of angelic figures (14:14-20), John repeats and enlarges the wisdom-saying he employed in the corresponding section, §*C* (13:9-10), concerning the patient endurance and fidelity of the saints. This time (14:12-13), however, the word is one of consolation, not of insistence on brutal trials. The beatitude (a proclamation of those specially blessed by God) concerns those who have proved their fidelity to Jesus by dying in his service ("in the Lord"). The Spirit himself endorses this divine declaration and goes on to explain it: the good works of the long suffering faithful are not temporary actions, but an endowment which remains with them in heaven, even before the last day of earthly time.[107]

[106]The contrast can be seen when one reads *1 Enoch* 95:3, where the just physically inflict torment on the wicked. Cf. G. W. E. Nicklesburg, "The Apocalyptic Message of *1 Enoch* 92–105," *CBQ* 39 (1977) 309–328, 312–315. Cf. also W. Klassen, "Vengeance in the Apocalypse of John," *CBQ* 28 (1966) 300–311, 309, 311. The "torment" inflicted by God's prophetic witnesses lies in their unwelcome preaching of repentance (11:3-10).

[107]The beatitudes (macarisms) throughout the NT do not look to one's social, economic, or other material condition as such. They concern how an individual or class—often one that is not valued highly by merely human standards—is preferentially regarded by God and stands as a model for others. In short, they proclaim his special, personal concern for a religious type.

The second major component (14:14-20) features four other angels in two pairs. Each pair contains one with a scythe and another who appeals to him, with a description of the results. The first pair deals with the harvest of grain, which stands for the just (as is evident from its contrast to the subsequent harvest of grapes). The second pair handles the harvest of grapes. As the amplification requires, the "grapes" are the wicked.

The first pairing of angelic figures opens (v. 14) with the image of a man, crowned, with a scythe. This figure can be none other than Jesus Christ, the Son of Man. At least implicitly, however, since v. 15 refers to "another" angel, he himself appears here as an "angel." He may be regarded as such because he is God's special emissary in judging mankind. More likely, however, one must allow for a certain "distancing" in apocalyptic language between a person perceived as physically, totally present and the same person as "represented," for example, by a kind of "stand-in." This mode of description respects the fact that, although the one seen is a real person, even a human being who is a divine person, that person is present only *in vision*.[108] With respect to Jesus Christ, whose "second coming" means both personal and physical contact with the faithful, such "distancing" is called for in an apocalyptic series of visions. The parousia (second coming) has not actually occurred; it is here configured symbolically. Particularly in a series of visions which looks forward to Jesus Christ's physical presence among the faithful, the apocalyptic prophet must exercise reserve in depicting him.

Addressing the man crowned (as presaging victory) and carrying a sharp scythe, another angel aproaches. His approach moves the picture from God's sanctuary (the place for those saved) to the figure on the cloud, who by implication has been given kingly power (cf. Dan 7:9). The harvest is ripe, and the one seated on the cloud (in the posture of judgment, not standing to receive kingly power) harvests the just from the earth.

Another angel comes from the sanctuary in heaven (from which God's retribution also emanates) with the same kind of instrument as that which the crowned man carried. This time, however, as the course of events will show, it is to implement requital.

[108]Cf. Giblin, "Revelation 11. 1–13," nn. 24, 62, and Acts 13:12-15. In Jude 5-7, Jesus is the Angel of Yahweh; *see below,* note 171.

The paired angelic figure comes ominously from the altar, and has authority over the fire. As the reader is expected to recall, an angel at the altar casts fire to earth at the introduction of the septenary of trumpets (8:3-5). This angel's voice, alluding to Joel 3:13, the Day of the Lord against the wicked in the valley of Jehoshaphat, next to Jerusalem, calls for the harvest of earth's grapes. In response, the second scythe-bearing angel harvests the grapes for trampling in the winepress of God's wrath. Outside the city (that is, in the valley of Jehoshaphat, outside Mt. Zion) the winepress is trampled. The unfordable stream of blood (the wine of God's wrath consisting in the lives of the wicked) symbolizes worldwide retribution, for the 1600 stadia represent four-squared times one hundred stadia. The number is awesome, but restricted, if only by the multiplication in terms of hundreds, definitely not in terms of thousands or ten-thousands. John's composition does not exult in this destruction, however much deserved, but contents itself with noting that the current is formidable, even impassable.

Section B' (15:1) Under the Seventh Trumpet

John sees another sign in heaven, great and marvelous (15:1). His words can evoke only the great sign in heaven which he mentioned in 12:1 and the counter-sign in heaven, noted in 12:3, both at the outset of §B. For the singular "sign" (*sēmeion*) plus the descriptive phrase "in heaven" occurs in Revelation only of these three phenomena. Thus, he counterpoises the great and awesome heavenly sign of §B', the seven angels with the seven last plagues, to the signs of §B which set the stage for heavenly warfare and the dragon's being cast down to earth. The anger *(thymos)* of the dragon (12:12) is now counterbalanced by the final anger *(thymos)* of God (15:1b).

15:1

[1]   And I saw another sign in heaven,
    a great and wondrous (sign):
    seven angels having the seven last plagues,
    (the last) because with them God's anger is fulfilled
    [completed].

Although quite brief, §*B'* proves strategically necessary to maintain the equilibrium of the total composition of 11:14b–15:8.[109] This sign amounts to the anouncement of God's final wrath against evildoers. The motif will be reintroduced at the end of §*A'*, as part of the "dovetailing" process of interlocking the septenary of the last plagues with the septenary of the trumpets. The septenary of the last plagues, however, will not be *activated* until the beginning of the final septenary (16:1). It is interesting to note that, although these seven angels "have" the last plagues when they are initially presented (scl., in §*B'*, 15:1), they are later (§*A'*, 15:7) "given" seven libation-bowls filled with them. The added reference to "libation-bowls" in §*A'* probably conveys the meaning that the plagues will occur in response to the prayers of the saints.

Section A' (15:2-8) Under the Seventh Trumpet

As in the corresponding, opening section under the seventh trumpet (§*A*, 11:15b-19), a heavenly canticle paired with the opening of God's sanctuary in heaven form the two, prominent features of §*A'*.

15:2-8

2 And I saw (something) like a crystal sea mixed with fire;
and those who were victorious
over the beast
and over his image
and over the number of his name
were standing on the crystal sea, holding God's harps.
3 And they sing the song of Moses, God's servant, and of the Lamb,
saying:
Great and wondrous are your works,
Lord God the Almighty!
Just and true are your ways,
O King of the Nations!
4 Lord, who will not be in awe of [fear] you,
and glorify your name?

---

[109]There is no need to change the order of the text, as Paul Minear does, *I Saw a New Earth* (Washington: Corpus, 1968) 328-329.

> For (you) alone (are) holy;
> for all the nations will come and worship before
> you;
> for your just decrees have been made manifest.

5   And afterwards I looked:
>   and the sanctuary of the tent of testimony was opened
>   in heaven,
6   and the seven angels who have the seven plagues
>   came forth from the sanctuary,
>   clothed in bright white linen,
>   and girt around their chests with golden sashes;
7   and one of the four living beings gave the seven angels
>   seven libation-bowls
>   filled with the anger of God who lives for ever and
>   ever;
8   and the sanctuary was filled with smoke
>   from the glory of God and from his power,
> and no one was able to enter the sanctuary
>   until the seven plagues of the seven angels were com-
>   pleted.

The canticle of §*A'* features the song of the faithful in heaven, who have overcome the beast (from the sea), the imperial image (idol) of the same beast, and what it stands for (that is, its name, the persecuting emperor doomed to frustration). John combines in this picture both the victory of the Christian faithful over the emperor and the triumph of God's people delivered from Pharaoh. The crystal sea is the heavenly ocean, an OT image of the firmament roofing God's creation, and its fiery nature evokes the Red Sea, the theater of Israel's deliverance during the Exodus. Accordingly, the victors' hymn is entitled the "Hymn of Moses and the Lamb." Its phrases combine a wealth of passages from Scripture.[110] As refashioned here, the OT texts serve strikingly to attribute the victory solely to the Lord's acting on behalf of his own people, though not at the expense of others. Its three portions (v. 3b, v. 3c, v. 4) highlight three titles and, in turn, God's works, his ways, and his just decrees. The last two portions are

[110]For example: Exod 34:10; Deut 32:4, Pss 88:6; 98:21; 111:2; 139:14; 145:17; Amos 3:13; 3:3 (*G*); Isa 2:2; Jer 10:7; 11:20; 16:19.

more tightly linked, celebrating as they do God's justice to the nations, his universal governance, which should prove salutary rather than condemnatory for the world at large. God's justice and fidelity are also proved, as the hymn of the victors supposes, in his fidelity to his witnesses, as earlier in the case of the two prophetic witnesses of 11:1-13.

Paradoxically, then, God's triumph in his Holy War against the forces of evil entails much more than wrathful requital of evil committed by mankind and more than reward for faithful service; it entails ample opportunity for repentance and conversion. Only at the very end of the end, the last plagues of Revelation 16, does God mete out one's ineluctable punishment. The theme of possible repentance first emerged with the three woes, identified with the last three trumpets. In the first (9:1-12a), unbelievers were tormented and were driven to hopelessness for a symbolic period of five months, but that period, however lengthy (see above, pp. 99-103) was not final. In the second (9:12b-11:14a) human beings remained unrepentant, even after a further, hellish plague (9:20-21), but most were amazingly converted by the heavenly triumph of God's faithful prophets (11:1-13). In the third, the appeal to repentance, announced by the angel with the everlasting, enduring Gospel (14:6-7) and coupled with threats of judgment (14:8-12), is uttered once again. Here (§*A'*), at the close of the third woe, the blessed themselves reaffirm the optimistic prospect, even as the portion of text (15:5-8) coupled with it prepares the reader for the execution of God's final wrath (cp. 15:1).

The complement to the canticle (as in §*A*) consists of the opening of God's heavenly sanctuary and a vision of his might. In § *A*, the ark of his covenant appeared, the palladium which indicated his efficacious presence in the Holy War. Now, in §*A'*, the "tent of testimony" appears. This evokes the desert sanctuary (preceding the temple) and, by the same token, God's abiding covenant with Moses (Exod 40:34-38). The heavenly sanctuary becomes inaccessible until the fulfillment of God's purpose (v. 8), probably to signify the exclusion of any deterring power of intercession. It remains inaccessible also because the decisive moment, marked by "It has taken place *(gegonen)*" in 16:17, pinpoints the same "theological moment" as the emergence of the new creation, the coming of the New Jerusalem (21:6, *gegonan)*, which replaces the heavenly sanctuary as God's abode with his people.

Worked into the midst of this scene of the opening (and effective closing) of the heavenly sanctuary are the seven angels who proceed from the sanctuary (vv. 6-7). They emerge in priestly attire, assisted by one of the four living beings who gives them the instruments of the wrath of God. The libation-bowls, recalling the instruments by which the prayers of the saints were offered to God (5:8), show that God's wrathful justice on the unrepentant and on the archetypes of evil (Babylon in particular) responds to those who pleaded to him to show his holiness and fidelity.[111]

§*IV. The Seven Libation-Bowls of God's Final Wrath (16:1-21)*

The seven last plagues stand as the third and last septenary of Part Two of Revelation. A number of features combine to establish not only connections with the foregoing septenary of the trumpets, but also links with the wider scenario of God's wrath against evil.

The septenary commences (16:1) with a loud voice from the sanctuary commanding the seven angels to execute God's wrath (cf. Isa 66:6). Even though the voice speaks of God in the third person, it may be his own or, better, that of the Lamb, whose wrath is that of the Enthroned (cp. 5:6 and 6:16; 19:5). In any event, it surely expresses God's wish (cp. Ps 69:25 and Zech 3:8). Perhaps a certain lack of clarity both here (16:1) and later (19:5) is designed to set in relief the very throne of the sanctuary declaring: "It has taken place *(gegonen)*" (16:17; cp. 21:5-6).

The first four angels smite in turn, as in the case of the trumpets, earth (v. 2), sea (v. 3), fresh waters (vv. 4-7), and the sun

---

[111]Compare "holy" *(hosios)* in 16:5 and 15:4, and both of these texts with the prayers of the martyrs in 6:10. Appropriately, the prayers of the saints are offered to God in "golden bowls *(phialai)* filled with incense" (5:8). An angel subsequently offers incense to God with respect to the prayers of all the saints (8:3-4) at the outset of the trumpet-septenary. The libation-bowls *(phialai,* as in 5:8) are employed to execute God's wrath in answer to these prayers (16:1-21). The priestly garb of the libation-bowl angels and also their coming from the sanctuary (15:1) thematically links these liturgical acts in the progression of Rev 4-22.

(vv. 8-9). The fifth strikes the beast's throne (vv. 10-11). The sixth (vv. 12-16) dries up the Euphrates, to prepare for a final engagement with an invading force from the east. Like the sixth element in the septenaries of the unsealings and of the trumpets, the sixth libation-bowl introduces a perspective enlarging that of the septenary in which it occurs. The enlargement or expansion consists minimally of v. 15, but may include vv. 13-14 and 16 as well, which contain imagery which will be developed in 19:11-21. Finally, the seventh angel pours his libation-bowl on the air (v. 17). At that moment, God declares the events fulfilled (v. 17b), and John describes the climactic catastrophe on earth, that affecting the World-City (vv. 18-21).

A. THE FIRST FOUR OF THE LAST PLAGUES (16:1-9)

16:1-21

1   And I heard a loud [great] voice from the sanctuary
    saying to the seven angels:
    Go, and pour out onto the earth
    the seven libation-bowls of God's anger!

2   And the first went away and poured out his libation-bowl
    on the earth,
    and an evil and foul ulcer appeared [came to be]
      on the human beings who had the mark of the beast
      and who worshiped his image.

3   And the second poured out his libation-bowl
    on the sea,
    and it turned to [became] blood, like that of a dead
    body,
    and every living thing died, everything in the sea.

4   And the third poured out his libation-bowl
    on the rivers and the sources of (fresh) waters,
    and they turned to [became] blood.

5   And I heard the angel of the waters saying:
    You are just, you who are and who were, the Holy
    One,
      in that [because] you have judged these actions
      [things];

6   because they have poured out the blood of holy men
             and prophets,
         and you have given them blood to drink;
         they deserve (it) [are worthy].
7   And I heard the altar saying:
         Yes, Lord God the Almighty,
         true and just are your judgments!

8   And the fourth poured out his libation-bowl
         on the sun,
         and it was allowed to burn human beings with fire,
9   and human beings were burned with searing heat [with
             great burns]
         and they blasphemed the name of God,
             who held power over these plagues,
         and they did not repent by giving him glory.

Allusions to the plagues preceding the Exodus from Egypt are
even more in evidence in the septenary of the bowls than in that
of the trumpets. The first plague, for instance (16:2), recalls the
sores of Exodus 9:8-12. John tailors the plague, however, to the
key motif of this septenary, requital against the godless devotees
of the beast from the sea (Roman imperial power) and his image
(the cult of the self-deifying emperor).

The plagues of the last septenary are not "numerically limited"
to the "one-third" stressed throughout most of the trumpet-series.
That fraction was a sobering, preparatory motif, as was the earlier "one-fourth" featured in the unsealings. As the second plague
suggests by speaking of "every living thing," a greater disaster
cannot be imagined. The "sea," however, represents not the inhabited world, but chaos, particularly as now devoid of life.

The third plague targets once more (as did the first) the human
villains in this cosmic cataclysm. When fresh waters turn to blood,
a pair of heavenly declarations acclaim God's judgment against
those who slew his saints (that is, all those genuinely faithful to
him) and particularly his prophets (his spokesmen).[112] This third

[112]Cf. A. Y. Collins, "The History-of-Religions Approach to Apocalypticism and the 'Angel of the Waters' (Rev 16:4-7)," *CBQ* 39 (1977)
367–381. Collins shows that John has *adapted* a traditional judgment-
doxology to produce an "eschatological vindication-formula," ibid., 369.

"libation-bowl angel" now comments upon what he has just done.[113] He addresses God as the Holy One *(ho hosios,* vv. 3-4, not *ho hagios),*[114] recalling the Lord's title, "Holy One" *(hoti monos hosios)* in 15:4, but in such a way as to bring out the corollary of God's salvific justice, namely, his judgment against evil. Repentance was still a viable option in 15:3-4. Now, however, certain human beings themselves have ruled that out. God's holiness, an expression of his kingly power (harkening back to the beginning of the seventh trumpet's message, 11:15-18; cp. 15:4) also denotes his unique personal integrity. Therefore, while it looks first and foremost to humans' well-being in redemption, it must entail as an alternative the ruin of the unrepentant. For God cannot compromise his very self. Responding to the angel's verdict, the (angel of the) altar approves (v. 7, also recalling 15:3-4) God's justice and fidelity in his decisions. The angel in charge

[113]Similarly, elsewhere, a given angelic action is interpreted by the same angel (18:21-24), or a given angel proclaims a document he holds (10:2a.5-7; 14:6-7), or the number of those sealed is (implicitly) spoken by the angel with God's seal (and by his attendants, 7:2-8) after he has expressly enjoined others to wait (7:1-2). The "altar" which verbally responds (16:7) is probably apocalyptic shorthand for the angel who offered incense at the altar and cast its fire to earth—but in a half-hour of complete *silence* (8:1, 3-5), including, of course, his own silence. Because the souls of the OT martyrs were under the altar before they were "raised" to don white robes (6:9-11), John writes "altar" in 16:17 to evoke that scene as well. Both the plea for vindication of blood and the omen of fire cast to earth are fulfilled in waters of blood. Fire and bloody water nicely complement one another in apocalyptic imagery (cp. the blazing *star,* Absinthe [Wormwood], and the *fresh waters* it poisons, in the scene of the third bowl, 16:10-11).

[114]Revelation predicates *hagios* ("holy") of the faithful ("the saints," *passim),* of heaven (20:9), and also of Jerusalem (both as symbolic of the world subsequently profaned, 11:2, and as the New Jerusalem, the bride of the Lamb, 21:2, 10; 22:19), as well as of God and Christ (though clearly here in a unique sense, 3:7; 4:8; 6:10). On the other hand, Revelation predicates *hosios* ("holy") only of God himself (15:4; 16:5). *Hosios* (like the Latin *fas)* conveys for John the idea of divine right, proper to God alone as the ultimate source of justice (cf. "because [you] *alone* [are] holy [*hosios*]," 15:4). *Hosios* (Heb *ḥasîd*) probably also connotes the fulfillment of God's covenant-fidelity *(ḥesed,* his faithful love, true to his word); cf. Hauck in *TDNT* V, 489–493, 492, 490.

of casting fire upon the earth (8:3-5) seconds the declaration of God's justice made by the angel of the waters.

This vignette (vv. 5-7) builds upon, advances, and thus synthesizes anew at least three more foregoing scenes (besides 15:3-4 and 11:15-18). In 6:9-11, at the fifth unsealing, God's faithful under the altar prayed for vindication of their blood. They received a heavenly reward and were told to wait until their number was fulfilled. By now, in John's end-time scenario, that moment has come—with the last plagues. Next, in 8:3-5, just after the oracular unsealings and before the actual trumpet-blasts heralding the great conflict, the prayers of the saints were offered to God and fire from the altar was cast to earth. Then, with the first trumpet, not only hail but also fire mixed with blood was cast upon earth (8:7) and, especially with the third trumpet (8:10-13), a blazing star, Wormwood, fell upon the fresh waters. Foregoing aspects of God's judgments on behalf of his loyal people find their further, clearer realization in the third of the last plagues. God vindicates his own holiness at the time he determines, which has allowed up to the final moment of these plagues an opportunity for genuine repentance. The final moment, to be sure, is staged in amplified, parade format which will entail still more "floats" to come. Theologically, however, it can consist of a complexive instant: the command (16:2) and its fulfillment ("It has occurred," *gegonen,* 16:17b).

The fourth plague smites the sun. Since the point of this plague is not darkness (as it was in the fourth trumpet-blast) but scorching of the unrepentant, other heavenly bodies are ignored. The motif of God's punishing his adversaries, attested earlier (notably in the first and third of the last plagues) now finds its final reason: blasphemous unrepentance. The note of unrepentance, which appeared first under the sixth trumpet (9:20-21) is now compounded with blasphemy: the beast's own bearing is blasphemous (13:1-6) as is any blasphemer's allegiance to him (cf. 16:2). The theme of blasphemous unrepentance helps crochet together the first four plagues with those that follow, particularly the fifth and seventh. The sixth plague, since it looks proleptically to 19:11ff., does not as clearly contain it, although it hints at the theme by referring to the beast and his ilk.

B. THE FIFTH OF THE LAST PLAGUES (16:10-11)

16:1-21

¹⁰　And the fifth poured out his libation-bowl
　　on the throne of the beast,
　　and his kingdom [realm] became darkened
　　and (people) gnawed their tongues from pain,
¹¹　and they blasphemed the God of heaven
　　　for their pains
　　　and their ulcers,
　　and they did not repent of their works.

Whereas the fifth trumpet (the first woe) released a demonic figure, the King of the Abyss (9:1-11) to plague mankind (except the faithful) with agony leading to despair, the fifth angel with a libation-bowl devastates a demonic figure's kingdom. This demonic figure, the beast (typifying the godless State) does not appear to be identical with the star fallen from heaven, the King of the Abyss, who suggests Satan himself, as do figures in the second and third woes (11:7; 12:9). This sea-born mutant amounts to Satan's institutionalized, earthly representative. The whole series of last plagues envisages God's termination of the godless State and its idolatrous devotees. Babylon, the pagan city of Rome herself, stands as the principal target, as will become evident with the pouring out of the seventh bowl. Nonetheless, since the beast also stands for the imperial establishment of Rome, it is fittingly dealt with here. Rome becomes a kingdom of darkness, suitable for the blasphemously unrepentant, a kind of hell on earth.

John has not finished his treatment of the beast even with this plague. On his broad canvas, each major eschatological adversary will be fully terminated in turn: first, Babylon (in the seventh plague, 16:17-21); then, in the narrative (19:11-21:8) which follows an interpretation of Babylon's fall (17:1-19:10), the beasts (19:11-21) with allied kings of the earth, Satan with his demonic horde (20:1-10), and Death and Burial (20:11-21:8).

C. THE SIXTH OF THE LAST PLAGUES (16:12-16)

16:1-21

¹²　And the sixth poured his libation-bowl
　　on the great river, the Euphrates,

and its water was dried up,
to prepare the way of the kings from the rising of the
sun.

[13]   And I saw (issuing)
from the mouth of the dragon
and from the mouth of the beast
and from the mouth of the false prophet
three unclean spirits, like frogs [toads].

[14]   They are, indeed, demonic spirits working signs
which go on their ways to the kings of the whole
inhabited world,
to gather them for the war of the great day
of God the Almighty.

[15]   Lo, I come as a thief!
Blessed is he who is awake
and watches his garments,
so that he may not walk naked
and (have people) see his shame.

[16]   And they gathered them at the place
called in Hebrew Armageddon.

The Euphrates was to John's geographic and biblical horizons
a mighty barrier at the edge of his view of the world. It helped
define the then most belligerent and threatening frontier of the
Roman Empire. When Rome shall have been plunged into the
darkness it deserved, still worse perils would be in the offing. Even
as God's final wrath is being executed on the evil empire John
knew, his purview must encompass all conceivable adversaries facing essentially the same divine judgment. Hence, he gazes ahead
as he pens what happens under the penultimate sixth of the last
seven plagues. The mighty barrier disappears to pave the way for
invaders from the populous East. In writing about the events following the outpouring of the sixth libation-bowl, he evokes part
of the picture following the sixth trumpet, the hellish horde from
the Euphrates (9:14ff.), and the sixth unsealing (6:12-17), the Day
of the Lord.

He articulates the scene according to his vision of three frog-
like, unclean spirits of deception. Although reminiscent of the
plague of Exodus 7:25–8:15, their source is the unholy triad of

the Dragon, the beast from the sea, and the false prophet (the beast from the earth), and all three function as false prophets. They entice the rulers of the inhabited world to gather for battle at Armageddon. In John's view, as borne out subsequently (19:11-21), this battle is not one of mutual annihilation by earthly armies. Rather, it is a wrongheaded, wrongly-inspired contest against almighty God himself. Deception is the cause of futile opposition to God and of prideful arrogance, and will prove to be equivalently self-destructive. The symbolic place alludes to Mt. Megiddo, a key pass from the east between northern Israel and the Palestinian coastal road leading to Egypt. It was the site of Josiah's defeat (2 Kgs 23:29), a disaster for Judah, and so burned itself into biblical imagination as a classic image of utter ruin in a futile contest (cp. 2 Chron 35:20-25).

Embedded in the expanded description of the invasion from the East is the unannounced word of the Lord (v. 15). His very warning comes abruptly, as will his actual advent, and he intends it to foster alertness (cf. Matt 24:43; 1 Thess 5:2). The point of the proverbial beatitude has been modified to fit the scene of a battle, after which the vanquished were further shamed by being led naked into captivity, like chattel. Hence, the watchman's proverbial concern for his household goods has been altered to address more embarrassing personal needs.

The *enlargement* (v. 15) of the sixth element in this third septenary of the major vision strikes one as exceptionally short and peremptorily immediate. The enlargement under the sixth unsealing looked to the preparation of the faithful community for the coming conflict and to their ultimate victory (7:1-17). John's ongoing prophecy and the prophetic role of persecuted witnesses after him filled the perspective of the enlargement under the sixth trumpet. Now, with the sixth plague, the enlargement spotlights the Lord's own coming on the day the Holy War is resolved.

D. THE SEVENTH OF THE LAST PLAGUES (16:17-21)

16:1-21

17   And the seventh angel poured his libation-bowl
        on the air.
        And a loud [great] voice came from the sanctuary, from
          the throne,

saying:
It has taken place [occurred]!

18   And there occurred lightnings and voices and thunders,
and a great earthquake occurred
such as had not occurred from the time a human being was on earth,
so extensive (was) this great earthquake.

19   And the great city was (split) into three parts,
and the cities of the nations fell,
and Babylon the Great was remembered before God,
for (his) giving her the wine-cup of the anger of his
wrath.

20   And every island fled,
and mountains disappeared;

21   and a great hail, like hundredweights,
came down from heaven
upon human beings,
and human beings blasphemed God at the plague of the
hail,
for its striking-force [plague] was extremely heavy
[great].

In John's bizarre cosmology, "air" does not seem to be just another element of the world inhabited by humans. Somewhat as the sun does (cp. 9:2), air encompasses every place humans can live. When, therefore, the air itself is smitten by the seventh angel (16:17a), the climactic plague has occurred, worse than any of the pre-Exodus plagues on Egypt.

The Godhead's own voice sounds forth with exceptional solemnity (v. 17b), both as "a great voice from the throne, out of the sanctuary" and as uttering "It has taken place" *(gegonen)*. Only twice in about forty-some uses of the verb *ginesthai* (to come to be / to occur / to take place) does John employ its perfect tense. Both times he does so of God's own voice in the context of a definitive declaration from the throne.[115] The two occurrences cor-

---

[115]The parallelism between the utterance in 16:17b and that in 21:6a (where the speaker is *clearly* the Enthroned himself) excludes the view that a "throne angel" voices 16:17a. *See below,* pp. 171, 174, and notes 37, 74, 87, and especially 123.

respond in such a way as to indicate contrary aspects of the same, final moment of judgment. Here, in 16:17a, the perfect singular appears: *gegonen,* "It has taken place"—namely, the final wrath against unrepentant blasphemers on earth, specifically, against Babylon. Later (21:6a), the perfect plural appears: *gegonan,* "They have taken place / come to be"—namely, the new heavens and the new earth, summed up in the descent from heaven of the New Jerusalem. The solemn context of the second instance of the perfect tense contains both the new creation and the final judgment, with the general resurrection and, consequently, the definitive end of the last eschatological adversaries, Death and Burial (Hades).

Repetitiously, the adjective "great" occurs in 16:17-21 an emphatic seven times. In John's Semitizing style, varied adjectives are rare. "Great" could be translated "loud" of the voice from the throne, "shattering" of the earthquake, "heavy" of hailstones, and so forth. Nonetheless, the monotonous repetition of this hackneyed adjective, "great," has the advantage of insistently, solemnly sounding the note of finality.

After the Enthroned has spoken, a threefold *(a, b, a')* pattern articulates the cataclysm (with the term "great" occurring twice in each portion). First *(a,* v. 18), the known grouping of lightning, voices, thunders, and earthquake—progressively built up, after 4:5, through 8:5 and 11:19—is heightened by describing the quake as unlike any other ever experienced by mankind. Second *(b,* v. 19), the Great City, Babylon, falls into three pieces, her fate fulfilling God's wrath. Here one finds the centrally-placed, salient feature of the whole patterned arrangement. Babylon represents all godless cities, which collapse along with her. Third *(a',* vv. 20-21), as even islands and mountains vanish (recalling the earthquake motif; cp. 6:12-14), "mankind" is again singled out (v. 21b, cf. v. 18b), precisely as suffering not "on earth" (cp. v. 18) but "from heaven" (v. 20). As the earthquake of v. 18 amplified the portents of 8:5 and 11:19, so the hailstorm here surpasses any other (including that of 11:19). The blasphemies, implying non-repentance (as well as the restriction of this cataclysm to those who are not among the faithful) endorse as a third occurrence in this septenary (cp. the fourth and fifth plagues) the unaltered character of the evil.

Retrospective and Prospective Observations

The first four sections of Part Two of Revelation form a coherent, cohesive panorama of almighty God's redemptive deliverance of his people. The Throne Vision (§I, 4:1–5:14) discloses God's plan for the fulfillment of creation through the redemptive action of the Lamb, the only one who is worthy to disclose the destiny of the world, especially for the benefit of the faithful. The septenary of unsealings (§II, 6:1–8:5) contains an oracular preview of the coming Day of the Lord and introduces the following septenary of trumpets to herald deliverance through God's Holy War. The trumpets (§III, 8:6–15:8) give portents of the final victory, the last three of them (as combined with the three woes) introducing both the escalated opposition, diabolical activity, and the prospects of repentance even for those subjected to diabolical rule. In particular, the voice of the seventh trumpet discloses the not-to-be-delayed mystery of God's triumph. The seventh trumpet comprises the great conflicts, first in heaven, then on earth, and concludes by introducing the septenary of angels with the final plagues. The septenary of the last plagues (§IV, 16:1-21), with appropriate brevity, concludes God's wrath with the World-City, typed as Babylon, and modeled largely after the evil empire as John experienced it, pagan Rome.

The total scenario, however, remains incomplete. For, in the first place, other adversaries must be done in as well in order to fill out the picture of God's absolute victory in the Holy War. Thus, foes of the living God like Death and Burial (introduced in the unsealings, 6:7-8), Satan himself (introduced cryptically in the first and second woes of the trumpet-series, and expressly with the third woe: 9:1; 11:7; 13:9, 12), and his mutants and agents, the beasts (13:1-18), have to be dealt with as well as the foe that was introduced last, Great Babylon, the whore (14:8). In short, all the adversaries have to be dealt with, and will be eliminated completely in an order inverse to that of their initial appearance. John will proceed to treat the three remaining adversaries (or sets of foes), namely, the beasts, Satan, and Death and Burial, in § VI (19:11–21:8), allotting a sub-section to each.

In the second place, the scenario of God's Holy War, true to its biblical archetype (the Exodus) must end not just with the defeat of oppressors or the annihilation of other enemies whomsoever (by the *ḥerem* or "anathema" of utter destruction), but with peaceful possession of the land which God bestows on his people. Hence, the necessary corollary to the destruction of Babylon, the Worldly City, is that there be manifested from heaven a really "New-World" City, the New Jerusalem. To do justice to the antithesis between these two kinds of worlds, John defers treating the remaining adversaries to 19:11–21:8, that is, to §VI, at the close of which he will mention the appearance of the New Jerusalem, and inserts as paired interpretation-scenes §§V and VII. The first of these (§V) will deal with Babylon, the whore; the second (§VII) will present Jerusalem, the bride. Each of these interpretation-scenes will be introduced by "one of the angels with the libation-bowls," clearly tying the interpretation to the climactic moment when Babylon's destruction has taken place and the New Jerusalem can replace it in a new creation. Towards the close of the first interpretation-scene (§V), even in advance of the actual appearance of the New Jerusalem (close of §VI) as well as of the angel's interpretation of the heavenly city (§VII), John correlates the disappearance of Babylon the whore (the three alleluias in 19:1-4) with the forthcoming appearance of the Lamb's bride (the final, thunderous alleluia, 19:6-8).

A concluding liturgical dialogue, grafted on to §VII, will bring John's Revelation—the entire book—to its literary close.

§V. Angelic Interpretation-Scene Regarding the Fall of Babylon (17:1–19:10)

This lengthy interpretation-scene (17:1–19:10) is counterposed to the concluding section of John's vision (§VII, 21:9–22:11) on several counts. Each is similarly introduced (17:1-3; 21:9-10) and similarly concluded (19:9a-10; 22:6, 8-9). The angel in question is one of those who executed God's final wrath. John himself is rapt in the spirit and transported to a special place, either to the wilderness, to view the whore of Babylon (17:3-6) or to a high mountain, to behold the virgin bride of the Lamb, the Holy City descending from heaven (21:9-11). Concluding passages also contain corresponding features, like assurances regarding words of divine testimony (19:9-10; 22:6) and a command not to worship the angel but only God (19:10; 22:9).[116]

The interior structure of the paired interpretation-scenes differs considerably, as does their length. To grasp the ambit of the lengthy, first interpretation (§V), note the following three sub-sections, delineated in greater detail in the following pages:

§*A. The Woman and Her Entourage* (17:3b-18)
§*B. Judgment Oracles and Lamentations* (18:1-24)
§*C. Jubilant Rejoicing* (19:1-8)

These three sub-sections, taken together, are framed by the opening and closing portions of the interpretation-scene (that is, by 17:1-3a and by 19:9-10, respectively).

To cover this first, ample interpretation-scene, the commentary will treat in turn its introduction, each of its three subsections, and its conclusion. The relevant text will be placed before each of these divisions. In the case of each of the three subsections, however, the text itself will be prefaced with a brief outline.

17:1–19:10

17 ¹   And one of the seven angels who had the seven libation-bowls

came and spoke with me, saying:

Come,

I shall show you the judgment of the great harlot
who sits upon many waters,

²   with whom the kings of the earth have committed fornication,

and from whose wine of fornication those dwelling on the earth
have become drunk.

³   And he led me in the Spirit to a wilderness [desert].

When John mentioned his ecstatic experience (literally: "I came to be / was in the Spirit") in 1:10 and 4:2, he referred directly to the Lord's voice. These two passages marked his inaugural vision, the beginning of Part One of Revelation, and then the be-

---

[116]Cf. C. H. Giblin, "Structural and Thematic Correlations in the Theology of Revelation 16–22," *Bib* 55 (1974) 487–504.

ginning of Part Two, the cosmic vision which followed from it. Revelation 4:2 was consequent on the Lord's invitation to ascend through an opened door in heaven. In the current text (17:3), however, and again in the later, corresponding interpretation-scene (21:10), an angel "transports" John "in the Spirit" to a given "earthly" locale. These two texts (17:3; 21:10), therefore, have a somewhat subordinate role within Part Two, and do not stand on a par either with 1:10 or with 4:2. The earthly locale in each case (a wilderness; a great mountain) helps set the tone for the interpretation. Babylon is devastated; the New Jerusalem descends from on high. In each case, the interpreter is one of the angels who had a libation-bowl filled with God's final wrath. Thus, John correlates both interpretations with the climactic "moment" of God's final judgment.

The angel's words introducing the great whore (vv. 1-2) recall Jeremiah's condemnation of Babylon (Jer 51:7, 13). In Revelation, the "many waters" (cf. 17:15) further allude to the restless peoples of the Mediterranean, and the drunkenness of the earth-dwellers suggests the madness of evil which arises from the harlot's immorality. The overriding theme of the interpretation, God's verdict of condemnation, is announced at the outset (v. 2a).

A. THE WOMAN AND HER ENTOURAGE

17:3b-6	1. John's vision of the woman	
17:7-18	2. John's astonishment and the angel's interpretation:	
17:8-18	a. of her entourage:	
17:8		x. the beast (on which she sits);
17:9a		a call for wisdom (regarding):
17:9b-11		y. its seven heads—as mountains on which she sits; as kings, plus the beast;
17:12-14		z. and its ten horns—their common cause with the beast against the Lamb;
17:15		x'. the waters on which she sits;

17:16-17   z'. the beast and its ten horns—their
                                common cause with the beast
                                against the woman;
17:18   a'. of the woman herself.

17:1–19:10

17 ³ And I saw a woman,
            seated on a scarlet beast,
                filled with blasphemous titles [names],
                who had seven heads and ten horns;
    ⁴   and the woman was clothed in purple and scarlet,
            and (was) gilded with gold and precious stones and
                pearls,
            and had a golden cup in her hand,
                filled with abominations and (the) filth of her forni-
                cation;
    ⁵   and on her forehead a name was written—a mystery:
            Babylon the Great,
                the mother of fornications and of the abominations
                of the earth.
    ⁶ And I saw the woman
            drunk with the blood of the saints
            and with the blood of Jesus' witnesses.
    ⁷ And seeing her, I was dumbfounded [I wondered a great
        wonder].

    ⁷ And the angel said to me:
            Why are you (so) dumb(struck)?
            I shall explain to you the mystery of the woman
                and (the mystery) of the beast carrying her,
                    which has the seven heads and the ten horns.
    ⁸ The beast which you saw
            was and is not and is about to come up from the Abyss
            and he is going to destruction,
                and those who dwell on the earth,
                    those whose names are not written in the book of life
                        from the foundation of the world,
                    will be dumbfounded
                        when they see (the facts about) the beast,
                that he was and is not and is passing (away).

9   This (is) the way for the mind which has wisdom (to use it):

The seven heads are seven mountains upon which the woman sits,

and (they are also) seven kings:

10   five have fallen, one exists, the other has not yet come,

and when he comes he must remain (only) a little while;

11   and the beast which was and is not (is) indeed himself an eighth,

and is from (the sequence of) the seven,

and is going to destruction.

12   And the ten horns which you saw are ten kings

who have not yet received a kingdom [kingly power],

but who will take power with the beast for one hour.

13   These have a single purpose

and give the beast their authority and power.

14   These will wage war with the Lamb,

and the Lamb will conquer them,

for he is Lord of Lords and King of Kings,

and those with him (are) called and chosen and faithful.

15 He said to me:

the waters which you saw,

where the harlot is sitting,

are peoples and multitudes and nations and tongues.

16   And the ten horns which you saw and the beast (as well)—

these will hate the harlot

and make her desolate and naked

and will devour [eat] her flesh

and will burn her with fire.

17   For God has put [given] (it) into their hearts

to execute [do] his purpose

and to exercise [do] a single [common] purpose

and to give their kingly power to the beast

until the words of God are completed [fulfilled].

18 And the woman whom you saw is the great city,

which has kingly rule over the kings of the earth.

The image of the woman, a caricature of the goddess Roma, dominates John's vision. The beast with seven heads and ten horns is the principal secondary image. Its color reflects the imperial status of the woman herself. The cup which she, in her flagrant finery, offers to the world is a blend of false worship (abominations) and moral vices (typified by fornication). That her announced title is a "mystery" should prompt the reader to decode "Babylon" as the world-metropolis, Rome (cf. 1 Pet 5:13). In turn, Rome, as John experienced it, is the type or metatemporal model of self-deifying political power. John climactically represents her as the persecutor of holy persons, notably the prophets ("Jesus' witnesses").

In response to John's numb shock[117] the interpreting angel first describes Babylon's entourage, particularly the beast and his special attributes, and then, quite briefly, the woman herself. The exposition, therefore, follows an order inverse to that of the angel's announcement (v. 7b).

The order of exposition, not only apropos of the way kings are presented in relation to the beast, but also by mention of the waters on which the whore sits (v. 15), which harks back to 17:1b rather than to v. 7b, suggests that the passage has been recomposed and amplified.[118] Directly contrasted with God, "who was and is and is coming" (1:4, 8), the beast (v. 8) appears as a demonic power limited to a period of brief domination upon the earth and doomed to destruction. Its adherents, excluded from eternal life, will be amazed at its demise.

John's appeal for wisdom (v. 9) precedes a multiple, allegorical exposition of the beast's seven heads and ten horns. After identifying the seven heads as the seat of imperial power, Rome (v. 9a), John speaks of them as a sequence of seven emperors (vv. 9b-11). Decoding them has taxed the ingenuity of commentators.[119] John may well not be referring to a specific "list" at all,

---

[117]S. Thompson, *The Apocalypse and Semitic Syntax,* 12, notes that this Greek word *(thaumazein)* actually bears the stronger sense of the Aramaic *š⁰mam,* "dumbfounded" (Dan 4:16[19]). John plays on the sense by repeating the verb in 17:8.

[118]Kraft, *Offenbarung,* 220, 224.

[119]For a review of the opinions, cf. Charles Brütsch, *Die Offenbarung Jesu Christi. Johannes-Apokalypse* (Zürich: Zwingli, Vol. 2, 1970) 240–245.

since he may have chosen the number seven to express a certain "fulness"[120] as, in the case of Daniel 7, there had to be "four" world-empires. In any event, Beasley-Murray correctly insists that this symbolism of sevenfold tyranny derives from ancient tradition and is not intended to be a taxative list of historical Roman emperors. One is reminded of the seven-headed monster of chaos. If one still opts for a numbered series, one would best begin it with Augustus Caesar (as according to Tacitus), omitting the dictator Julius Caesar, and ignoring the three military coups of A.D. 69 (the year of the three generals, Galba, Otho, and Vitellius), placing Vespasian (A.D. 69–70) as the sixth, his son Titus (who reigned for only two years) as the seventh, and Domitian, regarded as a "reincarnation" of Nero,[121] as the beast itself, a climactic eighth, summing up the whole imperial line. John's final composition, antedated to the time of Vespasian ("one exists"), envisages particularly the reign of Domitian (A.D. 81–96). That the beast has previously been identified as Nero (13:8) and stands here for Domitian poses no problem in apocalyptic symbolism. Apart from popular acceptance of Domitian as a "returned" Nero, the resurgence of threatening imperial power as wielded by Domitian aptly suits John's motif of the pseudo-parousia of pagan rule, doomed to destruction.

The ten horns, derived from the image of the beast in Daniel 7:7, 24 (the Antigonid Kingdom of Syria) lack the particular al-

---

[120]Beasley-Murray, *Revelation*, 256–257.

[121]Even Roman authors so regarded him; cf. H. B. Swete, *The Apocalypse of St. John* (London: Macmillan,[2] 1907) 221; cp. Revelation 13:1-18.

Vespasian was not a persecutor, but John's presentation of him as the sixth (if such is indeed the case) does not suppose that he was. The "Great Tribulation" which John elaborates as occurring "in the days of the seventh angel . . ." is a vision for the *imminent future*. This perspective is borne out by John's mentioning the "short time" of "the other" (scil., of the "seventh," *which he pointedly avoids numbering* in order to proceed immediately to the climactic "eighth"), 17:10-11. The climactic "eighth" may in part be clarified by the gnostic or, better, *magical* notion of the ogdoad. In Greek-Egyptian magic, the god standing over all the demons was named "Eight(hood)" (Greek *Ogdoas*, German *Achtheit); Reallexikon für Antike und Christentum* (Stuttgart: Hiersemann, I, 1950) 78 *Achtzahl*, I. Also, the beast itself is a kind of hydra, summing up all its heads.

lusions and development found in Daniel. In effect, they are in-struments of the beastly empire itself, and probably stand as a "complete set" (the number ten) of vassal and/or allied powers. As elsewhere in Revelation (e.g., 14:17; 19:19-21), numerous kings function in the service of imperial Rome. Using two, counter-balanced units (vv. 12-14 and 16-17), which straddle the world-wide perspective pointedly introduced by v. 15, John speaks of the combined intent of the beast and its royal allies. On the one hand (as later in 19:19-21), the entire hostile force with one pur-pose *(gnōmē)* attacks the Lamb and meets defeat (vv. 12-14). On the other hand, the same force will serve to execute God's own purpose *(gnōmē)* in bringing about the destruction of the harlot, Babylon. Evil lacks integrity. The harlot's seat of power and its scope proves to be intrinsically unstable and will demolish her.

Concluding the description (v. 18), John returns to the woman who holds temporary sway over powers destined to destroy her. That the actual fall of Rome did not occur according to this sym-bolic scenario is beside the point. Jeremiah's prophetic perspec-tive, for instance, concerning the fall of the Babylon he knew (Jeremiah 51) was not invalidated by the fact that Babylon fell "without a shot being fired,"as it were. That evil empire did, nonetheless, meet its doom. A fortiori, the symbolic perspective of John's apocalyptic prophecy should not be taken as a detailed allegory of historical occurrences. The Roman Empire stands in John's view of the world as a type of any self-indulgent, self-glorifying power that is opposed to God and his people, and there-fore faces disaster.

B. JUDGMENT ORACLES AND LAMENTATIONS

18:1-3	a.	A glorious angel pronounces a judgment-oracle against Babylon; he illuminates the earth.
18:4-8	b.	A voice calls from heaven for God's people to dissociate themselves from Babylon, ex-plaining this by a judgment-oracle.
18:9-19		c. The whore's moment of judgment is lamented by her former clients:
18:9-10		x. earth's kings;
18:11-17a		y. earth's merchants, and the traders;

18:17b-19   z. pilots, sailors, and travelers on the sea, and fishermen.

18:20   b'. A call to those in heaven to rejoice because of God's justice on their behalf.

18:21-24   a'. A mighty angel casts a millstone into the sea and explains his symbolic action with a judgment-oracle.

17:1–19:10

18 ¹ Afterwards I saw another angel coming down from heaven,
> having great authority,
> and the earth was illumined by his glory;

² and he cried out in a mighty voice, saying:
> Babylon the Great has fallen, fallen,
> and has become a dwelling-place for demons
>> and the ward of every unclean spirit,
>> and the ward of every unclean bird,
>> and the ward of every unclean and hateful beast,

³ for from the wine of (God's) anger at her fornication
> all the nations have drunk,
> and the kings of the earth have fornicated with her,
> and the merchants of the earth have become wealthy
>> from the power of her sensual luxury.

⁴ And I heard another voice from heaven, saying:
> O my people, come out of her,
>> lest you share in her sins,
>> and lest you receive (a share) of her plagues,

⁵ for her sins have reached the sky [touched the heaven(s)]
> and God has remembered her injustices.

⁶ Give her as she has given—and double (it)—
> a double portion in accordance with her works—
> in the cup which she has mixed pour her a double portion.

⁷ Give her as much torment and grief
> as she (gave) herself of glory and sensual luxury;
> for she said in her heart:
>> I sit (enthroned) as a queen,

and am not a widow,
and I will not see grief.

8   Therefore, in a single day her plagues will come (upon her):
pestilence [death]
and grief
and famine;
and she will be burned (up) in fire,
for mighty is the Lord God who judges her.

9   And the kings of the earth,
who committed fornication and lived in luxury with her,
will weep and wail over her
when they see the smoke from her fire(storm),

10   standing afar off because of fear of her torment,
(and) saying:
Woe, woe to you, O great city,
O mighty city, Babylon;
for in a single hour has your judgment come.

11   And the merchants of the earth
will weep and grieve over her,
for no one buys their merchandise any more: loads

12   of gold and silver and precious stones and pearls,
and linen and purple, and silk and scarlet,
and every (kind) of scented wood,
and every (kind) of ivory ware,
and wares of wood and bronze and iron and marble;

13   cinnamon, cardamom, incense, myrrh, frankincense;
wine, oil, fine-flour, wheat;
cattle and sheep;
horses and wagons
and (human) bodies, the lives [souls] of human beings.

14   Gone from you are the fruit(s) of your soul's desire(s),
and lost to you are all the shiny and splendid things,
and you shall not find them ever again!

15   Traders in these things,
who had become rich from her,
will stand afar off because of fear of her torment,
weeping and grieving,

16   saying:
Woe, woe, O great city,

you (who were) clothed in linen and purple and
scarlet,
and were gilded with gold and precious stones and
pearls;

17   for in a single hour all this great wealth was made
wilderness.
And every (ship's) pilot and everyone who sailed aboard,
and sailors, and those who worked the sea
stood afar off,

18   and they shouted as they saw the smoke from her
fire(storm),
saying:
Who was like the great city?

19   and they cast dust on their heads
and they shouted, weeping and grieving,
saying:
Woe, woe, O great city,
in whom all who had ships on the sea became rich
from her splendor;
for in a single hour she has become a desert [a wil-
derness].

20   Congratulate yourself at her (plight), O heaven,
and (you) saints and apostles and prophets;
for God has exacted from her in judgment
your (own, requested) judgment.

21   And a mighty angel lifted a stone like a great millstone
and cast it into the sea,
saying:
Thus, with violence,
will Babylon, the great city, be cast (down)
and will never again be found.

22   And the music [voice(s)] of harpists and singers
and of flute-players and trumpeters
will never again be heard in you;
and any (kind) of artisan of any (kind) of craft [art]
will never again be found in you;
and the sound of a mill
will never again be heard in you;

23   and light from a lamp
will never again shine in you;

and voice(s) of bridegroom and bride
will never again be heard in you.
For your merchants were the potentates of the earth;
for with your sorcery all the nations were deceived;
24   and in (you) yourself [in her] was found
(the) blood of prophets and saints
and of all those slaughtered on the earth.

John enunciates the judgment against Babylon in a complex-ive perspective. Although he uses three tenses, he focuses upon a single eschatological moment: the inflicting of God's judgment. In the framework of the concentric structure (see outline above), the opening *(a)* and closing *(a')* judgment oracles speak, respectively, of the past fall of Babylon and of its future disappearance. A voice *(b)* calls from heaven and, minding the immediate future, bids God's people to flee the city, which is marked for judgment. Balancing this (in *b'*), another voice calls to those in heaven to rejoice at the present time, the instant of God's salvific justice on behalf of the saints. The center *(c)* depicts the very moment of destruction as a current "single hour"—although, as will appear below, three tenses are used to describe the laments.

Three judgment oracles can be discerned *(a, b,* and *a')*. Each consists characteristically of the sentence (vv. 2, 6-8a, 21-23a) and the reason(s) for it (vv. 3, 5 and 8b, 23b-24); the order in *b* is concentric with the sentence placed in the middle. The salvation oracle in *b'* (v. 20) also echoes the theme of judgment. The first oracle *(a)* presents the angel as a striking representative of the Lord himself, illumining the earth (cp. Ezek 43:2). The threefold occurrence of *phylakē* (often used in the sense of "prison," or "watchtower," and here translated for the sake of consistency as "ward") in v. 2, should best be taken here (in line with *katoik-tērion,* "dwelling-place") to stand for a "roost" or "confined habitat." The abruptly introduced second oracle, which refers to the Lord God in the third person (vv. 5 and 8) and addresses "my people," probably voices the judgment of the Lord Jesus. The twofold punishment echoes the decisive or "superlative" penalty known from prophetic declarations like Jeremiah 16:18 and Isaiah 40:2b, as the woman's attitude reflects that of Babylon in Isaiah 47:5-9. Concluding the whole composition *(B),* the third judgment oracle *(a'),* balancing the first *(a),* adds the symbolic action of a mighty angel casting a millstone into the sea (cp. Jer 51:63) to dramatize the violent end of the world-city and its pleasures (cp. Jer 25:10). In addition, the final oracle speaks not of Babylon's own excesses but rather of her seducing the rest of the world and of her slaying not only the prophets and saints, but others as well. In the latter respect, she epitomizes the tyrannies of all time. Once again, then, John's metahistorical perspective features Babylon-Rome as a type transcending the factual, temporal limits of Roman imperialism.

Preceding the final judgment oracle, and corresponding in the overall structure to the voice from heaven in vv. 4-8 stands another, unheralded heavenly command to rejoice (v. 20; cp. Jer 51:48; 44:23). Once again, however, the reference to God in the third person in an unannounced utterance supposes that the voice be assigned to an angel (cf. 12:10-12a) or, as in the correlated judgment oracle (vv. 4-8) to the Lord Jesus. Here, as in 12:12, "heaven" stands for the angels, to which are expressly joined blessed human beings. God's judgment is shared by the saints, who had appealed for it (cp. 6:10) and were instrumental in effecting it (cp. 12:11).

At the center of this portion *(B)* of the interpretation-scene, John places a lengthy, ironic lament (note the theme of weeping and wailing, vv. 9, 11, 15, 19) drawn extensively from OT prophetic imagery, especially Ezekiel 26-28. The reader can readily distinguish three major stanzas (vv. 9-10, 11-17a, 17b-19), each marked at the beginning by specific reference to a region (earth, earth, sea), at the end by the refrain "Woe, woe . . . O great city . . . for in a single hour . . . . (with reference to her judgment or desolation)," and towards the middle by the verb "standing/will stand/stood." The central stanza is bipartite (vv. 11-13, 15-17a) bound together by close synonyms (merchants/traders) and a similar focus of attention (gold . . . scarlet, vv. 12a and 16b). It is punctuated, one may almost say centered, on the generically-stated lament in v. 14.[122] John significantly closes the

---

[122]In particular, v. 14 fits precisely where it is placed, between the lament of the merchants and that of the traders. In a generic way, and with a relish for literary flourish (for, in Greek, "all the shiny and splendid things" are *panta ta lipara kai ta lampra),* the "lyrical" lament refers

merchants' catalogue of marketed goods, more pointedly than does Ezekiel 27:13, by mentioning the degrading slave-trade. To Babylon-Rome's cruel treatment of human beings (cp. v. 24) and her corruption of them (cp. 17:2) John adds the exploitation of mankind that accounts for her luxury.

C. JUBILANT REJOICING

19:1-3 a. Three alleluias

19:1-3   —the first two from the heavenly multitude, celebrating God's judgment, and then Babylon's everlasting ruin;

19:4   —the last, endorsing the foregoing, from the elders and the four living beings as they worship the Enthroned One.

19:5   b. A message from the throne calling for praise of God by all his servants.

19:6-8 a′. A climactic alleluia celebrating God's kingly power and giving him glory for the forthcoming wedding of the Lamb.

17:1–19:10

19 ¹   Afterward, I heard (something) like a loud [great] voice of a large multitude in heaven
    saying:
      Alleluia!
      Salvation and glory and power (belong to) our God:
²   for his judgments are true and just;
      for he has judged the great harlot,
        who corrupted [destroyed] the earth with her fornication,
      and he has vindicated the blood of his servants
        from her hand(s).
³   And they said a second time:
      Alleluia!
      And her smoke will go up for ever and ever.

to the items detailed in vv. 12-13 and 16b-17a. See Beasley-Murray, *Revelation,* 267 n. 2 (refuting R. H. Charles).

⁴ And the twenty-four elders fell down and the four living beings, too,
and they worshiped God, the one seated on the throne,
saying:
Amen! Alleluia!

⁵ And a voice came forth from the throne,
saying:
Praise our God, all (you) his servants,
and (you) who hold him in awe [fear him], small and great!

⁶ And I heard (something) like the voice of a large multitude and like the sound of cascading [many] waters
and like the sound of mighty thunders,
saying:
Alleluia!
For (the) Lord our God, the Almighty has (used his) kingly power.
⁷ Let us rejoice and exult and give glory to him,
for the wedding of the Lamb has come,
and his bride has readied herself,
⁸ and she has been given pure white linen to be clothed in
—the linen, indeed, is the just deeds of the saints.

⁹ And he said to me:
Write (this down):
Blessed are those invited [called] to the Lamb's wedding-feast.
And he said to me:
These true words are God's.
¹⁰ And I fell before his feet to worship him.
And he said to me:
See (that you do) not!
I am your co-servant
and (the co-servant) of your brothers
who hold (fast to) the witness [of] Jesus.
Worship God!
The witness from [of] Jesus, indeed, is the Spirit of prophecy.

In response to the call for rejoicing in 18:20, but after concluding the whole scene of laments and judgment oracles (18:1-24),
John sets forth his auditory vision of a series of alleluias ("Hymn
praise to the Lord!") 19:1-8. All are located, as in the case of
every prayer in Revelation, on the heavenly plane. The first two
(vv. 1-2, 3) come from a great multitude, and go on to give specific reasons for praising God. The first celebrates God's salvific
glory in fulfilling his judgments, not against a plethora of persecutors (as in 16:7), but specifically against Babylon as the cor-
rupter of the earth (v. 2), completing with a victory-shout of praise
the thanksgiving-style echo of the "war-cry" at the outset of the
major engagement of the Holy War (cp. 11:18 in the context of
11:15-19). The persecutor par excellence has been requited. The
second praises God for the everlasting memorial of Babylon's annihilation. Revelation never presents the faithful as coming closer
to "gloating" over just punishment, and, even here, does so in
reference to "institutionalized evil," not to specific human persons. The royal court of elders and the four living creatures
representing creation worship God and voice a confirmatory
Amen with the third alleluia (v. 4). Preceding the final alleluia
(vv. 6-8) in the *aba'* format of this passage (19:1-8), John places
in central focus the voice from the throne (v. 5). The implied
speaker, who refers to "our God" in addressing God's servants,
may perhaps be taken as another divine person, either the Lord
Jesus or, preferably, the Spirit.[123] Jesus Christ's central position

---

[123]Kraft, *Offenbarung,* 243, gratuitously asserts that neither God nor
the Lamb (scil., Jesus Christ) speaks in Revelation. The voice from the
throne, however, conveys more than merely the image of a "throne angel's" utterance. For the expression occurs elsewhere, too, only in texts
of exceptional solemnity and theological emphasis (notably 16:17 and
the corresponding but clearer 21:5-8, esp. v. 6).

Perhaps, as in 21:3-4, preceding the clearly personal, divine voice of
20:5-8, the statement from the throne may be regarded as mediated by
an angel, much like the altar's voice in 16:7. Still, as in 16:7, one would
expect the angel in question to have been indicated previously, namely,
in conjunction with some action performed by him. One would do better to opt for the voice of the Lamb (as sharing the Father's throne and
as suggested by the phrase *"great* [powerful] voice") or for the voice
of one of the elders (since what is said recalls 7:15-16—but, in this case,
"throne" must be taken in the wider sense of "heaven, the throne-scene"

in relation to the throne has been stated in 5:6 and, elsewhere, he expresses his own special relation to God (3:21; cp. the single throne of God and the Lamb in 22:1). The substance of the message from the throne, "Praise our God," phrases more precisely for John's readers the foregoing, triple "alleluia" and the climactic "alleluia" which follows. The rest of the verse recalls Ps 135:1.

In a closing crescendo, a final alleluia breaks forth from the heavenly multitude (cp. 19:6 and 19:1). Underscoring first God's exercise of kingly power, they glorify God not for punishing the harlot (as in vv. 1-3) but rather for the positive counterpart of his sovereign rule, the forthcoming wedding of the Lamb to a pure, readied spouse. Thus, the body of this whole interpretation-scene announces at its end the advent of the new Jerusalem, which will conclude (21:1-8) the subsequent, narrative segment (19:11-21:8) and form the theme of the correlated interpretation-scene (21:9-22:9). In noting the bride's clothing, John seems to avoid the implication that something new has been provided for her (as was the case with the souls under the altar, 6:11).[124] Rather, he implies by her readying herself and by the unequivocal gloss or footnote-style reference to the "just deeds of holy persons" that she already needs no further authorization to fulfill her life's role. Equivalently, the bride of the Lamb is the Christian community which awaits only the final transformation of the wedding itself, the resurrection.

as the variant reading took it). In any event, the "great voice from the throne" is intended to be especially weighty and arresting, and its message provides the needed background for construing what the Enthroned says in v. 6a.

A final possibility, which I am strongly inclined to think makes the best sense, is that *the voice is that of the Spirit.* Its introduction is sufficiently vague, anthropomorphically: *"from* the *throne* [of God]," not a "body," *(see above,* notes 37, 74, and 87). What is more, the Enthroned's command to John (v. 5b, "these words are faithful [believable] and true,") corresponds quite precisely to the interpreting angels' affirmation of *divine* testimony—that of the Spirit of prophecy himself—both in 19:9 and in 22:6! Thus, the endings of §§V, VI, and VII cohere beautifully!

[124]Cf. Kraft, *Offenbarung,* 244.

Adela Y. Collins found it striking that no hymns occur in Revelation after the alleluias of Revelation 19.[125] Appropriate prayers occur, of course, in the epilogue, expressing earnest desire for the Lord's coming (22:17, 20b). No hymns or prayers, however, appear in the body of Revelation after these alleluias. To add any further hymns would have been anticlimactic, especially since, substantially, the Holy War scenario is essentially realized in the destruction of the earthly empire, Babylon, and the advent of its heavenly replacement, Jerusalem, the bride of the Lamb. Remaining eschatological adversaries must be dealt with in 19:11-21:8. But these are basically of a demonic or other-worldly character, and their main function has been focused in terms of the arch-adversary afflicting the saints, namely, Babylon. On her reign, as in the case of the last plagues ("It has taken place" [*gegonen*], 16:17) the terminal point of God's Holy War finds its adequate focus.

Formally concluding this entire, first interpretation-scene, vv. 9-10 contain key elements to be repeated at the close of the corresponding, second interpretation-scene. Thus, both passages refer to "these true words" as God's own (19:9b; 22:6a). Both also mention John's impulse to fall at the feet of the angel to worship him, and the angel's refusal, inasmuch as he is John's co-servant and that of his brothers the prophets, together with the angel's command to worship God (19:10; 22:8b-9). Other correspondences are looser, but recognizable, though one must allow for the enfilading of the close of the second interpretation-scene with the close of the whole book. Thus, both interpretations conclude by mentioning John's brothers as those who keep or hold fast to the words of prophecy, their witness deriving from Jesus (19:10) which, albeit less extensively, are identified as the words of this book (22:9-10; cp. 22:7). The command to write (19:9) is complemented by the injunction not to seal the words of this prophetic book (21:10). A beatitude figures in each conclusion (19:9 and 22:7), although in 22:7 it is uttered (appropriately without an announcement) by Jesus himself.

Nowhere else in Revelation besides the introductory and concluding portions of these two interpretation-scenes does John so

---

[125]A. Y. Collins, *The Combat Myth,* 234. She finds an explanation in the liturgy, as the locus for a proleptic experience of salvation.

consistently and extensively employ the same phraseology and sets of motifs, particularly in basically the same order. Accordingly, the two correlated interpretation-scenes help set in sharp relief the intervening narration (19:11–21:8), which treats both the annihilation of the eschatological adversaries which remain after Babylon and also the actual advent of the new creation.

§VI. Narrative Regarding Other Eschatological Adversaries and the New Creation (19:11–21:8)

To avoid needlessly compartmentalizing this section, one should address it as comprising three major divisions:[126]

§X. *The King of King's Victory over the Beast, the False Prophet, and the Kings of the Earth* (19:11-21)

§Y. *The Victory over Satan at the Climax of the Millennium* (20:1-10)

§Z. *Judgment from the Throne, with the Vanquishing of Death and Hades and the Advent of the New Jerusalem* (20:11–21:8)

In brief, the three divisions highlight Armageddon (*X;* cf. 16:13-14, 16), the Millennial Kingdom *(Y)*, and the Last Judgment *(Z)*.

One can discern the distinctiveness of each division by attending to the figures and motifs involved. Thus, in *X* one finds the horseman (-men) and conflicting armies (19:11a, 14, 18, 19, 21); the sword (19:15, 21); Christological titles given to the one on the white horse (19:11, 13, 16); and conflict with the beast, the false prophet, and the kings of the earth (19:19-20). In *Y,* and there alone, appear the motifs of "the thousand years" (millennium) (20:2-3, 4, 5, 6, 7) and "the first resurrection" (19:5-6). Emerging in *Z* are the Enthroned One (20:11; 21:5; cf. 20:12 and 21); the motif of a new heaven and a new earth (in particular, 21:1, 5); the end of Death and the Grave (20:13, 14; 21:4); the complementary themes of reward in terms of works (20:12, 13) and in terms of gratuitous inheritance (21:6-7b), each related to the theme of life and contrasted with the second death (20:12, 15; 21:6, 8).

---

[126]Cf. Giblin, "Structural and Thematic Correlations," 500–502.

These three sub-sections are severally interlaced. Single examples will suffice here to indicate their correlations:[127]

in X and Y, victorious confrontation with forces of deception (19:20; 20:3-8);
in Y and Z, throne-imagery related to the resurrection-theme (20:4-6; 20:12);
in X and Z, the characterizations "faithful and true" (19:11a; 21:5b) and the color white (19:11, 14; 20:11).

An overarching theme of all three sub-sections consists in the express mention of judgment (19:11; 20:4; 20:12-13) and in the reference (only here in Revelation) to the lake of fire and/or the second death—which amounts to the same punishment (19:20b; 20:6-10; 20:14-15 and 21:8). The second death becomes progressively clarified, as one can see in the light of the last text (21:8), where all the key elements occur: lake/burning/brimstone (sulphur)/fire/second death. As noted earlier, the major eschatological adversaries remaining after Babylon are liquidated in an order which is inverse to that of their first appearance in Revelation. Thus, the beast and the false prophet are done away with in X (19:20; cp. 13:1-8); Satan's activity is punitively terminated in Y (20:3, 10; cp. 12:3-18, and perhaps 11:7 and 9:11); and Death and the Grave meet the same fate in Z (20:13-14). "Human" eschatological adversaries, like the kings *et al* of the opposing host *(X,* 19:21), the mob of nations called Gog and Magog *(Y,* 20:8-9b), and immoral individuals *(Z,* 20:15; 21:8), also fall before God's judgment, the former groups mainly as victims of deception, the last group as fully responsible individual sinners.

Before the commentary on each of these three sub-sections, a more detailed outline of each one will be provided. This outline, in turn, together with the commentary, will help establish the inner coherence of each of these three major sub-sections.

X. THE KING OF KING'S VICTORY OVER THE BEAST, THE FALSE PROPHET, AND THE KINGS OF THE EARTH

19:11-16   *A.*   The Horseman Faithful and True Ready for Combat

[127]Ibid., 500.

19:11–21:8

19[11]   I saw heaven opened,
and lo, a white horse,
and the one seated upon it (was) called faithful and true,
and justly he judges and makes war.

[12]   His eyes (are) like a flame of fire,
and on his head (are) many diadems,
and he has a name, written, which no one knows but he himself,

[13]   and he is clothed with a garment dipped in blood,
and his name has been called "The Word of God."

[14]   And the armies in heaven follow him on white horses,
(and are) clothed in pure, white linen.

[15]   And from his mouth comes forth a sharp broadsword to smite the nations,
and he shall rule [shepherd] them with an iron rod,
and he shall trample the winepress of the wine
of the anger of the wrath of God the Almighty;

[16]   and he has on his garment [and] on his thigh a name, written,
"King of Kings and Lord of Lords."

[17]   And I saw a single angel standing in the sun,
and he cried out in a loud [great] voice
saying to all the birds flying in mid-heaven:
Come hither!
Gather for the great feast of God;

[18]   to eat the flesh of kings and flesh of generals,
and flesh of mighty men,
and flesh of horses and those seated upon them,

and flesh of all free men and slaves alike, both small
and great!

¹⁹ And I saw the beast and the kings of the earth and their
armies
gathered to wage war
with the one seated on the horse
and with his army.

²⁰ And the beast was taken prisoner,
and with him the false prophet,
who had done signs in his presence [before him],
by which he deceived
those taking the mark of the beast
and those worshipping his image.
Alive, the two were cast into the lake of fire burning
with sulphur.

²¹ And the rest were killed by the broadsword
of the one seated on the horse—
the broadsword coming forth from his mouth,
and all the birds were sated with their flesh.

"Openings in heaven" mark dramatic stages in John's narration. At the beginning of the major vision (4:1) a door lay open
(ēnęǫgmenē) in heaven, and John was invited to pass through this
opened door in order to receive the vision of the end-time. At
the beginning and end of the series of events heralded by the seventh trumpet, the heavenly sanctuary was opened (§II.A., 11:19,
ēnoigē. . . ; §II.A'., 15:5, *ēnoigē)* to reveal in turn the palladium of the Holy War and the preparation for the last plagues.
Now, in 19:11, concluding this imposing series of heavenly openings (with its insistent use of the aorist or perfect tenses of
anoigein), heaven itself has been laid open *(ēnęǫgmenē)* to disclose the parousia, the triumphant battle of Christ against the
forces of deception. His war is waged with sovereign justice. He
is faithful and true, that is, he enjoys the divine title of the
"Amen" (3:14; cp. Isa 66:16) as one who is fully reliable and has
"the last word." Appropriately, he is soon identified as the Word
of God (19:143). The phrase "faithful and true" also forms an
inclusion with the close of §VI (21:5b) where, in the scene of final judgment, God himself avers the statements concerning his
new creation. In addition, the phrase figures in the conclusion

of the two interpretation-scenes (§V, 19:9b—with a slight variation: "these true words are God's"; §VII, 22:6a) which "frame" this narrative section (§VI). The phrase not only helps delineate the structure of these three sections and render them more cohesive, but also conveys a sense of prophetic, divine finality.

In line with the pervasive thematic of the Holy War, the Messiah appears as a warrior. Actually, the combat itself is not described, for it is won by the Lord's mere word. Only its grisly results are indicated, and these largely in prospect. This apocalyptic realism may not appeal to our taste, but it derives from biblical imagery that fueled John's creative imagination, and proves almost necessary to describe the termination of the Holy War proper, namely the *ḥerem* or utter destruction of God's foes.

The Messiah himself is described in two subdivisions (*a* and *a'*) of the first portion of the text *(A)*, that is, in vv. 11-13 and 15-16. Each closes by referring to his name: the Word of God (v. 13), the King of Kings and Lord of Lords (v. 16). A name distinctly indicates its bearer's uniqueness as a person, and often does so in terms of his proper function. The name "which no one knows but he himself" is mysterious, but not altogether hidden. The relative clause indicates quite expressly that the name or title is unique, proper to the bearer alone. The context clarifies its meaning. Building up to the first, special title, the Word of God, John describes in language suggesting divine judgment his eyes like flaming fire (cp. 1:14; 2:18), his imperial status (many crowns on his head—which also prepares for the corresponding title in v. 16), and his clothing, dyed with the blood of God's adversaries (cp. Isa 63:1-6). As God's Word, he is the communicator of God's judgment.

Before the second title appears, i.e., at *b* (v. 14), John introduces a modification and development of the text from Isa 63:1-6. Here, the Lord does not enter this conflict alone. Along with him rides a heavenly army, the angels, not cuirassed in armor but dressed as for a wedding feast, in pure white linen (cp. 19:8). It is most unlikely that we are to understand the heavenly army as the saints themselves. For, elsewhere in Revelation, it is the angels who militantly execute God's decrees or who figure in belligerent engagements (e.g., that of Michael and his angels in 12:7-9). Significantly, even where the saints in heaven share in the victory of the angels, they do so passively (12:11).

With v. 15, John pursues his description of the Word of God by speaking of the sword from his mouth, equivalently the word of condemnatory judgment (1:16; 2:12, 16; cp. Isa 17:4; Isa 11:4 plus 49:2; 2 Thess 2:8).[128] In conjunction with this, John notes his messianic, judgmental authority, symbolized by the iron rod (cp. 2:27-28a), and recalls the blood-red garment of the victor (v. 15c; cp. v. 13a) when executing God's wrath (cp. 14:19-20). Written or embroidered on the garment covering his thigh is the second major title, which denotes universal supremacy. This title, "King of Kings, Lord of Lords" (leaving out the "and," by which John tells us to add the two parts of the title), when put into Aramaic, appropriately expresses a triple fulness, the number "777," which is the victorious counterpart of the number of the beast (which, again in Aramaic, is "666").[129]

In the center of the passage (*B,* vv. 17-18), in gruesome contrast with the wedding feast of the Lamb announced by the *angelus interpres* (19:9) lies the cry of the angel in the (noonday) sun who invites the birds to the God-given feast (a *Schlachtfest)* on the slain armies. Thus, John's literary composition places in sharpest relief in this whole sub-section *(X)* the *ḥērem* of Armageddon, even before it has presented the gathering of hostile forces.

Counterposed to the opening portion (*A,* vv. 11-16) by mention of armies opposed in war to the horseman and his army and, later, by reference to the broadsword coming forth from the Lord's mouth, the closing portion (*A',* vv. 19-21) describes the gathering of the foe and their complete defeat. John says nothing about the details of the engagement. He has already supplied the information needed to construe the use of weaponry and notes it again at the end of the passage. The broadsword from the mouth of the Word of God is what has slain the foe (vv. 15, 21). In effect, the victory is achieved without loss and even effortlessly.

---

[128]Although both John of Patmos and John the Evangelist predicate of Jesus Christ the term *Logos* ("Word"), their respective representations of his role as the Divine Communicator (and, concretely, in theophanic form, as the Divine Communication itself) differ considerably; one can hardly suppose that the Evangelist (or his co-author, the "Redactor") composed Revelation.

[129]Cf. Patrick W. Skehan, "King of Kings, Lord of Lords (Apoc. 19:16)," *CBQ* 10 (1948) 398.

Divine justice proves irresistible. The termination of the beast by fire fits with a long line of biblical penalties, like God's judgment on Sodom (Gen 19:24), and on the fourth beast in Daniel 7:11. The kings and their hosts become the prey of vultures, in line with the imagery of Ezekiel 39:17-20. Interestingly, John employs Ezekiel's description of the fate of Gog not of Gog's mythical army (which he refers to in *Y,* in connection with the defeat of Satan), but of the kings of the earth, allies of the beast (cp. 17:12-14). The beast (namely, the beast from the sea) and the false prophet (that is, the beast from the earth)—who was particularly responsible for deceiving humankind—are taken prisoner only to meet a worse fate: a living death in the lake of fire and brimstone. Thereby ends, after Babylon, the first of the remaining eschatological adversaries. In terms of clock-and-calendar time, of course, the end of Babylon and all the other adversaries will take place simultaneously, in an instant. Apocalyptic, however, requires sequences of particular visions and sequences of appropriately grouped visions in order adequately to present its theology. For it has no alternative to spelling out its relatively "pre-conceptual" theology in images, especially such as will move its readers to religious awe and a keenly felt hope for salvation.

Y. THE VICTORY OVER SATAN AT THE CLIMAX OF THE MILLENNIUM

20:1-3	A.	The Binding of Satan for a Thousand Years
20:4-6	B.	The Heavenly Kingdom of the Thousand Years, the First Resurrection
20:7-10	A'.	The Loosing of Satan at the End of the Thousand Years and His Destruction Along with Gog and Magog

19:11–21:8

20 ¹ And I saw an angel coming down from heaven,
  holding the key to the Abyss and a great chain on his hand,
 ² and he controlled the dragon, the primeval [ancient] snake,
  who is the Devil and Satan,
  and he bound him for a thousand years;

3
and he cast him into the Abyss,
and he locked and sealed (it) above him,
so that he might not deceive the nations any more,
until the thousand years be completed;
afterwards, he must be released for a little time.

4
And I saw thrones,
and (people) sat upon them,
and (power to execute) judgment was given them;
and (I saw) the souls of those beheaded
for the(ir) witness [of] Jesus
and for the word of God,
and (these were) they who had not worshiped the beast
or his image,
and had not taken his mark on their foreheads and
on their hands,
And they came to life,
and exercised with Christ kingly power for a thousand
years.

5
The rest of the dead did not come to life
until the thousand years were completed.
This is the first [prior] resurrection.

6
Blessed and holy is one
who has a share in the first [prior] resurrection.
(For) over these the second death has no power,
but they shall be priests of God and of Christ
and shall exercise kingly power with him for the
thousand years.

7
And when the thousand years will have been completed,
Satan will be loosed from his prison.

8
And he will come forth to deceive the nations,
those at the four corners of the earth,
Gog and Magog,
to gather them for the war—
whose number is like the sandy shore of the sea.

9
And they came up onto the broad surface of the earth,
and they surrounded the encampment of the saints
and the beloved city,
and fire came down from heaven and devoured them.

10
And the Devil, who (was) deceiving them,

was cast into the lake of fire and sulphur,
> where the beast, too, and the false prophet (were);
> and they will be tormented day and night for ever and
> ever.

Paramount in this sub-section is the thousand-year reign which the martyrs enjoy with Christ during the period when Satan is himself inoperative and even at the moment of Satan's final, frustrated assault. Since the central portion (*B*, 20:4-6) of this concentrically structured *(ABA')* sub-section stands in the limelight, it merits prior attention.[130]

John's vision recalls the scene of divine judgment in Daniel 7 (the thrones), but those seated on the thrones are here identified as martyrs, those who have died under persecution led by the false prophet. Moreover, they are directly associated not with the Ancient of Days but with Christ, and share in his triumphant, messianic reign. For them, the kingdom becomes an ongoing, physical reality, including even resurrection from the dead. At first, they are presented as "souls" (*psychai*, cp. 6:9). This helps set in relief their further transformation, within the same heavenly state of beatitude, to risen physical life (v. 4b, "And they came to life"). John makes clear to his reader that he is not speaking of the final, "general" resurrection (which he will narrate in 20:12-15) but of a prior state (v. 5). The *general* resurrection is "timed" to coincide with the end of the thousand years. At that point, the alternatives will be the second death (eternal hell) for the wicked (20:15; 21:8) and pain-free, eternal life with God for humans who have done good (21:3-4, 6-7). For these martyrs, however, the course of risen life will continue beyond the thousand years into the period of bliss for all those raised to eternal life. For this

---

[130]The central portion itself falls into three sections:

a) 20:4a (to ". . . and on their hands."), depicting the scene of judgment and then the martyred souls, with an account of their meritorious action (stated first positively, then negatively);

b) 20:4b-5, their resurrection and thousand-year reign, and then a negative statement indicating their special privilege;

c) 20:6 (*plus* "this is the first [prior] resurrection" from the very end of v. 5), containing the designation "first resurrection" and stating the beatitude, with clarifying *adjuncta* or additions, both negatively-phrased and positively-phrased.

"first" (or *"prior"*[131]) resurrection remains immune from the second death.[132]

The entire description corresponds not to some temporal, clock-and-calendar perspective or even to some kind of symbolically temporal, earth-bound computation of time.[133] Rather, it climactically expresses a state of heavenly reward which John has reiterated, with rephrasing, at least seven times in the course of the major vision:[134]

6:9-11	the robes given OT martyrs;
7:4-17	the 144,000 as later an innumerable throng of victors;
11:11-13	the efficacious resurrection-ascension of the twin witnesses;
12:11-12a	the victory over Satan by those faithful to their deaths;
14:1-5	the 144,000 celibates with the Lamb on Mt. Zion, who sing a victory-hymn before the throne;

[131]*Prōtōs* ("first," a superlative) is sometimes used for *proteros* ("former of two/prior"); cf. Zerwick—Smith, *A Grammar of New Testament Greek* (Rome: Biblical Institute,⁴ 1963) §151.

[132]Note the promises to the victor as given in the seven proclamations to the churches. All in all, these promises equate freedom from the second death (2:11b) with a share in the new Jerusalem (2:7b; 3:5; 3:12).

[133]Jürgen Roloff construes the millennium as a timeless sabbath (cf. *Barnabas* 15, 4-8; *2 Enoch* 33:1; cp. Ps 90:4); *Die Offenbarung des Johannes* (Zürich: Theologischer Verlag, 1984) 192. The major text Roloff cites, however, the *J* recension of *2 Enoch* 33:1-2, which may be a Christian insertion, speaks of an eighth, timeless period of a thousand years ("neither months nor weeks nor days nor hours") and does not develop a "sabbath" theme or period of "rest." Cf. F. I. Andersen, "2 (Slavonic Apocalypse of) Enoch," in J. H. Charlesworth, *The Old Testament Pseudepigrapha,* Vol. I (Garden City: Doubleday, 1983) 91-213, 156. The text of *2 Enoch* 33:1-2 attests, at the very least, a conventional apocalyptic use of the number "one thousand" to express an eschatological and, indeed, a "timeless" period, one not determined by clock or calendar.

[134]Cf. also the first part of Revelation: 2:11b with 3:5; 3:12a (which speaks of God's sanctuary before adding further a reference to the New Jerusalem); 3:21.

14:13	those who die in the Lord's service from the time of the beast's persecution and are therefore blessed, finding rest according to their works;
15:2-4	those on the fiery crystal sea [firmament] who praise God with the canticle of Moses and the Lamb;
20:4-6	the millennial kingdom.

When John mentions the martyrs in v. 4, he has in mind not only the fact of their deaths but also their prophetic function. One may take the first of the reasons for their death ("for their witness of Jesus") in the sense of the witness which they gave to Jesus or, better, as the witness which Jesus enabled them to give through his Spirit (cp. 19:10), just as the corresponding reason, "and for the word of God" refers to the message or commandments given by God (cp. 12:17). John does not indicate a second group (e.g., "confessors"). At the same time, however, John implies that the martyrs typify all the saints, certainly more than a delimited, single class. For those enjoying the "first resurrection" are described as the priestly kingdom. John's reference to this theme, which he drew from Exodus 19:4-6, has appeared twice before. In Revelation 1:5b-6, the community on earth described themselves in terms of the priestly kingdom (as those redeemed by Christ's blood). Later, in 5:9-10, the heavenly court predicated the priestly kingdom of a universal people which would reign over the earth, thus bringing out its eschatological scope. In 20:6, the only limitation called for is not a categorization according to class (e.g., martyrs, as contrasted with confessors, virgins, etc.), but merely one according to bodily existence in heaven as distinguished from bodily existence on earth. A typing of all blessed Christians in terms of one salient aspect (being a martyr) fits with John's previous use of one group, the celibates (14:1-5) to signify all those who have proved to be worthy followers of the Lamb. Moreover, the beatitude (v. 6) commenting on the first resurrection of these holy persons recalls the beatitude in 14;13, which spoke of those who died in the Lord. Their service of him and "their good works," which followed them, hardly designate in an exclusive way those actually killed during the beast's persecution.

Setting off the central portion (*B*, vv. 4-6) of the text are correlated passages regarding the tethering of Satan (*A*, vv. 1-3) and his being released to deceive the nations and meet his doom (*A'*,

vv. 7-10). One should recall that Satan himself attempted to attack the rest of the woman's children (12:17), but was apparently frustrated, standing on the sandy shore of the sea. He was reduced to working through his surrogates, the beasts. His assault through proxies was subsequently directed against the faithful on earth.

In 20:1-3 *(A)*, John employs another, different mythic image to describe essentially the same event, the de-activation of Satan in his "personally" directing the process of deception that entails idolatry and persecution. Satan is chained, bound, and sealed up in the abyss for a thousand years, but with the definite prospect of release for the climactic moment of conflict.

His release, activity, and undoing in 20:7-10 *(A')* at the end of the thousand years has to be construed in relation to his *new target,* not the faithful on earth, but those reigning with Christ as his priests in heaven *(B,* vv. 4-6). His very own deception of the nations takes on a cosmic if still "earthly" dimension in marshalling a mythical host, Gog and Magog, from the four corners of the earth. John has already made considerable use of Ezekiel 38–39 in depicting the Messiah's triumph over the beast, the false prophet, and the kings of the earth. John has reserved the more cosmic imagery, however, that of Gog and Magog, for this further dimension of the conflict with the Messiah's reign and realm. In doing so, John changes Ezekiel's single leader (Gog of Magog, Magog being Gog's mythical northern realm) to a characteristically paired set of adversaries, Gog and Magog (as he paired the beasts and also Death and the Grave). He also expands to the four corners of the earth the region from which they come. Furthermore, their army, for all practical purposes, is a demonic horde, for it "comes up onto *(anebēsan epi)*" the broad surface of the earth; that is, it comes from the abyss (cp. v. 3). Satan's deception of this innumerable, demonic, earthly mob is but the condition for an assault on a new target: "the encampment of the saints and the beloved city."

The second phrase, "the beloved city," is best taken not as differing from the encampment but as a synonym for it, introduced by an explanatory "and" (epexegetic *kai:* "and/that is/even/indeed"). Caution is in order in trying to identify this symbolic site. It must be related, if only because of the tightly-structured *(ABA')* context, to where "the saints" are placed in this sub-section *(Y)*, namely, in heaven. "Encampment" *(parem-*

bolē, signifying a military enclosure, cp. Heb 11:34; 13:11, 13; Acts 21:34, 37 etc.) fittingly suggests the objective of an armed assault. Furthermore, it reflects the imagery which John has used of the dwelling-place of those in heaven (cp. his use of the verb "to tent" in 12:2; 13:6; 7:5; 21:3) and of God's own dwelling ("tent," *skēnē* in 13:6; cp. 21:3).[135] This "beloved city" is not yet the Jerusalem come down from heaven to earth. As Mt. Zion stands for God's heavenly abode in 14:5 (cp. Isa 4:3-5), with a strong hint of the abiding city to be manifested as the New Jerusalem, so does the "beloved city" here.[136] The theme of the "first resurrection" provides the necessary theological continuum between the current heavenly abode of the saints and that which shall be made manifest in the new creation.

As elsewhere in apocalyptic (2 Thess 2:3-4; Mark 13:14; Matt 24:15) the climax of anti-God violence finds its archetype in an attempted or actual usurpation of a peculiarly divine domain, so, similarly, in Revelation 20:9. Here, however, Satan attacks the saints who enjoy with Christ his messianic reign in heaven. Actually, there is no contest—in the sense of physical contact. God destroys the opposing horde with fire from heaven (cf. Ezek 38:22) and casts Satan into the lake of fire and brimstone—all of which underscores the security of the saints in heaven and the non-termination of their status. Thus, the motif of the thousand years *does not delimit the messianic reign,* which will continue on into a new, manifest state once the new heavens and earth appear.

---

[135]Elsewhere, John uses *naos,* "sanctuary," except where he combines it with *skēnē,* "tent,": "sanctuary of the tent of testimony," 15:5. The *naos* (see above, note 37, and 11:1-2) designates "heaven" with the strong connotation of "perfectly safe, protective region."

[136]Mt. Zion, as "beloved," is equated with the city of Jerusalem in Ps 87:2-3; cp. Ps 78:6. Like Mt. Zion, John's "beloved city" defines a heavenly state in terms of an earthly locale. John so depicts heaven as he does here largely in function of his placement of the demonic but "earthly" army (v. 9). Actually there is no call whatever to press the imagery of v. 9 in such a way as to reduce the state of the first resurrection to the life of the Christian community on this planet, as St. Augustine did *(De Civitate Dei,* 20.7 ff.), understanding the millennium as the period of the Church's earthly existence from Pentecost to the Parousia.

Rather, it apocalyptically "times" the climactic moment of the destruction of Satan and the frustration of the worst conceivable form of violence directed against the divine Messiah and his faithful. Again, there is really no contesting the sovereignty of God.

Z. JUDGMENT FROM THE THRONE

20:11   *A.* The (Visual) Vision of One Seated on the Great White Throne

20:12-15 *B.* The (Visual) Vision of Judgment According to Works—the End of Death and the Grave

21:1-2   *C.* The (Visual) Vision of the New Creation and the Heavenly Jerusalem

21:3-4   *D.* The (Auditory) Vision of the Proclamation of Divine Rewards—the End of Death and Grief

21:5-8   *E.* The (Auditory) Vision of the Enthroned's Proclamations of the New Creation and of the Final Alternatives

19:11–21:8

20[11]   And I saw a great white throne
      and the one seated upon it,
        from whose face heaven and earth fled (away)
        and no place was found for them.

[12]   And I saw the dead, the great and the small
      standing before the throne.
      And books were opened;
      and another book, which is the book of life, was opened,
      and the dead were judged from the things written in
        the(se) books—according to their works.

[13]   And the sea gave up the dead which were in it;
      and Death and the Grave [Hades] gave up their dead,
      and they were judged—each (and every) one—
        according to their works.

[14]   And Death and the Grave were cast into the lake of fire.
      This is the second death, the lake of fire.

[15]   And if anyone was found not written in the book of life,
      (that one) was cast into the lake of fire.

21 ¹ And I saw a new heaven and a new earth.
>   For the former heaven and the former earth had passed
>   away,
>   and the sea exists no longer.

² And the holy city, New Jerusalem, I saw,
>   coming down from heaven, from God,
>   prepared as a bride adorned for her husband.

³ And I heard a loud [great] voice from heaven
>   saying:
>>   Lo, God's dwelling [tent] is with human beings,
>>   and he will dwell [tent] with them,
>>   and they will be his peoples
>>   and he himself will be God-with-them,

⁴   and he will wipe every tear from their eyes;
>>   and death will no longer exist,
>>   nor will grief or clamor or pain exist any longer,
>>   for the former things have passed away.

⁵ And the one seated on the throne said:
>>   Lo, I make all things anew.
>   and he said:
>>   Write (this down): These words are faithful and true.

⁶ and he said to me:
>>   They have taken place [occurred]!
>>   I am Alpha and Omega, the beginning and the end.
>>   I shall give—(quite) freely—to one who thirsts
>>   (permission) to drink from the fountain of the water
>>   of life.

⁷   The victor will inherit these things,
>>   and I shall be God to him
>>   and he shall be a son to me.

⁸   But for cowards, faithless, perverts, murderers, for-
>>   nicators, sorcerers and all (kinds of) liars—
>>   their share (lies) in the lake burning with fire and
>>   sulphur,
>>   which is the second death.

The literary structure in John's scenario of the final assizes consists of two sets of visions. The first set *(ABC)* is visual; the second *(DE),* auditory. In the first set, John recounts seeing the

Enthroned *(A,* 20:11), then the judgment of the dead and the termination of Death and the Grave *(B,* 20:12-15), and lastly the new heavens and earth, along with the New Jerusalem *(C,* 21:1-2). In the second set, he reports hearing first a voice from heaven *(D,* 21:3-4) and then three statements by the Enthroned One *(E,* 21:5-8). The auditory portions *(D* and *E)* of this subsection *(Z,* 20:11–21:8) successively recapitulate elements of the preceding, visual experiences *(A, B,* and *C).* Thus, *D* (21:4) recalls the end of death in *B* (20:12-15) and the passing away of the "former things" (namely, the former heaven and earth) in *C* (21:1), alluding to the "flight of heaven and earth" in *A* (20:11) as well. God's own statements from the throne *(E,* 21:5; cp. 20:11, 12) recapitulate and advance to their conclusion all the preceding portions, including *D* (cp. 21:3, 7).

The opening verse *(A,* 2:11) introduces the Enthroned in a majestic setting by himself. The flight of heaven and earth, recalling the theophany of God's act of deliverance in the Exodus (Ps 114:3-7), strikingly centers attention on the sovereign, victorious judge (the color of the throne being reminiscent of the color of the Messiah's steed at the opening of *X,* 19:11). It would be pedantically obtuse to ask how heaven and earth could disappear before the sea gives up its dead (20:13). The flight of heaven and earth dramatically fixes attention on God alone, and prepares remotely for the subsequent insistence on a new kind of creation (21:1, 4, 5). Similarly, it would be idle to try to determine whether John depicts merely a renewal of the physical creation (along the lines followed by Second Isaiah). In John's apocalyptic vision there occurs neither a return to paradise nor an ecological reworking of the current physical order. For a life without death, grief, clamor, or pain (21:4) supposes an entirely new created order, which John, building on 21:2, will symbolically present in the next section (§VII, the angelic interpretation of the New Jerusalem). John does not concern himself with physical geography but with the final destiny of mankind according to God's judgment and personal favor (grace).[137]

The picture of the general judgment *(B,* 20:12-15) prescinds from whether or not those who have enjoyed the heavenly millen-

---

[137]The transcendence of physical geography is evidenced in Jewish apocalyptic, too; cf. *2 Esdras* (*= 4 Ezra)* 7:39ff.

nium also appear before God. Suffice it to say that this judgment is a general one, for "great and small alike," and certainly does not exclude Christians (3:5). That the sea gives up its dead also serves to stress the universality of the final judgment. In the biblical tradition, death without proper burial (scl., in the earth) was held in particular dread (cf. 1 Kgs 13:22; 14:11; Jer 8:1-2; and cp. the disgrace inflicted on the twin witnesses, Rev 11:8-10). Furthermore, John stages this judgment only to indicate the principles on which rests God's final verdict for each person (20:13b, 15). Each is judged according to his works but also according to the reckoning of God's grace (the book of life, which records those effectively saved by the Lamb, cf. 21:27). John does not attempt to resolve the interplay of men's free will and God's grace. Nevertheless, the promises to the "victor" enunciated in the seven proclamations to the Churches and the "inheritance" (a gracious gift) promised to the "victor" in 21:7 suppose that the apparent duality does not entail a dichotomy. The Lamb's book of life, expressing "predestination" (cf. 17:8, "from the beginning of the world") according to the Lamb's own predestined self-sacrifice (cf. 13:8, "from the beginning of the world") shares with the Lamb's redemptive death the character of "predilection" and "prevenient grace" rather than "predetermination" according to some mechanically-conceived decree. The Lord's promise that the *victor's* name will not be erased from the book of life (3:5) conveys an implied warning that, unless one's works correspond to or "instrumentalize" redeeming grace, the "predestination" will not be achieved as intended.

John's sketch of the general judgment also covers the end of the paired eschatological adversaries Death and the Grave, who were the first to be introduced (in the fourth unsealing, 6:7-8). These two meet the same end as the others, the lake of fire (20:14; cp. 19:20; 20:10). This fate, a living death, likewise awaits the wicked (20:15; 21:8). Indeed, one suspects that John has deliberately added the two references to Death and the Grave (in 20:13b and 21:1f.) more clearly to link Z to the preceding sub-sections *(X* and *Y)* and to complete in inverse order the accounting for all adversaries both of the living God and of his redeemed people.

In *C,* 21:1-2, two correlated notions (note "I saw" used twice, vv. 1 and 2) describe a new set of events. In the remainder of Revelation, the new heaven and new earth seem to be summed up in the New Jerusalem itself, a city which, in effect, is a new world. One should bear in mind Isaiah 65:17-18, which provides a basis for this identification and serves as the springboard for John's description here, as well as for that which he pursues later (Rev 21:4; cp. Isa 65:19). The absence of the sea troubles some readers who enjoy its vast expanse and symphonic moods. They should remind themselves that, especially in the mythic or apocalyptic imagery of the ancient Near East, the sea stood for chaos and/or the abyss, the habitat of monsters threatening God and man alike. Given this background, its disappearance deserves special mention along with the passing of the former or "old" heaven and earth. Moreover, the sea (or "waters") sometimes stands as a third region (besides heaven and earth), notably with its connotation of chaos (cf. Gen 1:1-2), and calls for special comment. The heavenly city which God creatively provides to replace the former cosmos appears as a bride intended for the Redeemer (cp. 19:7; 21:9). She stands as the very antithesis, of course, of the woman *(gynē)* who is the whore, Babylon (17:2-6). Accordingly, John will later (21:9) describe her not only as the bride *(nymphē)* but also as the woman *(gynē)*—in the sense of the "wife"—of the Lamb.

The first paragraph *(D,* 21:3-4) of the auditory part of John's vision develops only the blissful consequences of the final judgment and the new creation. The speaker, who refers to God in the third person, is perhaps a throne-angel, although, as in 19:5, it may be the Lord Jesus. Inspired richly by OT passages like Isaiah 7:14; 25:8; Ezekiel 37:27; 2 Samuel 7:14, John tells of God's personal rapport with human beings. True to his universalistic perspective of humanity (e.g., the varied, reiterated phrase: "people, nations, tribes, and tongues") he represents the "people" of God in the plural, as "peoples," suggesting their complementary diversity. Racial and or national exclusiveness, so characteristic of much of Jewish apocalyptic, lies far from John's thought. God himself is Emmanuel ("God-with-us") among the varied throng of all the blessed.

The voice of God himself, uttered of course through the prophetic experience and writing of John, solemnly proclaims the final, encouraging news *(E,* 21:5-8). He has renewed everything, not by "developing" it—ecologically, as it were—but by fashioning a transfigured order of creation endowed with features of life which are proper to the resurrection of the just. In the first statement (21:5a), God himself reaffirms what the foregoing voice of Christ had described. By his second statement (21:5b), God solemnly reaffirms the whole vision. The words "faithful and true" serve also to form an inclusion with the opening description of the Word of God *(X,* 19:11). Moreover, together with similar phrasing in the close of each angelic interpretation-scene (§V, 19:9; §VII, 22:6), the phrase "[God's] faithful and true words" helps both to delineate each of the three closing sections (§§V, VI, VII) of Revelation and also to articulate their cohesiveness.[138] Lastly, God's definitive utterance, "They have taken place *(gegonan)!"* correlates the scenarios both of the final judgment and of the new creation with the previous, decisive moment of the final plagues (against Babylon) in 16:17b: "It has taken place *(gegonen)!"*[139]

The things which have occurred consist of the things renewed (cp. Isa 43:18-19) and, accordingly, the reliable and verified words of God.[140] As at the beginning of Revelation, although there in an oracle pronounced by the leader of the assembly (1:8), God refers to himself as Alpha and Omega. At this juncture, the self-identification is clarified as "the beginning and the end," namely, the source and end of all things.

Two aspects of God's final verdict conclude his declaration. The first (21:6b-7) stresses the reward, both as a matter of grace *(dōrean,* "freely"), fulfilling the promise of Isaiah 55:1, and as supposing human endeavor (21:7). The endeavor, implied by the term "victor," accords well with Paul's insistence that the ultimate success is not precisely a self-effected, human achievement but a gift, an "inheritance." A key quality of this inheritance,

---

[138]This point seems to have been missed completely by R. H. Charles, as Beasley-Murray points out in a similar connection, *Revelation,* 317 n. 1.

[139]Cf. C. H. Giblin, "Structural and Thematic Correlations," 502–503. Nowhere else but in 16:17 and in 21:6 does John use the Greek perfect, which is clearly a "definitive" tense, of the verb *ginesthai* ("to become/occur"), a word John writes at least forty times in Revelation.

[140]If *gegonan* ("they have occurred/taken place") referred only to the neuter plural "all things" *(panta)* in 21:5a as its supposed antecedent subject, one would expect the Greek verb to be in the singular.

if not, indeed, its substance, is a form of divine sonship. It may well be, however, that, to preserve the distinctive sonship of Christ, John has substituted for the phrase "father to him" the expression "God to him."[141] The second aspect of God's last word is a correlated condemnation to the second death for vicious human beings (21:8). This ominous warning must be voiced if only to retain the dominant, judgmental tone of this sub-section *(Z)* as a whole—in line with the two foregoing ones.

The short catalogue of vices stands not as a taxative enumeration but as a sweeping warning. These class-types of sinners reflect vices scored elsewhere, or elsewhere supposed, in Revelation. The cowards, who head the list, probably refer to those who fail in the courage expected of the one whose response to the Lord makes him a victor. The faithless represent much the same group, with emphasis either on loss of faith or on infidelity in general moral practice. The noun "perverts" hits not only at sexual aberration but also at the moral corruption which is particularly linked to false worship (cf. the typing of Babylon in 17:4-5 and cp. 21:27). Murderers and fornicators, sorcerers (religious charlatans) and liars seem to be linked with "perverts" as they are with "idolaters" in 22:15. Unrepentant murderers, sorcerers, fornicators, and, in addition, thieves, have appeared earlier (9:21) as immoral classes having a common anti-faith background, the cult of false gods (9:20). The ultimate sin, accordingly, is that of the liars, later (22:15) specified as "everyone who loves and does the lie." For the lie is the denial of truth, preeminently as the falsification of God and what is due him (as in the case of false prophecy, 16:13; 19:20; 20:10; cp. 2:2; 3:9). The followers of the Lamb are expressly free of the lie (14:5).

§*VII. Angelic Interpretation-Scene Regarding the Heavenly Jerusalem (21:9–22:11)*

This concluding section of the major vision (4–22) proves to be sufficiently definable even at its end if one recognizes that it

---

[141]Cf. Beasley-Murray, *Revelation,* 313. In this respect, Revelation would be in accord with John's Gospel, which reserves to Jesus (except for the idiom "sons [*huioi*] of light" in John 12:36) the term "son" *(huios),* and uses "children" *(tekna)* of those who, though begotten by God (John 1:12), are merely human.

dovetails with the conclusion or epilogue to Revelation as a whole. Thus, 22:6b (God's sending his angel), 22:7 (the unannounced voice of Jesus), and, substantially, 22:10-11 (the last words of the angelic interpreter) form the transition to the epilogue or conclusion proper. The latter is found in the dialogue of 22:12-20 and is followed by the closing, one-line epistolary salutation in 22:21.

Accordingly, the frame-passages of §VII, which are those in which the words of the *angelus interpres* of this vision (21:9–22:9) correspond closely with those of his counterpart in §V (17:1–19:10), consist of 21:9-10a at the outset and 22:6-9 at the end.

Apart from the frame-passages, then, the body of the scene may be outlined as follows, although some portions, especially at the outset,[142] are grammatically welded together. Each of the three stages of the angel's discourse, as John recounts it, pays attention to the light from God *(a, a', a'')* and to specific, mainly numerical aspects of the city *(b, b', b'')*. The major divisions *(A, B, C)* of the interpretation proper are given according to John's advertence to the angel's action:

21:10b-14	A.	*The Angel's Manifestation of the Holy City*
21:11	a.	God's glory as her brilliant illumination
21:12-14	b.	A general view of the walls and gates
21:15-21	B.	*The Angel's Measurement of the City*
21:16-21	b'.	Specific features:
21:16-18	x.	—the size of the city —its walls; the city itself (gold, pure [as] crystal);
21:19-21	y.	—the foundations of the city walls —its twelve gates; the city square (gold, pure [as] crystal).
21:22-27	a'.	God's glory as its light; no sanctuary
22:1-5	C.	*The Angel's Manifestation of the River of Life*

---

[142]In the Greek text, vv. 10b-14 contain a string of participles, although the interpretation proper begins in v. 10b with a verb in the indicative mood *(kai edeixen moi)*.

22:1-3a	*b''*. The river of life from the throne and the tree of life
22:3b-5	*a''*. God's illumination

Since §VII occupies a relatively smaller portion of John's apocalypse than did §V, the whole text may be provided immediately below. Its tight connection with the ending of Revelation, often labeled as an "epilogue," prompts the inclusion of the latter as well.

21:9–22:11

21 ⁹ And one of the seven angels who had the seven libation-bowls,

> those filled with the last seven plagues,

came and spoke with me, saying:

Come,

I shall show you the bride, the wife of the Lamb.

¹⁰   And he led me in the Spirit to a mountain huge [great] and high,

¹⁰   and he showed me the holy city, Jerusalem,

coming down from heaven, from God—

¹¹   She has God's glory,

> her brilliance like a splendid jewel [stone],
> like a diamond [crystal-jasper] jewel [stone].

¹²   She has a massive [great], high wall,

and has twelve gates,

> and upon the gates twelve angels,
> and names inscribed, which are those of the twelve tribes, (the) sons of Israel:

¹³   east, three gates,

> north, three gates,
> south, three gates,
> west, three gates;

¹⁴   and the wall of the city has twelve foundation-stones

and on them twelve names, (those) of the Lamb's Twelve Apostles.

¹⁵   And the angel who was speaking with me

had a measuring-stick, a golden reed,

to measure the city and its gates and its wall.

16   And the city lay four-square,
      its length as great as its width.
      And he measured the city with the rod: 12,000 stadia;
      its length, breadth, and height are equal.

17   And he measured the wall: 144,000 cubits—
      a human's measure, which is (also) the angel's.

18   And the material of the wall was jasper.
      And the city (itself) was pure gold,
      like pure crystal.

19   The foundations of the city wall were adorned
      with every (kind of) jewel [precious stone]:
      the first foundation (was) jasper,
      the second, sapphire,
      the third, chalcedony,
      the fourth, emerald,

20   the fifth, agate,
      the sixth, carnelian,
      the seventh, yellow topaz,
      the eighth, beryl,
      the ninth, topaz,
      the tenth, apple-green quartz,
      the eleventh, blue sapphire,
      the twelfth, amethyst.

21   And the twelve gates, twelve pearls;
      each gate was from a single pearl.
      And the square of the city (was) gold,
      pure as transparent crystal.

22   And I did not see a sanctuary within it,
      for its sanctuary is the Lord God, the Almighty, and the
      Lamb.

23   And the city has no need for the sun or the moon to shine
      on it,
      for the glory of God illumines it,
      and its lamp is the Lamb.

24   And the nations will walk about by its light,
      and the kings of the earth will bring their glory into it.

25   And its gates will not be closed (at any time) during the
      day,
      for there shall be no nighttime there.

26 And (people) will bring the glory and honor of the nations into her.

27 And nothing unclean will enter it,
or [and] one who does (what is) corrupt and a lie,
but only those written in the Lamb's book of life.

22 1 And he showed me a river of (the) water of life,
bright as crystal,
coming forth from the throne of God and of the Lamb.

2 In the middle of the (city's) square
and of the river (flowing) on each side
(was the) tree of life yielding twelve fruits,
producing its fruit for each month;
and the tree's leaves (were) for (the) health of the nations,

3 and no accursed (ailment) will exist any longer.
And the throne of God and of the Lamb will be in (the city),
and his servants will worship him,

4 and they will see his face,
and his name (will be) on their foreheads.

5 And there will be no night any longer;
and they have no need for light from a lamp and light from (the) sun,
for the Lord God will illumine them,
and they shall (exercise) kingly rule for ever and ever.

6 And he said to me:
These words are faithful and true.
And the Lord God of the spirits of the prophets
has sent his angel to his servants
to show what must occur soon [quickly].

7 Lo, I do come quickly.
Blessed (is) the one who keeps the words of the prophecy of this book.

8 And I, John, (was) the one hearing and looking at these things.
And when I heard and looked,
I fell down to worship at the feet of the angel showing me these things.

9   And he said to me:

> See (that you do) not!
> I am your co-servant
> and (the co-servant) of your brothers the prophets,
>> and of those who keep the words of this book.
> Worship God!

10   And he said to me:

> Do not seal (up) the words of the prophecy of this book,
>> for the time is near!

11
> Let the unjust man commit injustice still,
> and let the filthy be made filthier still;
> and let the just man do justice still,
> and the holy man be made holier still!

12
> Lo, I am coming quickly,
> and my reward is with me,
>> to repay each one according to [as is] his work.

13
> I am Alpha and Omega,
> the first and the last,
> the beginning and the end.

14
> Blessed (are) those who wash their robes
> so that there will be authorization for them
>> (to have access) to the tree of life,
> and (so that) they may enter the city.

15
> (Shut) outside (are) the dogs and the sorcerers
>> and the fornicators and the murderers and the idolaters,
> and everyone who loves and does a lie.

16
> I, Jesus, sent my angel
>> to attest these things to you, to the churches.
> I am the root and scion of David,
> the bright star of dawn.

17
> Both the Spirit and the bride say: Come!
> And let him who hears say: Come!
> And let one who is thirsty come;
> let the one who wishes receive life's water freely [*gratis*].

18
> I testify to everyone who hears the prophecy of this book:

If anyone adds (to the words of this prophecy),
   God will add upon him the plagues written in this
      book;
[19]   and if anyone subtracts from the words of the
      prophecy
         of this book,
   God will subtract his share
      in the tree of life
      and in the holy city—written about in this book.

[20]   He who testifies to these things says:
   Yes, I do come quickly.

Amen!
Come, Lord Jesus!

[21]   The grace of the Lord Jesus (be) with all (of you)!

The destruction of Babylon (16:17) and God's new creation, the heavenly Jerusalem (21:5-6a) occur, in a metahistorical dimension, simultaneously. God's negative judgment on evil coincides in the apocalyptic perspective with his positive, salvific reward for the saints. Again, the single moment of the convergence of requital and reward is marked by *gegonen* in 16:17b and by *gegonan* in 21:6. The paired interpretation-scenes dramatically reenforce this climactic moment, as it was first introduced at the end to the septenary of the last plagues (16:17b) by commencing with the intervention of one of the angels who held the libation-bowls which were filled with these final plagues.

Much as in the OT thematic of God's Holy War, destruction of the godless enemy serves as a necessary condition for God's granting the land to his people. His kingly rule is fully achieved only in its intended realm. In Revelation, however, where the new creation has replaced the former things, God's realm transcends any previous limitations, and entails a theophany, a manifestation of God himself among mankind. Appropriately, then, the angel leads John in a spiritual journey-experience to a high mountain to behold the holy city descending from God's abode. The introductory portion of the interpretation (vv. 9-10) is firmly knit (in the compound sentence, ". . . and he showed me . . .," v. 10b) together with the interpretation proper.

As he begins (*A,* 21:10b-14), and before he adverts to anything else, John speaks of the city as a manifestation of God's glory (*a,* 21:11). He comments on its brilliance *(phōstēr,* that is, its being something in which light is concentrated and thence radiates).[143] The term aptly suits the quality of a diamond (21:11b). The theme of pervasive light recurs in corresponding developments, namely, the *a'* and *a''* segments: "illumine" in 21:23 (cf. "light" in 21:24) and "illumine" in 22:5; the developments bear out the theme of God's enlightening presence.[144]

From outside, as it were, John describes his initial view of the city's imposing structure *(b,* vv. 12-14). Specifically, he mentions its massive wall (a feature which forms an inclusion between v. 12a and v. 14) and its gates (vv. 12b-13). In doing so, he employs the number "twelve" six times. That number, clearly symbolic of the realm constituted by God's people, will occur a total of twelve times in the rest of the interpretation proper (21:10b-22:5), and then only in the divisions *b, b', b'''*[145] The numerical incidence is hardly to be judged accidental in this well-honed passage. Besides, John employs the word "God" seven times within the same compass of text (21:10b-22:5).[146] If the *opening* of the

---

[143]Cf. H. B. Swete, *The Apocalypse of St. John,* 284.

[144]The use of *phōstēr* or *phōtizein* characterizes the subdivisions *a, a'* and *a''*. The only other time either word occurs in Revelation is when *phōtizein* is predicated of the glorious angel who declares the fall of Babylon, 18:1. The figure of the angel in 18:1 (equivalently "the Angel of Yahweh") is obviously described in terms borrowed from Ezekiel's vision of the coming of the Lord—for the time of destruction and for the time of his merciful return as well (Ezek 43:2-3). Once again, John beautifully balances the corresponding interpretation-scenes of §§V and VII, and does so with stunningly original theological effect.

[145]Thus, in *b,* 21:12-14, six times, notably of "names" (vv. 12 and 14); in *b',* 21:16-21, five times including multiples of distance (12,000 stadia and 144,000 cubits) and the ordinal "twelfth" (v. 21); and in *b'',* 22:1-5, once (22:2)—the twelfth occurrence—of the twelve fruits of the tree of life according to "each month" (but pointedly without saying "twelve" months).

[146]The seven occurrences are 21:10b, 11, 22, 23; 22:1, 3, 5, including the solemn expansions "Lord God, the Almighty" (21:22) and "Lord God" (23:5), which appear in the third and seventh positions, respectively (positions to which John always pays special attention in a num-

interpretation-scene, i.e., 21:9-10a is also counted, which seems reasonable given the fact that it introduces the *specific point* of this interpretation,[147] John also mentions seven times the other divine person, the Lamb.[148] Assiduous numbering of key terms is not peculiar to apocalyptic texts. It is attested, for example, in the covenant-formula as presented in Joshua 24:1-25.[149] Nevertheless, if only as a narrative conceit, it contributes to the fascinating coherence of a dialogue (as in Joshua 24) or dramatized vision (Rev 21:9-22:9) and witnesses to the writer's delight in challenging his audience's interest.

John does not describe the wall as a fortification, but as an imposing feature of the habitation for God's people, the faithful. For the wall soars up from its apostolic foundation stones, the men chosen by the Lamb. At the same time, its gates bespeak the continuation of the revelation to Israel in its integrity, the twelve tribes. The twelve corresponding angels on the gate-structure (*pylōn,* not *pylē* [gate-door]) apparently stand for the guardians (cf. Isa 62:6) of the Israel of God. John aligns the symmetrically disposed gates in an order of the compass (ENSW) which he probably adapted from the order of Ezekiel's vision of the measuring of the sacred area of the temple (Ezek 42:15-20),

---

bered series, as in the three septets of the unsealings, trumpets, and bowls). "The Lord God of the spirits of the prophets" occurs in what clearly lies outside the vision proper, as the angel concludes the interpretation-scene (22:6); the same is true of his command to worship God (22:9).

[147]As the conclusion (22:6, 8-11) significantly does *not* do.

[148]The Lamb *(to arnion)* appears in 21:9, 14, 22, 23, 27; 22:1, 3. The third occurrence (21:22) pairs him with the Lord God the Almighty as the (one) sanctuary (actually, as the replacement of a man-made sanctuary or even of "heaven" itself). The sixth (22:1) and climactic seventh (22:3) instances speak of "the (one) throne of God and of the Lamb" in such a way that the sixth points to the throne as the source of the water of life, and the seventh entails face-to-face worship of God.

[149]Cf. C. H. Giblin, "Structural Patterns in Jos 24, 1-25," *CBQ* 26 (1964) 50–69. According to S. David Sperling, ". . . Giblin's important study has demonstrated how the placement of significant words and the repetition of grammatical forms serve to tighten the structure of the chapter." S. David Sperling, "Joshua 24 Re-examined," *HUCA* 58 (1987) 119–136, 122. Sperling dates Joshua 24 early in the reign of Jeroboam II (ca. 786–746 B.C.E.); ibid., 136.

although John's vision contains no sanctuary *(naos)* and, a fortiori, no temple *(hieron)* or temple-wall. Even so, he does not follow the circular order (NESW) which Ezekiel used in his placing
the tribal gates of the city (Ezek 48:30-35). Again, an OT image
has been "reborn" in the Apocalypse of John as John endeavors
to communicate the vision of a new kind of Israel which transcends any distinction between sacred and profane places.[150]

The second stage *(B,* 21:15-27) commences with a transitional
verse (21:15). The angel's measurement will be given in human
terms (v. 17b) in order to render the symbolic dimensions somewhat comprehensible to John's readers. Although the subsequent
description, as announced here, covers the city, its gates, and its
walls, not all it contains (especially vv. 18b and 21b, the "golden"
features) falls strictly under the concept of measurement, even
though it includes other numerical notations (vv. 19-21a). The
basic point announced, as perhaps suggested by the precious metal
of the measuring rod, is an appropriate description of the glorious components of the city. Unlike the opening description *(A.b,*
21:12-14), the current one *(B.b',* 21:16-21) takes its standpoint,
as it were, from the inside.

The first two measurements (vv. 16 and 17-18a) of the city as
a perfect cube and of the wall are the only ones which comprise
multiples of twelve, and may therefore be grouped together (as
under *x* in the outline). Twelve, multiplied "indefinitely" by a
thousand, symbolically expresses the city's indefinite extent without rendering it amorphous. Interestingly, the 12,000 stadia
(furlongs, actually somewhat over 600 feet each for a total of
about 1,500 miles) are a hundred times greater than Herodotus's
estimate of the size of Babylon.[151] John adds a third dimension,
its equal height. He may be suggesting a pyramid, which would
suit a city envisaged as situated on a mountain—or rather, as a
"holy hill." More likely, however, he intends to evoke the image
of a gigantic "Holy of Holies," which was a perfect cube, over-
laid with gold (1 Kgs 6:20). Although John subsequently insists
(21:22) that the city *contains* no temple-sanctuary, the Lord God's

---

[150]Notwithstanding Ezekiel's entitling the city "Yahweh is there"
(YHWH šmh), the specific "locale" of God remains the sacred precincts
of the temple (cf. Ezek 48:35; 43:1-7a).

[151]Herodotus, *History of the Persian War,* I, 178.

presence and that of the Lamb account for the special holiness of the entire habitation of the saints (21:10b.22-27) and their throne is at the source of its religious life (22:1-5).[152]

The second symbolic measurement (vv. 17-18a) describes the height of the city wall. The 144,000 cubits (about eighteen inches each, for a total of 216,000 feet) is obviously symbolic, as one will recall from the number used both for the innumerable, marshalled host represented as the Christian fulfillment of Israel (cp. 7:1-8 in the light of 7:9-17) and for the victorious, not numerically restricted faithful who follow the Lamb (14:1-5). The mind-boggling dimensions help indicate that the dwelling which it appropriately encompasses contains the Israel of God, probably in astronomical numbers. "Jasper," the material of the city wall, seems to be a kind of flashing rock-crystal or, equivalently, in evaluating John's imagery (4:3; 21:11; and 21:19), a diamond.

Punctuating the measurements and the enumerations in x (21:16-18) and y (21:19-21) are comments on the unblemished glory of the city (21:18b) and its central square—or main thoroughfare (21:21b). In both cases, the "sovereign metal," gold, is further described in such a way as to suggest a kind of transfiguration beyond the expectations of merely human experience. A not dissimilar apocalyptic description occurs in Mark's account of Jesus' transfiguration (Mark 9:3), where the transformed Jesus' garments "become glistening white, exceedingly so, such as no fuller on earth could whiten in this way." It is inadvisable, however, to force John's text by construing the comparison with "pure (transparent) crystal" to mean "transparent gold."

[152]Cf. Kraft, *Offenbarung,* 270–271. Kraft's construing the holy city, however, as the antithesis of the tower of Babel (Gen 11:1-9) requires more data from the text and more argumentation. To help, one might note that the city's inhabitants are "peoples" (plural, 21:3) but without the further, hitherto customary variations of "tribes, tongues, nations/races"; *see above,* note 58. The variations might prove counterproductive at this point, indicating not a universal pluralism but rather a divisive diversity. John does take care to note the entry of the "nations/races" and their leaders (21:24, 26). In 22:2, "the healing of the nations" comes from the medicinal leaves of the tree of life (a healing of divisions as well as of any other defects?). The dominant impression remains that of a place which is diametrically contrasted with the *city* of *Babylon,* not with the (albeit symbolically related) *tower* of *Babel.*

The enumerations in 21:19-21a (in the major portion of *y*) deal with the foundations of the city wall (vv. 19-20) and with the city's gates (v. 21a). Identification of many of the jewels set in the foundations has taxed the most scholarly commentators.[153] The one first mentioned, jasper, seems to be the equivalent of our "diamond"—at least in terms of the appreciative awe which John expects of his reader. Since it heads the list of twelve, it can hardly be less impressive than any other precious stone, and John delights in mentioning it elsewhere (4:3; 21:11-18). *Diamas,* the Greek word from which we derive "diamond," does not appear in John's vocabulary. The remaining stones are listed below. The ancients seem to have particularly valued the *hue* of stones, and, judging by Pliny the Elder, the sea-green and blue hues. In a number of cases, of course, the intensity or shading of gems also became a factor in one's appreciation of their beauty, and consideration of their suitability for various uses (engraving for signet rings, for instance) likewise affected personal preferences. Attempts to recapture John's intent are at best approximate. In the order of the text, but with consistent attention to the Greek, and beginning with the second stone listed, the gems are:

2) sapphire: perhaps lapis-lazuli;
3) chalcedony: turquoise;
4) smaragdus: emerald (cp. 4:3);
5) sardonyx: like agate, red, but lighter; a light reddish-brown, much in demand for making cameos;
6) sardion: carnelian, a fiery, blood red, perhaps equivalently a ruby, though sought for engraving (cp. 4:3);
7) chrysolite: yellowish, a form of beryl;
8) beryl: sea-dipped green;

[153] H. B. Swete's investigation of this problem may still be the best and the most concise *(The Apocalypse of St. John,* 67–68 and 290–294), so the lineup given below depends heavily on his comments. Swete's major ancient source is Pliny the Elder's *Natural History,* 37.20. U. Jart, "The Precious Stones in the Revelation of St. John XXI, 18–21," *StTh* 24 (1970) 150–181 is quite unclear. Also, she seems to suppose that John is making a selection of stones which could be engraved as were signet-rings. In spite of 21:14, one doubts that such was the key factor in his numbered catalogue, especially if the criterion were merely the kind of precious stones which mere human beings were able to engrave.

9) topaz: a golden-hued green (cp. Ps 119 [LXX] 118):127, where the Greek has: "I love your commands above gold and topaz.");

10) chrysoprasos: lighter than beryl; apple-green quartz;

11) hyacinth: blue or violet sapphire (cp. 9:17, the color of blue smoke);

12) amethyst: purplish, of greater brilliancy than hyacinth.

If it does nothing else, this list of jewels may impress the reader by captivating his imagination concerning the beauty and subtle variety of the dwelling which John says God has prepared for his people(s). There remains, to be sure, much more to the purpose of John's concise enumeration of these precious stones. They may well imply, as one may surmise in line with the reflections of Clement of Alexandria,[154] the variety and unity of apostolic tradition (cp. 21:14). They also seem to mirror, albeit in a transformed way (in designation and/or order) the unique badge of the high priest's office (Exod 28:15-21) to judge as God would for the benefit of the people. John may also be developing a "paradise motif," in line with Ezekiel's catalogue of stones (Greek text) in Ezekiel 28:13 and, at the same time, the prophetic promise of a city, equivalently a civilization, remade by the Lord (Isa 54:11-14; Tob 13:16). Some have held that John deliberately reverses the order of precious stones associated with the signs of the zodiac,[155] either to dissociate himself from pagan speculations about the divine city or, conversely—as a compatible paradox—to show that pagan aspirations are found in a new way in his own theological vision. None of these lines of interpretation contradicts any other, and all of them taken together seem compatible with John's penchant for resynthesizing OT hopes and even pagan motifs in his Christian perspective.

Turning to the twelve gates (21:21a), John succinctly notes their identical quality (twelve pearls) but also, characteristically, their supranatural (and suggestively "supernatural") dimensions. They are no vain adornment (as were Babylon's pearls, 17:4; 18:16). These features, which the reader already knows correspond to the twelve tribes (21:12-13), thematically complement the preceding

[154]*Paed.*, II.12, §119, noted by H. B. Swete, ibid., 293-294.
[155]See the judicious discussion by Beasley-Murray, *Revelation*, 324-325.

elaboration (21:19-20) of the twelve-apostles motif (21:14). As earlier (Revelation 7), one Israel of God emerges through complementary aspects: the old (the tribes of Israel) and the new (the Apostles). John also seems to be concerned, at least in 21:19-21a, to balance motifs of unity ("a single pearl," v. 21a) with diversity ("every [kind of] stone," v. 19a).[156]

Within the second stage *(B,* 21:15-27) of John's exposition, the concluding portion *(b',* vv. 25-27) picks up the more dominant theme of the divine, illuminating presence. Gold, gems, and pearls (cf. *a',* vv. 15-21) merely reflect the light, even when they shimmer with it. Only God's glory and the lamp that is the Lamb (21:11, 23) or the one throne that is his and that of the Lamb (22:1) can account for the source of light and of life.

Inspired by Isaiah 60:1-20, John expatiates on the light-filled city to which purified nations will flock. The allegedly "poor order" of John's text, vis-à-vis Isaiah's,[157] results from rearrangements and rephrasings John had to employ to make his theological vignette concise. He needed both to stress the indwelling, personal source of the city's light and also to depoliticize and denationalize the contributions of nations and their kings. Thus, he places God's glory as the source of illumination and the Lamb as its medium or instrument (the lamp) between absence of sun and moon (Isa 60:19-20) on the one hand and the presence of *illumined,* not subjected nations (cp. Isa 60:5-7, 11, 12, 14) on the other. The Jerusalem which John beholds has never been oppressed or conquered, for it is God's new creation. The kings are not paraded as conquered (Isa 60:10-11) or as bearing tribute (Isa 60:5-7); rather, they contribute their glory. Negations occur several times (vv. 23a, 25, and 27) in order to set in relief the glory of God and the glory (that is, the outstanding praise) of others (vv. 23b and 24a, v. 26) and then the personal purity from sin of those who have access to the city. Accordingly, "unclean" in v. 27 can-

---

[156]This "conceptualization" (scil., of unity in diversity) is not fanciful. Apocalyptic imagery seems to balance the same aspects elsewhere, as in Luke's account of the pentecostal phenomena in Acts 2:1-40, esp. vv. 1-11. Cf. C. H. Giblin, "Complementarity of Symbolic Event and Discourse in Acts 2:1-40," *Studia Evangelica VI* (TU 112; Berlin: Akademie-Verlag, 1973) 189–196, 192–195.

[157]So Kraft, *Offenbarung,* 273.

not be taken in the ritualistic sense of Isaiah 52:1 and 35:8, though it must retain its basic sense of "common," that is, "profane, not sanctified." The correlated causes of exclusion are doing what is corrupt (an "abomination," any serious moral offense, usually typified by sexual aberrations) and, above all, the lie (the opposite of truth and justice, which must characterize those attuned to God's very being).

The third stage of the interpretation (*C,* 22:1-5) is introduced by John's again adverting to the angel's action (22:1, "And he showed me," cp. 21:10b, 15). Once more, this distinct stage then comprises two components. As in the second stage, they are grouped in an order which inverts that of the first stage (the overview). First *(b' ',* 22:1-3a) John presents the water of life and the tree of life situated near it; second *(a' '* , 22:3b-5), he speaks of the worship and kingly rule of God's illumined servants. Both portions contain at their outset John's notation of the throne of God and of the Lamb (21:1b, 3b), the source of life and health and the focal point of worship. The divine oneness of God (the Father) and the Lamb (his Son) is stated in terms of functional theology; that is, an identical role or dignity is ascribed to both.[158]

---

[158]A good illustration of functional theology is Jesus' declaration according to John 10:27-30: ". . . and no one snatches (them) [i.e., the sheep as the Father's gift] from the Father's hand; I and the Father are one [*hen*]." The "oneness of being" (neuter *hen,* not masculine *heis* being used to render the predicated numeral "one") is, in the context, basically functional. Jesus and the Father exercise together the same sovereignly protective power. If the reader then *develops* John's theology by employing philosophical categories and judgments (viz., concerning "being," "essence," "nature," and the like), he is moving, albeit legitimately, into the area of "ontological" theology. Thus, however, one's theological thinking moves into another *mode* of abstraction.

Failure to acknowledge the distinction between the modes of thought of functional theology and of ontological theology can pose needless problems to the theological exegete. The interpretation of John 14:28: ". . . because the Father is greater than I (am)," is a case in point. The language is that of functional theology. For Jesus, who has just previously demonstrated his self-humbling service in the footwashing although (and because) he is the disciples' Teacher and Lord (13:12-17), speaks in John 14:28 *as this man,* God's Son-and-Servant, who is fulfilling his mission in the journey back to his Father. He is *not* speaking "as man (i.e., as

The same was true earlier, at the outset of *B.b'*, 22:1, where John identified the (one) sanctuary as "the Lord God, the Almighty, and the Lamb."

The "throne" of God and of the Lamb does not "localize" them, for John excluded such definition when he spoke of the absence of the sanctuary (21:22). Rather, the throne signifies the majestic personal presence both of God and of the Lamb as the single source of the water of life and the one authority worshiped by the saints. John has considerably altered, then, Ezekiel's vision of the life-giving river that flows from God's temple (Ezek 47:1-12; cp. Ps 36:7-9). The river, of course, is unsullied, recalling the earlier emphasis on purity and clarity (21:18b, 21b; cp. 21:27).[159]

The tree of life is situated in close proximity to the city square or its main artery and also to the river of life, from which it obviously draws its strength. John's staging, notwithstanding its attempted precision, remains somewhat ambiguous. E. Delebecque's translation of the location given in v. 2a may be a more exact alternative: "Between the esplanade and the river, in the middle, in the interval, a wood (or tree) of life."[160] In any event, John locates the tree of life quite near both the river of life and the symbolic "throughfare" for the city's population. He probably has in mind a single tree (not a forest or a line of trees, as in Ezekiel 47:12, which he here adapts). No doubt John is also thinking of a new form of the tree of life in Eden (Gen 2:9). John's tree symbolizes year-round life and health for God's universal people, "the nations." For *all* of those who enter the city (21:27; cp. 21:24b, 26) belong to the Lamb. The number "twelve," here used of the ongoing productivity of the tree of life (cp. Ezek 47:12), appo-

existing in his human nature)" or "as God (i.e., as existing in his divine nature)" but as *this man* who is uniquely God's Son and is on his mission. His language is not "merely deferential," nor, on the other hand, is it philosophical; it is the language of functional theology.

[159]Some see in the river an allusion to the Milky Way, as they find elsewhere John's reworking the signs of the zodiac. How this interpretation of the river can be squared with John's relating the river to the tree of life remains, to say the least, unclear.

[160]Cf. E. Delebecque, "Où situer l'Arbre de la vie dans la Jérusalem céleste? Note sur Apocalypse XXII, 2," *RevThom* 88 (1988) 124–130, 129.

sitely concludes the use of this number befitting God's people by its twelfth and last occurrence in this interpretation-scene. The absence of any curse alludes to Zecharaiah 14:11. In John's context, it denotes absolute security not just from ailments but from any kind of distress.

The concluding portion (*a'* ', vv. 3b-5) of this third stage *(C)* of the interpretation repeats, in line with *a* and *a'*, the primary emphasis on the city's light as derived from God alone. The traditional priestly blessing of Numbers 6:22-27 is eminently realized in John's vision:

> "The Lord bless you and keep you:
> The Lord make his face to shine upon you,
>   and be gracious to you:
> The Lord lift up his countenance upon you,
>   and give you peace."

For John, this blessing of the Israelite people extends to all nations (cf. v. 2) and consists in a direct vision of the Lord by all who uniquely belong to him (v. 3b). Since God's illumination remains constant, there is no need for a human implement (a lamp—here, clearly not to be identified with the Lamb, mentioned earlier [21:23] as the divine instrument of illumination) or for the merely natural source of light (the sun). Darkness is unknown (v. 5a; cp. 21:25b). Clearly, "night" denotes not precisely physical darkness but anything unfavorably associated with it, like ignorance and wrongoing.

That God and the Lamb share the same throne helps convey the sense that the pronouns "him" and "his" in vv. 3b-4 look primarily to the Godhead, but without compromising the divinity of the Lamb. "His name written on their foreheads" recalls the iterated idiom defining one's unique relationship to God both as a member of the Christian community and as an individual person (7:3; 9:4; 14:1). Similarly, it distinguishes the Christians' personal relationship to the Lamb from the pagans' subservient relationship to the beast (denoted by a "brand," *charagma,* 13:6; 14:9; 17:5; 20:4). There is nothing demeaning in the Lord's servants' bearing his name on their foreheads. The image suggests, rather, the headband worn by the high priest, which declared its bearer "holy to the Lord *(qdš lYHWH)."* It is not unlikely that John alludes here to the priestly character of God's people, which he expressly combines with their kingly rule (as he does here, v. 5) thrice elsewhere in Revelation (1:5b-6; 5:9-10; 20:4-6).[161] Worship of God is expected of all humans (14:6-7; 15:4). Worship of the beast or of false gods but parodies it (9:20; 13:4, 8, 12, 15; 14:9, 11; 16:2; 20:4); indeed, worship of any creature, even an angelic co-servant, is forbidden (19:10; 22:8-9). Significantly, the heavenly court of the elders and even the four living beings also worship God (19:4), but do so by "falling down," that is, by prostrating their faces to the ground (4:10; 5:14; 11;16; 19:4), whereas here the saints apparently look upon God "face to face" (20:3b-4a), with their allegiance marked on their foreheads.

After the first four-line sentence (vv. 3b-4) of this concluding portion (*a''*) of stage three, John pens the last four-line statement (v. 5). The view towards the throne (vv. 3b-4) finds its complement in the light emanating from God himself and accounting for the glorious, royal status of his worshippers. Their promised "kingly rule over the earth" (5:10) has become in its fulness an everlasting reign in the new heavens and new earth, which are summed up in the new Jerusalem created by God.

The close of this second of the two paired interpretation-scenes contains many phrases already discussed apropos of the first (see above, pp. 159–160). Two new elements distinguish it, however. First, v. 6b contains amplifications that look especially to the *beginning* of the whole apocalypse. Second, other features, like vv. 7 and 10-11, are fitted into the close of this second interpretation-scene in order to tie it to the *closing portion* of the whole apocalypse. In this way, not usual considering the technique John used earlier to link major sections of his vision in 4–22,[162] John enfilades the closing interpretation-scene with the conclusion or "epilogue" of his work.

---

[161]Cf. E. Schüssler-Fiorenza, *Priester für Gott,* 384–389. The priesthood of the saints is not ministerial, as the use of the word for worship *(latreuein* [7:15; 22:3b], not *leitourgein)* helps show. Moreover, the saints' activities entail demonstrations of praise, but not, for instance, such "serving" actions as the offering of incense (5:8; 8:3-4).

[162]U. Vanni, *La Struttura letteraria, passim.*

THE CONCLUSION TO THE BOOK OF REVELATION (22:7, 12–21)

The conclusion to the entire apocalypse may be termed an "epilogue" only in the sense that it strikingly corresponds to the "prologue." For it forms an integral part of John's whole unified and coherent composition. Detailed connections will appear in the commentary given below. A prominent characteristic of the epilogue in relation to the prologue lies in its reintroduction of dialogue in a liturgical setting of the community to which John writes. It is conceivable either that John himself wrote this dialogue or that, as seems likely in the case of the prologue, certain additions befitting his composition were inserted by his intended audience. In the epilogue, however, the community redactor or editor seems to have executed his task more deftly.

The outline immediately below should orient the reader to the interplay of the concluding dialogue proper. Since this dialogue dovetails with the end of §VII, however, the text of the epilogue has been placed above (pp. 201–202), along with the closing portions of §VII.

22:6	First Portion of the Close of §VII (the angel speaks)
22:6a	—the conclusion closely paralleling the end of §V
22:6a	—added remark looking back to 1:1
22:7	Unannounced Voice (Jesus Christ speaks)
22:8-11	Second Portion of the Close of §VII

22:8	—John's impulse to worship the angel
22:9-11	—the angel reproves John (the angel speaks—twice)
22:12-13	Unannounced Voice (Jesus Christ speaks) —with title
22:14-15	Community Response (community spokesman speaks) —declarations of blessedness and condemnation
22:16	Jesus' Voice Confirming His Angelic Message to John —with two titles
22:17	Community Exhortation (community spokesman speaks)
22:18-19	John's Anathema Against Falsifiers of His Prophecy
22:20a	Jesus' Voice (reported) Confirming John's Declaration
22:20b	Community's Prayerful Response (congregation speaks)
22:21	John's Closing Epistolary Salutation

A few words are in order to clarify the manner in which John has interlocked the end of §VII with the conclusion of his whole apocalypse. The final words of the angel at the very *end* of the conclusion of the *first* interpretation-scene (§V, 19:10b: "The witness from Jesus, indeed, is the Spirit of prophecy") are restated, substantially, by the *beginning* of the conclusion of the *second* scene (§VII), following the declaration regarding genuine testimony: "And the Lord God of the spirits of the prophets . . ." (22:6a). Restating the angel's final words enables John to supplement the closing line (v. 9) of the second interpretation-scene with an admonition (v. 10) regarding the entire apocalypse: "Do not seal up the words of the prophecy of this book." Thus, he effects an immediate transition to the end of his whole book. At the end of §V, prophetic declaration was grounded both in God himself (19:9) and in the testimony given by Jesus through the Holy Spirit, the Spirit of prophecy. At the end of §VII, John theocentrically links the function of the same Spirit, as exercised through the faculties of prophets, to the Lord God (the Father).

In apocalyptic perspective, God's word to the prophets is further mediated by visions, notably as given by angels, whether as individual, supra-human persons and/or as "stand-ins" for a divine person. God's sending his own angel to his servants to show what must occur soon (quickly, *en tachei*) plainly links 22:6b with the opening verse of Revelation (1:1). Thus, at the outset of the conclusion of §VII, John ties together his composition as a whole. God originates and completes the revelation.

Dramatically underlining the angel's remark about "the things that must come quickly/occur soon," John adds, without announcing it, a word which must be attributed only to Jesus: "And behold, I do come soon/quickly!" (v. 7). Jesus' second coming sums up the scope of the whole panorama which John has provided, with all its elaborated series of visions. The whole apocalypse does not deal with the end of this world so much as with the fulfillment of Christian faith and hope in Jesus Christ.[163] His coming also assures the reward for those alerted to it by John's prophecy, as the added beatitude declares (v. 7b).

By adding v. 7, John knits together with the conclusion of his apocalypse the conclusion of this particular interpretation-scene, for Jesus subsequently reaffirms this statement in the epilogue (twice: 22:12 and 22:20a). Likewise, the phrase, "one who keeps the words of the prophecy of this book" (v. 7b) closely links this unannounced statement to the angel's next words (vv. 9-10, the second portion of the close of this interpretation-scene) so that v. 7 can introduce the epilogue proper in a deftly-executed, "dovetailing" way, without shattering the context. Insistence upon "(hearing) the prophecy of this book" and on respecting its integrity will occur again, within the rest of the epilogue, in vv. 18-19. Furthermore, John's introduction of Jesus' statements in v. 7 knits together the end of his apocalypse and its beginning.

---

[163]The same is true of other outstanding examples of NT apocalyptic. J. Lambrecht, *Die Redaktion der Markus-Apokalypse* (Rome: Pontifical Biblical Institute, 1967) 263-297, 293-294, establishes for Mark 13 the structural and theological centrality of the Lord's coming and the gathering of his chosen ones (Mark 13:24-27). In 2 Thess 2, the major topic, "the parousia of our Lord Jesus Christ and our being gathered together to meet him" (2 Thess 2:1) is tightly unified, determined by a single definite article.

For the beatitude in v. 7 forms an inclusion with the first beatitude in Revelation, which occurs with the title to the work (1:3, hard upon 1:1-2).[164]

Notwithstanding perceptive and detailed studies on the dialogue in John's epilogue,[165] it remains difficult to assign precisely the various "speakers" at the close of John's apocalypse. Jesus intervenes in 22:7 to affirm and focus the point of the message from God's angel (notably, its amplification in v. 6). John then reintroduces himself to connect both of the foregoing. His impulse (v. 8) to worship the angel, a matter on which he had already been corrected (19:10), becomes more intelligible here as a somewhat

---

[164]The first beatitude (1:3) and the sixth (22:7) correspond in that both deal with an expected response to the reading of the book, namely, keeping the words of the prophecy written in it. The second and fifth (14:13 and 20:6) speak of a heavenly reward prior to the general resurrection, and both contain an important temporal reference: *ap' arti,* "from now on," and *chilia etē,* "a thousand years." The third and seventh (16:15; 22:14) contain a reference to guarding (keeping) or to washing one's own clothes: respectively, to avoid the shame of nakedness at Armageddon and to be able to have access to the tree of life and to enter the (holy) city.

The fourth beatitude (19:9) highlights the *invitation* to the wedding-feast of the Lamb. Fittingly, it is the only beatitude in which *no explanation* is stated—either negatively or positively, either in a causal clause or in a purpose clause, or in helpfully explanatory *adjuncta* (like the Lord's unannounced word in 22:7a, or the negative and positive clauses of 20:6 b, which describe the priestly kings' present and future privileges). Although the fourth beatitude stands alone among all seven, and in the center of the arrangement, the pattern *(ABCDB' A' C')* is not concentric. One can hardly argue, therefore, for its having "central importance." Nonetheless, it does stand out as a uniquely arresting statement of God's "grace" or blessing. One might also moralize that the persons invited had better respond appreciatively (cf. Luke 14:15-24; Matt 22:1-14) and be properly attired (Matt 22:11-14). Note Rev. 19:7-8, esp. 19:8b, and also the *third* and *seventh* beatitudes—which seem to be underscored in the *progression* of the entire series and deliberately to "upset" a concentric order! For, in the tight pattern *ABCDB' A' C'*, it is *only C'* that is "misplaced."

[165]Cf. M. A. Kavanagh, *Apocalypse 22:6-21 as Concluding Liturgical Dialogue* (Dissertation excerpt, Gregorian University: Rome, 1984) 125–140.

confused response to the two speakers in vv. 6-7.[166] After correcting John (v. 9), the angel goes on to enjoin him to let his book stand open, not only so that all his co-servants can read it, but because it is intended for the present, the end-time's climactic fulfillment, which is "under way." Almost certainly, v. 11 continues the angel's last words and states what is yet ("still") to happen before the Lord's words of judgment, which alone mark the "very end of the end." Both injustice and immorality must needs continue until the final verdict, and the same holds for justice and holiness. John's apocalyptic perspective, like that elsewhere in the Bible[167] supposes progressively diverging moral opposites. Even evil is conceived as coming to fulfillment. Jesus again interposes (vv. 12-13) to indicate the moment which terminates this process, as only a divine person can determine its end (v. 13; cp. 21:6-8; 20:12).

After Jesus reenters the dialogue (vv. 12-13), the statements of reward and punishment in vv. 14-15 are best assigned to another speaker, probably, for the first time in the epilogue, to a spokesman for the community. The length of this response makes it unlikely that the whole community voices it in concert (contrast, for example, v. 20b). Besides, Jesus' express reintroduction of himself ("I, Jesus, ..." v. 16) seems to suppose another interlocutor in the immediately foregoing verses (vv. 14-15). The combination of blessing and curse in vv. 14-15 has a juridical ring. The beatitude, for instance, speaks of "the right to the tree of life," and amounts to a declaration of acquittal in judgment, here

---

[166]In this connection, I retract my former view, published in "Structural and Thematic Correlations," 495–497, concerning the "escalation" of the *angelus interpres* in Rev 22.

[167]Cf. *2 Baruch* 3:4-9; *1 Enoch* 91:3-10; *2 Esdras* 14:15; Dan 12:4b (both LXX and Theodotion, though in different ways); 12:10; Gen 15:16; Rom 2:5; *Didachē* 16:4. Cf. C. H. Giblin, *The Threat to Faith. An Exegetical and Theological Re-examination of 2 Thessalonians 2* (Rome: Pontifical Biblical Institute, 1967) 131–135, 214–216. The author now retracts his view that Paul wrote 2 Thess, but considers that the interpretation he offered for the pseudepigraph remains basically sound; cf. Giblin, "2 Thessalonians 2 Re-read as Pseudepigraphal: A Revised Reaffirmation of *The Threat to Faith.*" *The Thessalonian Correspondence,* ed. R. F. Collins (BETL LXXXVII; University Press: Leuven, 1990) 459–469.

phrased as a blessing.[168] The corresponding curse, translated as a declarative sentence, may also be taken as imperatival ("Shut out . . . !"). For, though it deals with more specific, moral matters than does 1 Corinthians 16:22, it seems to recall that Pauline anathema, and fits the general liturgical context supposed both by Paul's statement in 1 Corinthians 16:22 and by the dramatic situation of this epilogue (cf. especially 22:20b, in which "Come, Lord Jesus!" is the Greek translation of the Aramaic *Marana tha* of 1 Cor 16:22b). Also, Revelation 22:15 lacks a verb, but employs an adverb, *exō*, which may be considered imperatival ("Outside!").[169] In either case—declarative or imperatival—the statement mentions an already-known list of vices, but with a new twist. The "dogs," which head the list, may refer generically to sinners or to the worst kinds, those who hate the Gospel (Phil 3:2). More likely, in the light of the list in 21:8, "dogs" at least includes "cowards, faithless, and perverts."[170]

For the third time, Jesus himself speaks (v. 16), indicating here that the angel conveys his testimony to the Churches. This statement effectively covers, therefore, both major parts of Revelation, notably including the seven proclamations, if the figure of Christ in the inaugural vision is equivalently an angelic "stand-in."[171] At the very least, it would include the last *angelus interpres,* and thus represent Jesus as being of equal authority with "the Lord God of the spirits of the prophets (who) sent his angel (to

---

[168]Cf. Beasley-Murray, *Revelation,* 339.

[169]The Greek (*A* recension) of Jgs 3:19 has Eglon dismiss his attendants with an adverbial phrase *(ek mesou)* similar to the adverb *exō:* "Out!" (or, politely construed: "Depart!"). In Rev 22:15, the sense would be: "Out(side) with the dogs . . .!" regardless, of course, whether any were present or not, since the statement would carry a judicial tone balancing that of the beatitude and would be pronounced in a necessarily stylized, liturgical setting.

[170]A connotation of pederasty (cf. Deut 23:18) may also be present in the use of the tag, "dogs"; Kraft, *Offenbarung,* 279–280.

[171]*See above,* note 108.

Jude 5–7, noteworthy for its apocalyptic cast of thought and its allusions to intertestamental apocalyptic, probably presents Jesus as the "Angel of the Lord"; Jarl Fossum, "Kyrios Jesus as the Angel of the Lord in Jude 5–7," *NTS* 33 (1987) 226–243, 227, and esp. n. 72, on Rev 10:1 and 14:14.

John and) to his servants. . . ." (v. 6b). Jesus goes on to recall his victorious role (the bright star of dawn, cp. 2:8, perhaps here with the messianic overtones of Num 24:17) as the Davidic Messiah (the "root" being understood as the "sprout," Isaiah 11:10, coupled with the affirmation of lineal connection, "scion/lineal descendant [*genos*]"). As the title he predicated of himself in v. 13 highlighted his divine prerogative, so these two titles indicate his human status: the risen, Davidic Messiah.

Once more, in v. 17, the expected sentiments of the community are articulated by its spokesman. In voicing their yearning, the speaker presents himself both as a prophetic figure, uttering what the Spirit says, and as a representative of the community, proleptically seen as the bride, those prepared by good works (19:7-8) to become the wife of the Lamb, that is, to become the city of God. As the presider of the community acknowledged (v. 14) the blessing of the tree of life, he goes on now to exhort the thirsty, surely one and all of his hearers, to come and receive freely (cp. 21:6b) the correlated blessing, the water of life (cp. 22:1-3).

To whom vv. 18-19 are to be assigned remains a bit puzzling. One should probably opt for John himself, who would here be writing his prophetic "signature" (cp. 1 Cor 16:21, followed by the prophetic sanction in 16:22, and also the personal warning in Gal 6:17). This is further suggested by the pronoun "I" together with the specific, threefold reference to "this book." The prophet, John, attests the authenticity of his own words. John states the unchangeable nature of the divine communication in language reminiscent of Deuteronomy 4:2 ("You shall not add to the word which I command you, nor take from it. . . .") and of Deuteronomy 12:32; Proverbs 30:5-6.[172] John is concerned with heretical distortions. His sanctions echo the penalties intended for the wicked (v. 18b), especially as the alternative to the state of risen life (v. 19b). Repeating the word "testify," John then reports in v. 20a the Lord's own word. Thus, he ratifies his own testimony in accordance with the insistent theme of the whole epi-

---

[172]W. C. van Unnik observed that Rev 22:18-19 adapted a well-used formula by playing on words (scil., by using *epitithenai* [twice] instead of *prostithenai* in v. 18); "De la règle *mēte prostheinai mēte aphelein* dans l'histoire du Canon," *VigChr* 3 (1949) 1-36, 35.

logue as enunciated by Jesus himself (cp. vv. 7, 12-13, and 16). When v. 20a is taken as John's report of the Lord's endorsement, the community's ("choral") response in v. 20b becomes a bit clearer. Its "Amen" covers not only the Lord's promise, as quoted by John, but also John's own "prophetic signature" in vv. 18-19. The community voices prayerful acceptance of John's entire communication and, at the same time, its earnest desire for the consummation which, through John, the Lord Jesus himself has promised.

In Pauline style, though without the personal touch Paul usually adds, John pens his closing salutation (v. 21). John makes his own, however, Paul's salient point: "the grace of the Lord Jesus," that is, the personal favor of God proved in and through the death and resurrection of Jesus Christ. John's final salutation anchors the greeting with which he opened his book (1:4).

APPENDIX: THE COHESIVE THEMATIC OF GOD'S HOLY WAR OF LIBERATION

Detailed arguments have been set forth[173] to show how the opening three chapters of Revelation are linked with the rest of John's apocalypse. For instance, features of the prologue are recalled in the epilogue: the angelic intermediary sent to John (1:1; 22:16), beatitudes regarding those who observe what John has written (1:3; 22:7), the self-predication of God and of Jesus as Alpha and Omega (1:8; 22:13), and the motif of imminence (1:3; 22:6b-7, 12, 20). The inaugural vision is correlated to the major vision by John's being called to attention by the same trumpet-like voice (1:10; 4:1) and by a progression to emphasis on the things to come hereafter (1:19; 4:1).

At the same time, a distinction obtains between two major parts: the first in 1:9–3:22, the second in 4:1 to the close of the interpretation-scene in 22:11. John's visionary experience as well as his assigned task as a writer differ in each part. In the first, he is on earth; in the second, he ascends to heaven (4:1) and is later symbolically transported to other, earthly sites (17:3; 21:10). In the first part, he writes the seven churches (1:11). Later, in penning his heavenly vision, he is enjoined to consume the open, proclaimed document and further to widen the scope of his proph-

---

[173]Cf. especially Ugo Vanni, *La Struttura letteraria,* 107–115, 116–119.

ecy.[174] Furthermore, the nature of the septenaries also requires a distinction between these two parts. The septenary of proclamations to the churches (2–3) does not have the same form or function as do the three numbered septenaries of the unsealings (6:1–8:5), the trumpet-blasts (8:7–15:8), and the libation-bowls (16:1-21). The proclamations are not interlocked with another septenary, as are the septenaries in Rev 6–16. In some minor respects, they have characteristics similar to the latter. For the third and seventh as elsewhere in numbered sets of seven carry special emphasis; the third proclamation for emphasizing the motif of war and "food" (2:12-17), the seventh for its final word from the "Amen" (3:14) and its astounding promise to the victor (3:21). Also, the sixth introduces proleptically a future, wider prospect, namely, that of a worldwide test (3:10). Nevertheless, the form (particular edicts, containing judgment and/or salvation oracles, with commands to heed and promises to the victor) and even the rhythm of the integrated series[175] preclude considering the septenary in Rev 2–3 as structurally joined or equated with those contained in the heavenly vision.

Although the two major parts (1:9–3:22; 4:1–22:11) need to be distinguished, they should not be separated or thematically uncoupled. The first looks to a set of particular situations; the second, to a worldwide scenario which is only announced in the first part (3:10). The temporal perspective emphatically widens (again, as suggested in 3:10: "going to come" *mellousēs erchesthai)* with the beginning of the second part ("what must happen hereafter,"

---

[174]Amplification of the scope of John's prophecy may be inferred from the addition of the word "many" to the fourfold listing and the substitution at the end of "kings" *(basileis,* suggesting a more imposing array) for "tribes" *(phylai)* in the fourfold listing (10:11). Furthermore, "again/once more/anew" *(palin)* suggests a renewal or further determination of the same matter (in this case, of John's prophetic function) rather than a distinct, changed commission. Note the only other use of *palin* in Revelation, scil., 10:8, where the particular *personal relevance* of the proclaimed scroll is brought home to John. There is no need at all to suppose the beginning of a new part of Revelation (vis-à-vis either the inaugural vision or the unsealed scroll). Supposing a new, major division, moreover, would truncate the trumpet septenary and the sequence of three woes and would sunder the cohesive thematic of Revelation.

[175]*See above,* pp. 80, 99.

ha dei genesthai meta tauta—developing 1:19). Indeed, the course of the major division eventually discloses a period of time, "the days of the seventh angel. . ." (10:7) of which John writes prophetically, but which apparently extends beyond that of his own ministry (as the Spirit's words apropos of the twinned witnesses suggest, 11:1-13).

Most important, a consistent thematic, that of God's Holy War, pervades John's entire composition. This thematic serves to confirm the structural unity and coherence of Revelation and to impart to it a distinctive and dominant theological emphasis. The following survey delineates its over-all articulation, especially as encompassing the prologue and the first part of Revelation as well as the major vision.[176]

John's epistolary greeting (1:4-5a) includes the wish of messianic peace, but takes as its standpoint the heavenly vision he has been given, which the theme of God's Holy War pervades. To construe his greeting in this way explains his stress on God's coming, his reference to the angels of the divine presence, who later appear as the seven angels with trumpets,[177] and his designation of Jesus Christ as the ruler of the kings of the earth. The prayerful response acknowledging the status of the faithful as a priestly kingdom may suggest both the character of God's people before his decrees are presented, as at Sinai,[178] and also a foretaste of the gathering of the elect as described in Matt 24:31.[179] More clearly, the closing verse of the prologue (1:8) oracularly declares the Lord's coming (cf. the greeting, 1:4) as that of the God of armies.[180]

---

[176]More detailed expositions already given in the commentary or in its introduction (especially under heading IV) are here supposed.

[177]*See above,* notes 37, 74.

[178]the text which John employs amounted in Exod 19:4-6 to a *promissory* covenant, whereas John presents it as realized through Jesus' death. John does not present himself as Moses, but as a co-servant of the community, although he alone experiences the trumpet-blast (1:10; cp. Exod 19:6) which precedes the theophany.

[179]The moment of the parousia is certainly present in John's thought, as the very next verse (1:7) indicates; cp. Matt 24:30.

[180]Cf. Karl Matthäus Woschitz, *Erneuung aus dem Ewigen: Denkweisen—glaubenweisen in Antike und Christentum nach Offb. 1-3* (Freiburg i. B.: Herder, 1987) 144 and n. 76.

John's opening visual description of the Lord (1:12-16), following Vanni's analysis,[181] is set forth in three small portions. The first (vv. 12-13) presents the Son of Man in priestly attire. The second (vv. 14-15) describes him, in effect, as Son of God, combining features of the Ancient of Days with aspects of the angelic figure Gabriel ("man [mighty one] of God"), but stressing fire in its pure state (cp. 2:18, not just as torches, Dan 10:6) and also the sound of God's own glory (cp. Ezek 1:14; 43:7). The third portion (v. 16) relates the Lord to the seven churches (which stand for the "fulness" of the earthly Church). It is this portion, particularly relevant to the following proclamations, which depicts the Lord as an imperial figure ready for combat. Not only does he hold in his hand the seven stars, like the figure of worldwide power on imperial coins, but his very utterance is a two-edged sword, and his countenace radiates the full power of the sun.

The Lord's imperial bearing is borne out by the seven imperial edicts he dictates. As the angel-guardians of *places,* the angels mentioned at the beginning of each missive may readily be conceived to have a kind of "military" role, like those of the angel of Persia, of Michael, and of the angel (Gabriel) speaking to Daniel (Dan 10:12-13) or also of the angel sent to Jerusalem (1 Chron 21:15). They may at least be construed to have a disciplinary function. In the Qumran War Scroll, the angels are associated with the embattled people (1QM X, 10-11; XII, 1-8; XIII, 10), especially as directing them in their struggle (1QM XVII, 6-7). Later, in John's major vision, angels seal the tribes marshalled for the actual engagement of God's Holy War (7:2-8). Here, they surely contribute to the image of a solemn assembly which, though on earth, stands under constant heavenly guidance.

Each of the written communications recalls imperial or royal prerogatives of the risen Lord, if not in his self-identification (2:1; 2:12; 3:1; 3:7) or in the body of the message (2:10; 2:16; 2:23), then at least in designating the one he rewards as "the victor." The term "victor" must suppose a kind of forthcoming battle or combat, and fits with an address from one's *imperator.*[182] Every

---

[181]Vanni, *L'Apocalisse,* 123-136.

[182]In the case of a merely earthly ruler, like Julius Caesar, the promise would, no doubt, deal with land and booty, as implied in Suetonius, *Lives of the Caesars,* I, 70.

other use of this word (or its verbal form) in Revelation bears out this inference. Although satanic forces achieve a partial "victory" by slaying God's witnesses (11:7; 13:7), and although the first horseman may represent merely ongoing belligerence in the world (6:2), the dominant victory is that of Jesus Christ, the Lion of Judah (5:5) as fully achieved in God's Holy War (12:11; 17:4). The faithful prove to be sharers in God's victory (12:11; 15:2; 21:7). All the opening decrees, then, announce this triumph, specifying in most cases aspects of life in the new creation (2:7, cp. 22:2, 14; 3:5, cp. 20:12, 15) or also the heavenly (millennial) kingdom (2:11, cp. 20:6; 3:5, cp. 7:13-17; 3:12, cp. 21:2) and/or victory shared with the King of Kings and Lord of Lords (2:26-28, cp. 19:15; 2:17, cp. 19:12-13).[183]

In view of God's Holy War, the Lord's army must be chaste or undefiled. John expresses this requirement in a new way, and on two counts. On the one hand, he mentions the theme of chastity expressly apropos of the already triumphant army of the Lord, the 144,000 celibates (14:1-5). This chastity, a state of being undefiled by idolatrous worship and the moral vices it fostered, appears in John's theological perspective as the *end-result* of an integrally Christian life in a hostile environment. John does not regard it as an ascetical act required by ritual, even though the OT ritual concretized the solid belief that one's own life-energy was to be dedicated completely to God's service in his combat. Instead, he views it as the crown of a whole life of dedication to the Lord. On the other hand, John finds the theme of *anticipatory* purification in fulfilling the current demands of the imperial warrior-priest, the risen Lord. The liturgy of the Lord's Day, which "dates" John's vision, requires purification by confession of sins *(Didachē,* 14). The first part of John's vision builds on that theme of needed purification.[184]

John does not develop the Eucharistic celebration in terms of the liturgy of the sacrament. It is not unlikely, however, that he alludes to it under the symbol of a banquet which the Lord him-

---

[183]The victory promised the lax Laodiceans (3:21) if they change their ways should astound any reader: they will share the *same throne* as God and the Lord Jesus! The underlying notion, of course, is the regal status of those in heaven (20:6) and in the New Jerusalem (22:3-5).

[184]Vanni, *L'Apocalisse,* 94–96.

self occasions (in the climactic seventh missive, to the Laodiceans, 3:20). One is hardly to suppose that, in 3:20, the Lord invites himself to a banquet already in process. Furthermore, the "engraved pebble" (2:17) of the third proclamation alludes to a banquet invitation. The paired mention of "hidden manna" (2:17) in the same, third missive's promise to the victor may imply the Eucharist, if only as an anticipation of the heavenly wedding-feast.[185] John demonstrates clearly, however, that he is concerned with establishing the basic theme of the Eucharist, namely, thanksgiving for creation (4:9, the "Sanctus" of the four living beings, seconded by the elders), thanksgiving for redemption through Christ's death (7:12, where the angels join the four beings and the elders in seconding the victory-shout of the triumphant saints), and thanksgiving for God's universal messianic reign (11:16, where the living beings and elders respond to the victory shout of heavenly voices at the sound of the seventh trumpet). As a prophet and apocalyptist, even within the parameters set by St. Paul (1 Cor 14:26-33, 37-40), John has an important preparatory function in the community's eucharistic liturgy. One may wryly observe, however, that the *Didachē*'s prescription to "suffer the prophets to hold Eucharist as (long a time as) they will" *(Didachē* 10, 7) was taken quite readily by John,[186] or was occasioned by others with similarly abundant capacity for discourse.

The major vision commences with John's being summoned by the same voice, like that of a trumpet, to ascend through the opened door in heaven. The throne vision, though serene, indicates that the initiative for God's Holy War of Liberation lies with

---

[185]That the Eucharist was regarded as a mysterious manna is evident from John 6, though the theme in the Fourth Gospel is developed differently. In Revelation, since all the other promises to the victor have a fully eschatological sense, referring to one's final status in heaven and/or the new Jerusalem, the "hidden manna" probably refers directly to the wedding-feast of the Lamb, and would only *connote* the Eucharist as an anticipation of that event, i.e., as celebrated with a view to Christ's coming (cf. the anticipatory *achri hou elthē* [subjunctive] in 1 Cor 11:26).

[186]In length, John's Apocalypse is over twice as long as the dogmatic sermon *(logos paraklēseōs)* known as the Epistle to the Hebrews, and about 83% as long as the shortest Gospel, Mark. It is conceivable that a major *portion* of Revelation (like the longer part, Rev 4–22, which is two-thirds the length of Mark), could be read on a single occasion.

God and the Lamb. God does not "rouse himself," as in OT imagery. Nonetheless, his throne stands as the source of the lightnings, voices, and thunders appropriate to a theophany. These presage the amplified epiphanic manifestations which will occur at strategic points throughout the elaboration of the thematic of the Holy War: in 8:5, under the seventh unsealing; in 11:19, after the seventh trumpet, with the appearance of the ark of the covenant; in 16:18, with the seventh libation-bowl containing God's final wrath (the *ḥērem* on Babylon).[187] The seven lampstands, God's spirits (4:5), are subsequently predicated of the Lamb (5:6), recalling the eyes of the Lord which go throughout the whole world to show his might in the Holy War (2 Chron 16:9). These seven spirits later appear as "the seven angels who stand before God" and who are given seven trumpets.[188] The crystal sea of the dais (4:6a) may well be that which later reappears as the sea of deliverance for the victors of the New Exodus (15:2). The four living beings praise God as the holy Lord God of the heavenly armies *(ho pantokratōr),* and the twenty-four elders acknowledge his dominion over the world as its creator (4:8-11). In effect, this is an instance of the *tᵉrû'āh* or battle-cry, recast as a thanksgiving (cf. also 7:12 and especially 11:17). The principal agent of the forthcoming action is the Lamb, introduced precisely as the victorious royal Messiah, the Lion of Judah (5:5), who alone can open the sealed book of destinies.

Before the Holy War, it was customary to recall with praise God's saving actions on behalf of his people.[189] In Revelation, this prayerful recognition is voiced by the elders, the living beings, and the angels, and extols not only God's creation of all (4:8-11) but also his redemption of a worldwide group, making them a priestly realm destined to rule over the earth (5:8-14). The prayers of the saints are also raised symbolically in the incense offered by the elders (5:8). The Lamb, his seven horns symboliz-

---

[187]The term "lightnings" *(astrapai)* never occurs alone; "thunders" *(brontai)* occur also in 6:1 (of the voice of the first living being), in 10:3-4 (where the seven thunders speak but are then silenced), and in 14:2 and 19:6 of a heavenly victory-shout; "voice(s)" *(phōnai)* occur by themselves scores of times.

[188]*See above,* p. 72, 93f.

[189]As in 2 Chron 20:5-12; cp. 1QM X-XIII.

ing universal power (5:6), inaugurates the disclosure of the Holy War both by taking the scroll from the right hand of the Enthroned—whose decrees it obviously contains (5:7)—and then by unsealing it (6:1-8:5). This action renders unnecessary, of course, the human need for special consultation of the Lord prior to the conflict (e.g., Jgs 20:23, 28; 1 Sam 14:37; 23:2, 4), the purpose of which was to acknowledge divine control over the whole course of forthcoming events.

As explained in the commentary, the unsealings serve as portents for the actual engagement. After the general theme of ongoing victory (6:1-2) and the associated vignettes of continual disasters (war, social injustice, and death in various cruel forms, 6:3-8), the plea of the martyrs (6:9-11) articulates the requirements of God's justice for an *end*-time. Their prayer of complaint finds an encouraging answer not only in their being rewarded in heaven for the time being, but also and especially in the sixth unsealing, which discloses quite neatly and clearly the thematic of the Holy War of the Enthroned and the Lamb (6:16-17). In contrast to the terror inflicted on all classes of earthdwellers (6:12-17), the army of God's people is protectively marshalled by the angels in the calm before the storm (7:1-8), and is then viewed proleptically as an innumerable, triumphant throng of purified victors. These are destined for heaven and for its earthly fulfillment in a new creation, as the various blessings predicated of them attest.

At the seventh unsealing, the angel of the altar silently performs a symbolic sacrificial act in offering to God the prayers of the saints and then casting fire upon the earth. The seven trumpets, progressively orchestrated by John's compounding three woes with the last three trumpets, herald the actual engagement. Notably in the first three trumpets, fiery elements of creation respond as heaven-sent agents of destruction. In the fourth, heavenly sources of light are themselves smitten. In the fifth, a fallen star unleashes a horde from under the earth, and in the sixth, a power from God's altar calls for the unleashing in due time of a chastising army from beyond the Euphrates. Thus, spatial and temporal elements of God's creation and elements from heaven, from below the earth, and from the borders of earth's civilization become the agents of God's wrath. John's perspective is even more vast than that in Deborah's vision of God's creation as engaged in his battles (Jgs 5:4, 20). Under the sixth trumpet blast, in John's "enlargement" of the perspective, the Angel of the Lord, a figure straddling earth and sea, clarifies the immediacy of the climactic phase of the engagement (10:5-7).

It is the seventh trumpet which announces without delay the advent of the world-encompassing kingly power of the Lord and of his Anointed. The actual coming of the God of armies is stated by the heavenly court of elders in 11:16 (with the significant omission of "to come," *erchomenos,* in the title repeated from 1:8 and 4:8). The palladium of God's Holy War appears (11:19) in conjunction with this declaration. The cosmic dimensions of God's War of Liberation are brought to a conclusion by the annihilation of Babylon (the *ḥērem)* through the final septenary of the last plagues (16:1-21) and, in appropriate order, by the termination of the other eschatological adversaries (19:11-21; 20:1-10; 20:11-15). This negative, destructive conclusion of God's War coincides with its positive intent, the advent of his new creation, the New Jerusalem for "his peoples" (21:1-8): "It has/they have occurred," *gegonen,* 16:17b; *gegonan,* 21:6. The special interpretations (regarding Babylon, 17:1-19:10, and then the New Jerusalem, 21:9-22:11, cp. 19:6-8), each of which is conveyed by one of the angels who executed God's final wrath, serve to highlight the twofold conclusion to the Holy War and clarify its theme as one of complete liberation.

Lastly, the epilogue (22:7, 12-21) reaffirms key features of the Holy War: purification (22:14) achieved by fidelity throughout the conflict, the Lord Jesus' being the Davidic, imperial conqueror (22:16), and the community's prayer for his speedy, triumphal coming (22:20).

The seven sections of Part Two of Revelation (4-22) call for an *over-all simplification in three stages.* Thus, the following grouping confirms the narrative progression which these seven sections articulate, but at the same time sets forth clearly the eschatological perspective of the whole, in terms of the beginning, the middle, and the end:

Stage One: The Preview (4:1-8:5; i.e., §§I and II—the book and its unsealings).

Stage Two: The Engagement (8:6-15:8; i.e., §III—the trumpets and the "septet" following the seventh trumpet). Here, the emphasis falls on the Great Tribulation (so announced in 7:14),